THE CRITICAL DECADE

THE CRITICAL DECADE

CULTURE IN CRISIS

NICOLAS TREDELL

CARCANET

For Angela

First published in 1993 by
Carcanet Press Limited
208-212 Corn Exchange Buildings
Manchester M4 3BQ

The essay 'Euphoria, Ltd' first appeared in the Casebook *Issues in Contemporary Critical Theory* (1987), ed. Peter Barry, and is reprinted by permission of Macmillan.

A CIP catalogue record for this book is available from the British Library.
ISBN 1 85754 015 8

The publisher acknowledges financial assistance from the Arts Council of Great Britain

Set in 10pt Sabon by Bryan Williamson, Frome, Somerset
Printed and bound in England by SRP Ltd, Exeter

Contents

Introduction

The 1980s saw a revolution in literary studies in England and the United States – a revolution which, indeed, challenged and partly dispersed the very notion of 'literary studies', broke down the assumptions, the procedures and the boundaries which had come to characterize such studies in the mid-twentieth century. It was a critical decade for literary studies in at least four senses: it was a time of crisis; it was a turning-point; it was a period in which criticism displaced the literary texts which had previously been seen as its *raison d'être*; and it was a decade in which literary studies became subject to fierce criticism of its preconceptions and protocols from those nominally working within the field itself. It is, of course, no accident that all this took place at a time of crisis – political, social, cultural, economic, ecological – on a global scale.

The essays in this book examine key aspects of the critical decade and its aftermath. Originally written *à chaud*, as specific engagements with particular books, topics and writers, in the main they have not been substantially altered: to change them would be to lose the sense of the heat, the intensity, which crucial moments of that decade could generate. Only in the chapter on Raymond Williams has a certain degree of hindsight been allowed, since the original obituary essay has already been published, in expanded and adapted form, as a book (see Bibliography).

If the essays which comprise this volume were provoked by particular moments, the issues with which they deal are not ephemeral: they persist, with inevitable differences of emphasis and context, in the debates of the 1990s. This Introduction offers a broad outline of those issues.

To begin with, there is the issue of the validity of the concept of literature as a distinctive and perhaps uniquely valuable kind of writing.

The belief that such a concept *was* valid underpinned literary studies in England and the United States in the mid-twentieth century; indeed, it was a concept that was so much taken for granted that it was hardly seen *as* a concept. In England, an ideology based upon it was most powerfully articulated by F.R. Leavis. In this book, the essay 'Anti-Philosophers' focuses on Leavis, and compares and contrasts him with Derrida, as ably explicated by Jonathan Culler. It was still possible to believe in the early 1980s (and not only, as it were, from the backwoods) that the Leavisian model – a 1930s' job with an increasing amount of Victorian upholstery and a modest degree of 1950s' styling – had some mileage in it yet. Now Leavis belongs irretrievably to the past, to that foreign country where they do things differently. But it is important not to lose sight of the compelling power, as well as the constricting pressure, of his period of dominance. And Leavis's texts, released from their moralistic baggage, may now be disseminated, *à la* Derrida, in ways that could prove fruitful.

The essay 'I'm Not Complaining' considers not F.R. but Q.D. Leavis, and examines what can now be seen as a sustained campaign in her work – from the early 1930s to the start of the 1980s – against certain kinds of feminism: a campaign that can be related to her own ambiguous role as an unackowledged legislator of a kingdom ostensibly ruled by a tanned, open-necked, presumptuously *macho* male potentate.

The attack upon the category of literature and upon the remnants of Leavisism was to be focused, in England, by the controversial book *Re-Reading English* (1982). 'Hegemony by Other Means' considers that book, in a careful but unsparing way. 'Rotten Reconstruction' is no less careful or unsparing in its treatment of *Reconstructing Literature* (1983), a book which was an implicit riposte to *Re-Reading English* but which exposed the intellectual bankruptcy of those who imagined they could rely on the old British defences – dismissiveness, proudly paraded ignorance, puerile humour – to combat the new challenges. With friends like this, literature needed no enemies.

The attack upon established literary studies mounted by the re-readers had three main elements. One was a general promotion of 'theory'. At first this seemed to promise a new conceptual and procedural rigour in literary studies, and it certainly disseminated and developed a range of interesting ideas. But after a time, its triumphal march turned into chaos, a clash of erudite armies and of urbane and uncouth guerillas. The quest for the grand theory which would explain the secret of life, the universe and everything (even that third-rate and marginal activity called literature) got lost in a maze of broken mirrors or a hypermarket of intellectual styles. The essay 'Post-Theory' explores the way in which theory's vaulting ambition o'erleaped itself, falling upon the other, and tried, imperfectly, to turn into art.

The second element of the attack upon established literary studies was sociological and political. It involved an exploration of the historical development of the category of literature and the disciplines of literary studies, and pointed to their possible ideological, political and social functions, particularly as instruments of bourgeois hegemony (presumed to be a bad thing). The essay 'The Politicization of English' seizes on this issue. The radical force of this element of the attack can perhaps best be measured by the fact that the attackers named in that essay have now, almost to a person, become professors and are thus, presumably, enjoying some of the benefits of bourgeois hegemony. In the 1960s there was, as the Sartre/Barthes essay mentions, an idea that radical political commitment entailed an attempt to change one's daily life in such a way as to put into practice, in a necessarily imperfect manner, those principles which would inform a future socialist society. The idea had a brief shelf-life: but it implies a test which should be applied to those who preach revolution from the comfort of their studies and salaries. How would they really behave in a revolutionary situation? Could they live in a society which stripped them of their status, denied them differential rewards? But of course such scenarios are unlikely to arise.

The third element of the attack on established literary studies was in the hermeneutic zone: it involved a challenge to established ways of interpreting texts in terms of authors, themes, truth-to-life, universal and transcendent values, and organic unity. This could be linked, in certain perspectives, with the sociological attack: for example, it could be charged that what were offered as 'universal' values were in fact 'bourgeois' values (for example, the desire for upward mobility). The hermeneutic challenge began to be mounted by structuralism, which might be seen to rewrite 'universal values' as 'universal structures' and thus to retain one aspect of the established dispensation, but which put into question notions of the 'author', and of 'truth-to-life' in any immediate sense. But it was poststructuralism and deconstruction which made the hermeneutic challenge unignorable. Poststructuralism and deconstruction are a frequent presence – or trace – in these essays: significantly, it is the study of Raymond Williams from which they are most absent:

Williams's refusal, or failure, to respond publicly to poststructuralism and deconstruction in anything more than an oblique way is, like his similar near-silence on psychoanalysis, an index of both constancy and circumscription. Stephen Heath has well described the 'éblouissement' of reading Roland Barthes (*Vertige du déplacement*, 1974, p.11), and it was Barthes above all who conveyed the dazzle of poststructuralism, the sense of being displaced from one's fixed positions into a whirl of indeterminacy and adventure. In time, of course, poststructuralism brought its own fixities, yet the moment of Barthes should not be forgotten. In this book, the essay 'Sartre/Barthes' compares and contrasts him with that older and immensely influential French writer Jean-Paul Sartre, whose work, for all its errors and excesses, remains exemplary. The essay 'Euphoria, Ltd' addresses poststructuralism and deconstruction more generally to mark out their limits – limits which are now, in the 1990s, coming to be more widely recognized. Nevertheless the essay does not suppose that the insights of poststructuralism and deconstruction could, or should ever, be annulled.

Poststructuralism and deconstruction provided powerful new interpretive techniques which could seem, at first, to reanimate the study of literature and to conserve and enhance the traditional canon. It was in this spirit that deconstruction was taken up by J. Hillis Miller, as the essay 'Deconstructive Débâcle' shows. But in the United States the restriction of deconstruction to this role was to be violently exploded by the revelation that Paul de Man, in whose ideas and personal integrity Miller, and many others, had invested heavily, had written many literary articles for a newspaper which had collaborated with the Nazis during the wartime occupation of Belgium. 'Deconstructive Débâcle' also explores Miller's unhappy response to that revelation and to the subsequent controversy. In a sense, however, the attempt to confine deconstruction to the canon was always inappropriate. For the writ of deconstruction and poststructuralism had always extended far beyond the literary, to encompass, indeed, the totality of culture – even though they proscribed the idea of 'totality'. In this, poststructuralism and deconstruction did open the possibility, which some critics later took up, of an alliance with that analysis of culture conducted, in a rather different idiom, by Raymond Williams. The essay 'From a Tight Place' looks at Williams's attempts to develop a theory of culture and also considers his study of drama, his view of television, his novels, his concern with the ideas of the 'country' and the 'city', and his socialist commitment.

Related to the debates on literature and culture, and indeed sometimes functioning as an intermediate term between the two, is the issue of the concept and the category of the aesthetic – its history, its characteristics, its validity: it is that history which Terry Eagleton tracks so energetically in *The Ideology of the Aesthetic*, and his exploration is considered in the essay 'Politic Evasions'.

Considerations of the nature of present-day culture have focused especially on the notion of postmodernism: on its definition, on its differences, or not, from modernism, on its relationship to other cultural modes, on its social and political significance, on its artistic production. 'Goodbye to Dada' discusses one of the most remarkable contributions to these questions, that of the American Marxist Fredric Jameson. In the United States, modes of thought have recently emerged which might be seen as variants of postmodernism, or updated programmes of pragmatism, or a mixture of both. 'Zapping the Foundations' assesses the vigorous anti-foundationalism of Stanley Fish, and 'Pragmatic Protocols' considers the thoughtful proposals for the reading and teaching of literary and cultural texts developed by Robert Scholes.

Literature, theory, poststructuralism, deconstruction, culture, the aesthetic, postmodernism, pragmatism: all of these topics might be seen to be subsumed in the master *topos* of politics. That would be the view of a Jameson or Eagleton. The questionable achievement of mid-twentieth century literary criticism – especially perhaps, in England, through F.R. Leavis – was to create an ideology that licensed a principled or pusillanimous disengagement from politics, but which also allowed one to feel that one was, at some deeper level, contributing to truly radical change. That notion began to crumble in the 1960s, as students struggled to read Henry James while footage from Vietnam screamed from their television screens. But it was the partisan research into the history of literary study as a discipline which really gave impetus to the attempt to fuse politics and letters. If literary studies was already covertly politicized, why shouldn't it be overtly so? 'The Politicization of English' challenged the idea, then gaining ground, that literary studies should become, centrally and explicitly, a 'site of struggle' in which politics were always to the fore. Since that essay first appeared, politicization has proceeded apace, in both England and the United States; in the latter, the problems which it has caused have become focused in terms of a debate about 'Political Correctness' – a focus which is regrettable in so far as it obscures the real issues and obstructs perfectly proper attempts to discourage racist and sexist language and behaviour on the part of tutors and students. The crucial question is whether the university should remain what Edward Said – hardly a politically quiescent critic – calls 'the Utopian space' where all kinds of questions can be explored. As Said points out: 'For it to become a site where social and political issues are actually either imposed or resolved would be to remove the university's function and turn it into an adjunct to whatever political party is in power' (*Culture and Imperialism*, 1993, p.xxix).

The objection to politicizing literary studies is often rewritten, and then dismissed, as an objection to the particular politics – left-wing – which are being promoted. But there are other grounds of objection, not least the argument that politicization may serve as – in the 1980s and early 1990s, has served as – an evasion of the truly difficult political questions. It is this argument which is pursued in the examination of Terry Eagleton's 'political' rhetoric in 'Politic Evasions'. For the crucial fact is this: as what used to be literary studies has become more left-wing, the world has become less so. The critical decade concluded with the collapse of Communist regimes in Eastern Europe, and the dissolution, not so long after, of the Soviet Union. Only bloody repression prevented what might well have been a similar collapse in China. This is not, of course, the end of Marxism as an intellectual system and a programme of research – though in so far as it ever was an inspiration to large-scale collective action, it is difficult now to imagine it ever becoming so again. The collapse of Eastern Europe and the Soviet Union is an epochal, world-historical change, the political and intellectual repercussions of which have already been immense. In a sense, it may be unfair to say that Marxism and socialism have been tried and failed; but it certainly looks that way to a lot of people, and that perception cannot be explained away as merely an ideological mystification.

A caveat against triumphalism has to be entered. The release of subjected peoples from those cruel, austere regimes is a great liberation. But one possible consequence of that liberation – or, more precisely, of the repression that preceded it – may be regretted: the death of a dream, of a vision of human possibility. Near the end of Graham Greene's *The Power and the Glory* (1940), the lieutenant who has pursued the whisky priest experiences, on the eve of the priest's execution, a sense of loss and disorientation: 'He felt without a purpose, as if life had drained out of the world' (1971 edn., p.207). Greene's propagandist point is easily grasped. But might not one also see that situation now reversed, the death of communism producing a sense of loss and disorientation on a much more profound level than that experienced by those old Cold Warriors who, having seen the evil empire subside into a dependency of Western Europe and the United States, try to demonize a liberalism that has long ago lost its nerve. Marxism was the greatest secular challenge to the capitalist order ever mounted – indeed, in the modern world, the greatest challenge of all, given that religion, especially Christianity, has found capital pretty easy to live with. If that has gone, and we are left with the society of the simulacrum and the spectacle, which skims across misery and despair in an endless play of excitation and consumption – the simstim world so vividly evoked in William Gibson's novels – then matters are critical indeed: but it is in the nature of this crisis that it will not be recognized as such. The essay 'Modern Tragedy' looks at the considerations on the past record, present condition and future prospects of Marxism and socialism by one of the most intellectually accomplished and astute of English Marxists, Perry Anderson. That essay has an elegiac tone which is doubtless, in part, a submission to the dying fall of the *fin-de-siècle* in a time which has seen the baulking of large hopes. As a prophylactic, Anderson himself invokes Gramsci, and his famous axiom could well seem apposite at present: pessimism of the intellect, optimism of the will. One might not slice it quite like that, however, but counsel, rather, a pained appraisal of the sources of hope.

Prominent among sources of hope are those surges of cultural and political activity on the sites where the writ of Western Man once ran rampant – but where, partly thanks to that activity, it does not do so quite so surely today. Those surges – comprised, in fact, of multiple, diverse, sometimes retrograde currents – can provisionally be named as feminism and post-colonialism, the latter being understood as that process by which, in Salman Rushdie's words, 'the empire writes back to the centre' – or, more precisely, in which the ex-empire may obliquely address its old captors in seeking to generate its own accents and auditors. To cite these as sources of hope may be seen, with good reason, as appropriative: a repetition in politically correct idiom of old demands that woman save and succour the weary male and that the New World redress the balance of the Old. The charge strikes home. But it is a charge which, in a sense, could itself be seen as an appropriation of feminism and post-colonialism, implying as it does that those movements *can* easily be appropriated, that their power of radical disturbance can be contained within the colossal hand of the Patriarch. To make this point, however, raises another spectre: that of romanticism. This magically transforms feminism and post-colonialism into supernal forces that are ineluctably stronger and purer than the powers which oppose them. It forgets that the Patriarch does still, after all, have a colossal hand, and can fire smart bombs from his fingertips; it denies that the Patriarch is within us as well as without us.

It is this amnesia and denial which the demanding, psychoanalytically informed feminism of Jacqueline Rose works against; the essay 'Women's Wager' looks at that feminism in relation to some other versions of feminism and to the haunting figure of Sylvia Plath – that haunting being related precisely, as Rose argues, to Plath's intense, vertiginous investment in fantasies and figurations that mark European and North American culture. The implication of Rose's book is that there can be no easy appropriation of feminism, even by feminists; the implication of Edward Said's *Culture and Imperialism* is that there can be no easy appropriation of post-colonialism, even by post-colonialists. The history and legacy of sexism and imperialism demand an arduous and anxious working-through. But to try to evade that history and legacy, to retreat into defensive denial – a response all too evident in some recent strident defences of 'Western tradition' – is also to renounce rich possibilities. The last essay in *The Critical Decade* explores Edward Said's bold cartography of culture and empire and the prospect of new world maps which it opens.

1 Anti-Philosophers: Leavis and Derrida

'Give up literary criticism!' This was the 'stern admonition' that Wittgenstein once delivered to F.R. Leavis (*The Critic as Anti-Philosopher*, p.176). Leavis, of course, had no intention of giving up an activity that he saw as central to life, but in later years, while continuing to denounce theoretical argument, he grew increasingly concerned to justify his claims for literature's centrality. This led to his paradoxical stance as an 'anti-philosopher' – and indeed as an anti-sociologist, anti-psychologist and anti-historian – who vigorously engaged with philosophical, sociological, psychological and historical issues, while rejecting the usual terms of debate for those issues.

The Critic as Anti-Philosopher (1982) is not the book Leavis would have produced had he lived and retained his faculties. The intention was to follow *The Living Principle* (1975), focused on T.S. Eliot, and *Thought, Words and Creativity* (1976), focused on Lawrence, with a third volume focused on Wordsworth. Instead we have a book which consists, apart from an essay on *Daniel Deronda*, of previously published pieces, but these were widely scattered and it is good to have them brought together. The earliest piece, from 1933, states the classic case against *Work in Progress* – later to become *Finnegans Wake* (1939), and a key text for poststructuralist criticism – as having an organization that is 'external and mechanical' rather than informed by a vital principle (p.123). An essay of 1953 wittily dissects the American 'Great Books' programme, pointing out that, despite its democratic pretensions, very few could cope with its immense reading list, which in any case largely ignores American imaginative literature. In two pieces from the 1970s, Eugenio Montale's *Xenia* is accorded the remarkable distinction of being the one work written after 1930, and the only foreign-language work besides

Anna Karenina, to achieve major status in Leavis's canon. There are good essays on Blake and Wordsworth, weaker ones on Hardy and Hopkins, and poised evaluations of Coleridge, Arnold and James as critics. Most notable of all, however, and an unusual item in Leavis's *oeuvre*, is 'Memories of Wittgenstein', in which Leavis displays the skills of a novelist in vividly evoking Wittgenstein, himself, and a vanished Cambridge. The account of their first meeting – Leavis had followed Wittgenstein out of a social gathering to remonstrate about his rudeness to another guest – is memorable:

> I caught him up on the Barton Road... and, with my hands on my lapels as if (I later realized) I were about to take my coat off, said: 'You behaved in a disgraceful way to that young man'. He looked at me in surprise: 'I thought he was a foolish young man'. To which I returned, emphatically containing myself: 'You may have done, you may have done, but you had no right to treat him like that. You've no right to treat anyone like that'. It was my turn to be surprised. Putting his hand on my shoulder, he said: 'We must know one another' (pp.131-2).

This mixture of respect and combativeness continued throughout a human relationship which could be said to exemplify Leavis's relationship with philosophy as a discipline. It continues right into the last of his essays published in his lifetime, 'Mutually Necessary', which also closes this book. This is strident and ranting: but it is a final, unrepentant reiteration of Leavis's 'anti-philosophical' stance.

That stance is, in a sense, more necesssary than ever in the 1980s. Not only philosophy, but psychology, sociology, semiology, history and politics are invading literary studies. Demands like those of the 'Great Books' programme are now implicit in many first degree courses. It is important to realize that Leavis's elevation of literary studies is partly responsible for this. His consistent affirmation of the supremacy of literature as a mode of truth – the statement from 'Mutually Necessary' that 'the surest insight into human nature, human potentiality and the human situation is that accessible in the great creative writers' (p.192) is characteristic – gave those in literary studies (and Leavis certainly led the way here) the confidence to pronounce on topics which were supposedly the concern of other disciplines. This inevitably provoked challenges from outside. But greater challenges came from those within literary studies who, in exploring other disciplines in order further to understand the distinctive nature of their own, and to supplement its insights, realized that literature might be, in some respects, wanting: that, for example,

Lawrence's account of the mining industry in *Women in Love* might not stand up too well in the light of historical research.

Though Leavis's claims for literature were bound to provoke such challenges, he failed to provide adequate means of meeting them. He was right to reject conventional philosophical argument (of which, admittedly, he had rather a narrow idea) to sustain his case, but wrong to refuse, until very late in life, to adopt other methods of general explication. It was only with *The Living Principle* that he began to find a method of formulating his position (a suitable method being an important part of that position) which allowed both sustained exposition and close attention to literary texts. But he had little time to develop this further, and his rhetorical energy in defending a non-theorized approach to literature, even as he himself grew increasingly interested in theoretical issues, fitted in all too well with that British cultural complacency which in other ways he so strongly opposed. This meant that when the assault of new theoretical perspectives from abroad began, very little immediate resistance, at least of an intelligent kind, could be mustered.

The task for the future is to draw out the theoretical implications of Leavis's work (including the implications of his way of writing theory), while at the same time – and necessarily, since Leavis's theory is so often implicit in his practice – making a sustained revaluation of his close reading and of the canon he established (though not primarily in order to establish an alternative canon). Recent commentaries on Leavis have leant either towards eulogy (William Walsh) or hostility (Catherine Belsey). Geoffrey Strickland, in *Structuralism or Criticism* (1981) starts in the right direction when he contrasts Leavis and Barthes, but he stays too much under Leavis's spell. So the task lies ahead. Its magnitude is a measure of the magnitude of Leavis's achievement.

'Give up literary criticism!' is an injunction that Jonathan Culler has echoed in urging us to stop producing interpretations of literary texts and study instead the interpretative conventions which govern such productions. In practice, this is likely to mean producing interpretations of texts not by novelists and poets but by critics and philosophers. Culler's latest book, *On Deconstruction* (1983) exemplifies this. A sequel to *Structuralist Poetics* (1975), it is more austere, further removed from literature, than its predecessor. If we feel that Culler has sacrificed himself as a literary critic for this book, there can be no doubt that his ability to assimilate and elucidate a wide range of complex material has created, as in *Structuralist*

Poetics, a valuable resource, not only for literary critics, but also for the attentive general reader.

Culler challenges the distinction between structuralism and post-structuralism as too simple (though arguably it remains a useful simplification), and proposes instead to locate deconstruction within the issues raised by the recent critical interest, for example in the work of Stanley Fish and Wolfgang Iser, in readers and reading. Reader theories, Culler points out, are self-contradictory in that they appeal to a reader's experience but also aim to prescribe the nature of that experience. Feminist critics, for instance, may appeal to the experience of 'reading as a woman', but meet the difficulty that women often read as 'men', adopting the interpretative strategies of male-dominated criticism. Reader theories have to create a hypothetical reader who plays the lead role in a narrative of the desirable reading process, a 'story of reading'. This reflects a division within reading: to read is to play the role of a reader (there are, of course, many different roles). There are other difficulties. Most stories of reading have a happy ending, in which the reader-hero comes to understand and transcend his or her own experience, but can we really stand outside our own interpretative procedures in this way? What is 'in' the reader, what 'in' the text? Is text or reader 'in control'? Cruces of this kind relate to those which concern deconstruction.

For Culler deconstruction means, first of all, Derrida; and Culler identifies, in Derrida's work, three main aims. First, to reverse philosophical hierarchies – for instance, centre/margin, norm/deviation – in which the first term is superior to the second; such hierarchies – male/female is a vivid current example – inform our social and political systems so that to reverse them is, necessarily if indirectly, to challenge those systems. The second aim is rigorously to trace the genealogy of philosophical concepts, while demonstrating how that genealogy, like a family tree, constitutes itself by what it leaves out as well as by what it includes. Thirdly, deconstruction seeks to show that philosophical discourse is self-subverting by identifying its rhetorical features and the contradictions in its key concepts. In these respects, Derrida, like Leavis, is an anti-philosopher. His stance is even more paradoxical than Leavis's, however, because he is a philosopher and not a literary critic and because, as Culler stresses, his deconstructionist discourse inevitably employs the methods it challenges and acknowledges its own ineluctable implication in rhetorical modes and contradictions, its own 'deconstructability'.

Derrida has given particular attention, in studies of Plato, Rousseau, Husserl, Lévi-Strauss, and Condillac, to an especially pervasive concept in Western culture, 'phonocentrism': the hierarchy speech/writing in which speech is the natural, immediate source of a writing which is artificial, removed, secondary. Derrida suggests, however, that speech is as artificial as writing. The meaning of a spoken utterance, as of a written one, depends not on an intended meaning in the mind of a speaker, but on the language-system within which the utterance occurs and on other sign-systems by which the immediate context of the utterance is interpreted. Since both written and spoken utterances rely for their meaning on signifying conventions, and not on an originating consciousness, they share the quality of iterability, or repeatability: the capacity to function independently of their original producer and context. Spoken utterances, for example, can be quoted by others in conversation, or, today, recorded on tape. As repeatability has traditionally been the definitive characteristic of writing (the material marks on paper or other surfaces being merely a means to that repeatability), Derrida argues that speech, since it shares this characteristic, is a kind of writing.

In Rousseau's description of writing as a 'supplement' to speech, Derrida uncovers an interesting contradiction. A supplement is an addition to a totality – a dictionary, for example – which reveals that totality as lacking, but still remains external to it. This process of supplementarity is endless: a new edition of the dictionary, assimilating its supplements into a new totality, will soon be revealed as incomplete by further supplements. Similarly the many attempts in Western culture, of which Rousseau's is one, to affirm, in writing, the priority and fullness of speech, imply an original deficiency in speech which makes such written affirmation necessary. A further example is the kind of literary criticism – F.R. Leavis's, for instance – which affirms the organic wholeness of certain texts. If those texts are self-complete wholes, why is a supplementary discourse needed to affirm this?

Literary criticism is one example of the process that Derrida, playing on the etymological link between 'graph' and 'graft', calls 'grafting': the repetition or reinscription, in different contexts, of written or spoken utterances. Critics transfer, or graft, passages from the texts they discuss into the context of their own prose. Grafting also occurs in creative work: *The Waste Land*, for example, grafts all kinds of utterances into a new context, and subsequent poetry and prose has re-grafted these into further contexts. Direct quotation is the most obvious form of grafting, but it also occurs in parody, allusion, the transfer of structural and rhetorical modes, and so on. Since, for any utterance, new contexts can always arise, and since any attempt to describe exhaustively the range of possible contexts creates a new context which is not included in the description, meaning can never be finally determined.

The attempt to determine meaning by referring to an originating presence – a speaker present in his utterance, an author present in his text – exemplifies, for Derrida, the 'metaphysics of presence' which has dominated Western thought. This metaphysics is flawed, from Derrida's viewpoint, because 'presences' can always be reinterpreted as secondary constructs; we can always argue that it is language which creates the notions of, for example, an 'I' that speaks, or of a world of discrete objects – as it can be argued that reader theories appeal to a 'reader' which in fact they construct. Moreover, for Derrida as for Saussure, language is a system of differences without positive terms: the meaning of a word depends, not on a natural and direct link with a referent, but on all the other words from which it differs. A word is never simply present, but always relates to absence. Language is characterized by *différance*, Derrida's neologism which fuses the meanings of 'difference' and 'deferral': it is difference that makes utterances meaningful, but, since utterances can always be grafted into new contexts, the delivery of a final meaning is always deferred.

In Western culture, the ultimate deliverer of final meaning, the transcendent signified, is God. In Derrida's terms, God is the prime motif of the 'logocentrism' of the West: the stress on the Logos, origin ('In the beginning was the Word...and the Word was God', John 1:1), presence, and final meaning. God is also, of course, the Father; and Derrida has assented to the link which feminists have suggested between 'logocentrism' and 'phallocentrism' – the emphasis on the phallus, the Father, the husband, the male.

How have these ideas affected literary criticism? Culler picks out four main aspects. Firstly, deconstruction calls into question critical concepts such as 'text', 'reader', and indeed 'literature' itself. In a deconstructionist perspective, 'literature' is constituted by a process of exclusion – a canon leaves out much more than it puts in – which depends on hierarchies such as centre/margin and is reinforced institutionally, for example through syllabuses for English degrees. Secondly, deconstruction is a source of themes which can be traced in texts, such as writing, the deferral of meaning, the inversion of hierarchy. Thirdly, it provides an example of reading strategies: it demonstrates, for instance, how to read in a way that brings out the contradictions, the self-subverting activity of literary texts. This is how J. Hillis Miller uses it in *Fiction and Repetition*, his study of seven English novels. Finally, deconstruction offers a source of suggestions about the nature and goals of critical enquiry. Should such inquiry proceed by – to quote Leavis in *The Critic as Anti-Philosopher* – 'a scrutiny of the data' (p.23), or should it inquire instead into the processes by which it is decided, implicitly or explicitly, what the 'data' are and what 'a scrutiny' in fact involves? And how can the goal of critical inquiry be the definitive meaning of a text if the delivery of such a meaning is always deferred?

In the last part of *On Deconstruction*, Culler surveys some of the critics who have adopted deconstructionist approaches, discussing, for example, Walter Michaels's explorations of the contradictions in Thoreau's *Walden*, the work of Paul de Man, and Barbara Johnson's very interesting analysis of *Billy Budd* as, in her words, 'a dramatization of the twisted relations between knowing and doing, speaking and killing, reading and judging, which make political understanding and action so problematic' (quoted Culler, p.239; Barbara Johnson, *The Critical Difference*, p.108).

F.R. Leavis is excluded entirely from Culler's book, but it is interesting to ask how Leavis's work relates to deconstructionist concepts. We can see that Leavis defined a canon by a particularly rigorous process of exclusion depending on hierarchies such as norm/deviation and serious/nonserious (*Wuthering Heights* is a 'sport', *Tristram Shandy* is 'trifling': *The Great Tradition*, 1972 edn, pp.39, 10n.3). He also relied heavily on a speech/writing hierarchy, affirming, for example, that it was the fact 'that people talked' which made Shakespeare possible (*Critic as Anti-Philosopher*, p.127), and on a 'metaphysics of presence', an appeal to what is evidently *there*. His texts display the processes of both supplementarity (as noted above) and of grafting – the grafts of Lawrence which he so frequently makes are very interesting in this respect. But let us turn things upside down, and look at Derrida from Leavis's standpoint: Derrida then appears as the ultimate victim of the Cartesian split between the analytic mind and the phenomenon that it analyses. Derrida, of course, would see the 'analytic mind', the 'I that thinks' as a verbal construct, not as an ontological ground, and would regard rational analysis as incapable of operating in the non-contradictory way to which it lays claim: yet to doubt one's own grounds and procedures to this extent is not, in Leavis's terms, the break from Descartes that Derrida implies, but the extension of Cartesian scepticism to its reckless limit. The analytic, sceptical method, cut off from the totality of experience, cannot approach the real; that can only be approached, though never fully and exhaustively known, through the distinctive activity of language in 'great literary works'. And this activity is not one to which the criterion of contradiction, drawn from rational analysis, can appropriately be applied. In this respect, the critic must remain an 'anti-philosopher'.

2 I'm Not Complaining: Q.D. Leavis and Woman's Estate

In her autobiography, *Journey to the North* (1970), Storm Jameson praised Q.D. Leavis's devotion to F.R. Leavis and his career, 'to which she subordinated her own without, so far as I ever heard, a sigh' (p.234). Since Q.D. Leavis's death in 1974, we have heard of at least one sigh: Boris Ford, in a supplement to her *Times* obituary (26 March 1981, p.16), quoted from a letter in which she expressed resentment at not being credited as co-author of *Culture and Environment* (1933) and *The Great Tradition* (1948), and claimed to have written much of the latter, including its first chapter and all the footnotes – arguably its most impressive parts. This prompts the curious reflection that what we now think of as traditional English studies, which is currently under feminist attack as male-dominated, was shaped, to a significant extent, by a lady in man's disguise. A picture of the oppressed woman concurring in her own oppression starts to emerge. The picture is complicated, however: M.C. Bradbrook's memoir of Q.D. Leavis in *The Cambridge Review* presents a formidably dominating figure, while John Carey's account of the Leavis's collaboration in *The Listener* comes close to offering us the stereotype of the mild-mannered husband forced into aggression by an overpowering wife. The matter remains sketchy and anecdotal: an adequate account and assessment of Q.D. Leavis lies in the future. Provisionally, however, we can point to the contradiction in Q.D. Leavis's career between self-subordination and forthright aggression. In view of this, it is interesting to consider the attitudes to women – and feminism – in her work.

Some of these emerge strongly in her *Scrutiny* contributions in the 1930s. She accepts, on the authority of Margaret Mead, that 'many qualities and habits of feeling which we think sex-linked are the arbitrary results of social forms' ('Caterpillars of the commonwealth unite!', p.214); she also shows herself, however, a vigorous opponent of 'permissiveness' and a doughty defender of the values of home-keeping and child-rearing, stressing the duties and responsibilities of women and regarding humility as a virtue. For example, these are her remarks on Naomi Mitchison's novel *We Have Been Warned* (1935) and Amabel Williams-Ellis's novel *To Tell the Truth* (1933):

> In neither... can one find any trace of humility. To most of us... a woman who has brought up several children decently and kept a family sound and united on anything less than sixty shillings a week is an object of profound respect... To Mrs Williams-Ellis, however, she seems to be no more than a symbol of capitalist exploitation, while to Mrs Mitchison she only means reflections of the 'How horrible to have to live in such poky little rooms... Silly of her not to have found out about contraception' type. ('Lady Novelists and the Lower Orders', pp.128-9)

To counter what she regards as these fashionable misrepresentations, Q.D. Leavis adopts a tactic, popular in feminist criticism today, of citing as superior, in its expressiveness and veracity, a non-literary text by 'ordinary' women: *Life as We Have Known It* (1931; Virago, 1982), a collection of letters from Co-Operative working women to a General Secretary of the Co-Op Guild. It is interesting to note that the writers of these letters surely belong to that 'generality' typified, for Q.D. Leavis in *Fiction and the Reading Public* (1932), by Joyce's Gerty MacDowell, whose sensibilities have been ruined by cheap fiction (1979 edn, pp.195-6).

Disdain for feminism emerges in the diagnosis of Dorothy Richardson's 'pervasive weakness' as 'the feminine self-consciousness that has to find an outlet in some form of assertion or demand'. Q.D. Leavis goes on: 'The demand for mass rights can only be a source of embarrassment to intelligent women, who can be counted on to prefer being considered as persons rather than as a kind, just as they will wish to work out individual solutions to their problems' (*Scrutiny*, 4:3, p.330). This would be an explosive statement in some circles today. Equally provocative, given the current fashion of endowing women writers with status largely on grounds of gender, is the opening of her review of Ruth Adam's *I'm Not Complaining* (Chapman & Hall, 1938; Virago, 1983): 'It is pleasant to be able to recommend a novel by a woman novelist in strong terms' (*Scrutiny*, 7:1, p.81). She acknowledges that Ruth Adam is a feminist, but one whose heroine, Madge Brigson, 'makes feminism respectable if not interesting'. Q.D. Leavis admires, however, Madge's fundamental scepticism about political groups and causes: this was, of course, a characteristic Leavis stance to the end, and maintained with particular firmness during the 1930s when the pressure to 'commitment' was strong – as it is, once again, today.

Q.D. Leavis's greatest sally against a certain kind of feminism is her review of Virginia Woolf's *Three Guineas* as a 'let-down for our sex' and a self-indulgent 'release of sex hostility' (*Scrutiny*, 7:2, p.204,205). She stipulates that any female author who advocates 'equality of opportunity' for the sexes must have 'a highly developed character...a respectable intellect...[freedom] from mere sex-hostility...an at least masculine sense of responsibility...that capacity for self-criticism which [is] a mark of the best kind of masculine mind' and, above all, be 'capable of justifying her existence in any walk of life' (p.209). She vigorously affirms the compatibility of domestic responsibilies and mental development:

> I feel bound to disagree with Mrs Woolf's assumption that running a household and family unaided necessarily hinders or weakens thinking. One's own kitchen and nursery...is the realm where living takes place...The activities Mrs Woolf wishes to free educated women from as wasteful not only provide a valuable discipline, they serve as a sieve for determining which values are important and genuine and which are conventional and contemptible. (pp.210-11)

Clearly, domestic responsibilities did not hinder Q.D. Leavis's thinking about *The Great Tradition*. Though the notion of the author as the source and guarantor of a text's meaning has come under strong attack in recent years, our response to that seminal book would undoubtedly alter somewhat if we took Q.D. Leavis as its joint – or as seems possible, main – author. Particularly, perhaps, in regard to its view of women. Take, for instance, the statement, understandably singled out by feminist criticism as darkly exemplary, that George Eliot's mind was 'in no respect disabled by being a woman's' (*Great Tradition*, p.100n.). This is in a footnote – and Q.D. Leavis, by her own testimony as reported by Boris Ford, wrote all the footnotes.

The distinct impatience with feminine 'silliness' evident in her *Scrutiny* contributions recurs in *The Great Tradition* in the sharp put-downs of certain kinds of femininity – as represented by Rosamond Vincy in *Middlemarch*, for instance. Was it Q.D. Leavis who wrote, of Rosamond: 'the reader certainly catches himself, from time to time, wanting to break that graceful neck' (p.84)? Obviously, lacking substantive evidence, such questioning could degenerate into a pointless guessing game; but it does highlight the problematic status of women in *The Great Tradition* – and in the 'great tradition'.

Q.D. Leavis had her own, strong ideas of a desirable femininity to oppose to both 'silliness' and what she saw as irresponsible feminism. This is evident when she praises Ruth Adam's attitude, in *I'm Not Complaining*, as that of 'an uncompromisingly intelligent woman, contemptuous of the unreal – sentimentality, idealism and any kind of emotional silliness' (*Scrutiny*, 7:1, p.82). M.C. Bradbrook suggests that in Q.D. Leavis's later work on the Victorian novel, an ideal of the Victorian heroine starts to develop, drawn from both fiction and fact – Esther Summerson in *Bleak House*, that 'exemplary woman of letters', the hard-pressed Mrs Oliphant ('Introduction', *Autobiography and Letters of Mrs Oliphant*, 1974, p.9). It is notable that in her introduction to Mrs Oliphant's *Miss Marjoribanks* (1866), Q.D. Leavis cites with approval the Victorian novelist's 'campaign against false Victorian values in regard to women' (1969 edn, p.15), but stresses her rejection of female emancipation as represented by the contemporary Women's Rights movement and John Stuart Mill.

Q.D. Leavis's ideal of the heroine is summed up in her final lecture, 'The Englishness of the English Novel', delivered in 1980. The lecture is, in a sense, a confirmation in the 1980s of the gloomier predictions in the early 1930s of *Fiction and the Reading Public*. She might have called it: I told you so. Though her condemnation of modern novelists is wholesale – Graham Greene, Angus Wilson, John Fowles, and others, are all struck from the bright book of life – her remarks on the female variety are especially pointed. Looking characteristically to the past, she identifies in English literature the type of the 'Protestant heroine', exemplified by 'high-minded young women who with dauntless courage act upon the findings of the individual conscience' (p.163). This type starts with Shakespeare's girl heroines (sometimes forced, like Q.D. Leavis herself, into male disguise) and continues through Clarissa, Jeanie Deans, Fanny Price, Dorothea Brooke, Laura Fountain (in Mrs Humphry Ward's *Helbeck of Bannisdale*, 1898), Anna Tellwright. These are compared unfavourably to the submissive Catholic heroines of European novels such as Balzac's *Eugenie Grandet* (1833) or Manzoni's *The Betrothed* (1827).

Now, however, this heroine has vanished, and the great tradition of major and minor women novelists who, from the eighteenth century, did so much to sustain and develop her, seems to have ended. Today's women novelists appear to Q.D. Leavis determined to renounce their English heritage for 'an international women writers' movement...characterized by a jargon that is the opposite of wisdom or maturity' (p.169). With her habit, already well-established by the time of *Fiction and the Reading Public*, of generalizing from cursory evidence, she uses a publisher's catalogue to support her claim that women novelists now aim to glorify the egotistical pursuit of self (including sexual)-fulfilment. Their work is contrasted unflatteringly with a novel of 1938: *I'm Not Complaining*, by Ruth Adam. Clearly that book, reviewed long ago in *Scrutiny*, had stayed with her; it is 'memorable for, among other things, its abnegation' (p.170).

Q.D. Leavis's abnegation – which seems to have been combined, to an extent yet to be determined, with considerable, if covert, power – was supported by a strong idea of a desirable femininity, with which she opposed both docile submissiveness and committed feminism. On the one hand, this idea of femininity was a very literary one, as her final lecture makes clear; she seems to have identified as strongly with her favoured heroines as those despised readers of popular romances identified with theirs. On the other hand, it was based on the practical experience of combining domestic responsibilities with intellectual endeavour. It seems possible that the complexities of her position bear some relation to the discourses of literary criticism which she, a formative and formidable influence, helped to construct. But such an investigation should not discount her critique of feminism: as she pointed out – it is a constant Leavis theme – there is a complacency, not only of conservatism, but of enlightenment.

3 Hegemony by Other Means

Culture abhors a vacuum. Is this why English culture, for so long notable, or notorious, for its insularity, has in recent years so uneasily resisted, has indeed sometimes avidly welcomed, the dazzling iconoclasms and dramatic inversions of structuralism and, more especially, of poststructuralism? Did it sense its own hollowness and try to fill it with imported commodities? In any case, the result is clear: Empedocles has thrown all things about, and we dwell now in fruitful chaos. This holds great risks and opportunities; *Re-Reading English* (1982) epitomizes some of the risks.

From the viewpoint of a socialist commitment and a materialist criticism, this collection of essays prescribes, with varying emphases, drastic remedies for today's 'crisis' in English studies in higher education: remedies which could have far-reaching effects, especially since the academy has, at present, an excessive influence on literary culture. Peter Widdowson, the editor, outlines these remedies in his Introduction. It is necessary to examine the history and current practices of English studies and literary criticism; challenge concepts of literature, the text, and literary value; study, along with 'literary' texts and without necessarily making qualitative distinctions, 'non-literary' texts and other media such as film and television; and draw on the methodologies, concepts and findings of fields of study like history and sociology.

Part I of the book, 'History, theory, institutions', is, apart from Brian Doyle's essay, the more restrained. Tony Davies offers some witty insights into how the approved teaching methods of seminar and tutorial compel the literary academic, whatever his ostensible theoretical perspective, to employ, in discussion with his students, a 'commonsense', empirical, fragmentary approach to his subject. A critical survey of poststructuralism, commendable for its compressed clarity, is provided by Peter Brooker, who points out, not with approval, that, at present, the 'commonsense' approach offers reasons for reading books, and reading English, which poststructuralism cannot yet give. John Hoyles considers Marxist and radical theories of literature, from Lukács and Adorno to Williams and Eagleton, and advocates the development of a radical poetics, building on Bakhtin's sociological poetics, in which literature is an agency of radical change precisely because it is a source of liberating pleasure. There are also explorations of the influence on English courses of the Open University and the Council for National Academic Awards, and a fascinating piece by Michael Green on the Birmingham Centre for Contemporary Cultural Studies, which argues that Cultural Studies should not freeze into an academic discipline but retain a critical, challenging role, especially towards the orthodoxies of English, history, and sociology. All these essays, while naturally provoking disagreement at times, are stimulating and judicious. One hopes that it will not lower Peter Humm's status with his radical colleagues to say that this is also true of his comparison, in Part II of this book, between the flow, bizarre juxtapositions and open-endedness of television, and postmodernist fictions such as those of Barthelme and Brautigan.

These quieter presences, however, serve less to restrain than to legitimate the strident, hectoring voices which dominate *Re-Reading English*. These can be heard mainly in Part II. Their tone, with one quaint exception, is captured to the point of caricature (but it is vehemently in earnest, unfortunately) in this sentence of Tony Bennett's, which includes most of the obligatory terms:

> From the point of view of a thoroughgoing materialism, the text is a site on which varying meanings and effects may be produced according to the determinations within which the work is inscribed – determinations which are never single and given but plural and contested, locked in relations of struggle. (pp.234-5)

Let us, however, attend to these voices: they speak of what could be the future.

Brian Doyle's revelation of the 'hidden history of English studies', though in Part I, belongs in spirit to Part II. English studies, Doyle argues, had their origins in courses on English culture and character which were developed as a means of social control, of imposing a false sense of national unity. As higher education grew more professionalized, English emerged as an autonomous discipline which concealed its ideological structure beneath a fetishized notion of the text and of literary value. Doyle's reductionist approach turns those who fostered English studies into the hapless agents of bourgeois hegemony, and dispenses with the need to confront notions of the text and of literary value as serious ideas in their own right; they are sufficiently explained, and exploded, by exposing their ideological function.

Opening Part II in earnest, Catherine Belsey, whom no one could accuse of lacking ambition, directs her reductionism against F.R. Leavis. Leavis claims to *discover* certain values in the novels of the 'great tradition', but in fact, Belsey argues, he is *selecting* a range of novels which can be made, by a critical discourse that restricts the plurality of their meanings, to conform to the values that he believes, erroneously, to be his own (they are, of course, constituted by ideological discourses). To compound his sins, Leavis, in presenting his discriminations between novels as discriminations between the subjectivities of their authors, creates a hierarchy of subjectivities. Ultimately, his critical discourse rests on the bourgeois myth of the transcendent human subject existing prior to all discourse and all social (as distinct from individual) hierarchies.

The conversion of Leavis's criticism into an ideological product means that we no longer have to take his judgements and values seriously, except as proof of his hopeless entanglement in bourgeois mythology. But Belsey's reductionist sword spares her own discourse, and she creates, if not a hierarchy of subjectivities, certainly a hierarchy of discourses, leaving us in no doubt, for example, that her feminist reading of *Daniel Deronda*, though not claiming finality, is superior to Leavis's banal interpretation. And of course, her whole essay constitutes a ranking of her critical discourse above Leavis's. She ranks it higher not because she can show, in the theoretical perspective in which she condemns Leavis, that it is superior, but because she judges it to be morally preferable. She rejects the Leavisian critical discourse not only, as she would have us believe, because of its rational contradictions, but on moral grounds. This comes home when she hints darkly that the phrase 'judgment of relative human value' in *The Great Tradition* should, when the book was first published in 1948, have been 'spine-chilling', 'in the context of the judgement of relative human value which led to the concentration camps' (p. 128).

Antony Easthope, like Belsey, attacks the notion of the transcendent human subject, this time in the criticism of poetry. He scorns the notion that poems give us the living voices of their authors: poems are sternly defined as nothing but artifice, in which language creates an illusion of human presence. He analyses a sonnet by Sidney in these terms. But Easthope's whole case rests on the absurd supposition that the unradicalized reader conflates his experience of presence in reading a poem with the empirical conviction that the poet is actually, if rather mysteriously, there: the error of the dog peering down the gramophone horn. In fact, that experience of presence is characterized precisely by its knowledge of an absence; the poet is not there, and the reader knows it; if he did not, he would not be reading but experiencing vision or hallucination. Easthope talks about poetry like a medieval priest detailing, with disgust, the physiology of women, and his aim is similar: to combat the seductions, the seven veils of poems, those dangerous snares on the path of (political) righteousness. His reductionism, like Belsey's, starts from an unacknowledged, unexplored moral stance.

The essays of Derek Longhurst, Carole Snee, and Wendy Mulford deal more directly with pedagogic matters. Longhurst wants to displace the myth of Shakespeare as the source of 'timeless' values and as England's national poet by making students examine the modes of cultural production in Elizabeth and Jacobean times and consider the varying interpretations of Shakespeare which have been made in criticism, teaching, the theatre, and on television. Snee advocates a problem or topic-centred 'period study' where 'any "texts" studied have an initial common status' (p.166), and close-reading techniques can be applied to them all. She tries to 'close-read' a government report, with predictable results: government reports, characteristically, don't offer any very interesting local life for inspection. Mulford recommends exploring the social and political force constituted by the writers of a period, and as an example looks at Elizabeth Robins's suffrage propaganda novel *The Convert* (1907), and at the work and organization of the Women Writers' Suffrage League. All these contributors skirt round issues of literary value (though Mulford's interesting essay approaches them, then draws back). But they may find that their students, subjected to these new regimes, become, like Robert Graves, a trifle temperamental. Most students will know already, not from bourgeois ideology but through their experience of reading, that they prefer some authors to others, and they may well ask: Why shouldn't we study those, instead of plodding through government reports or suffragette pamphlets? The reply that social and political change is more important than reading 'good' texts evades the real issue, which is: Why is such change so important? To explore this would mean starting to talk, once again, about values and experiences; and that might well lead to considering 'good' texts (*Measure for Measure*, say) as complex engagements with values and experiences that subvert the simplicities of commitment.

The joint essay by David Craig and Michael Egan follows an antique drum. They not only prefer some authors to others, but express their approbation in terms like these: 'images of striking sensuousness...grows organically...concrete enactment' (pp.213, 214). The correlation they assert between the presence of these qualities in a text and its (left-wing) historical veracity cannot deflect the diagnosis: they are terminal cases of left-Leavisism. But Tony Bennett's concluding essay lasers through this cancer, urging us to study how the meanings of texts are differently produced by critics in different historical circumstances, and to mobilize texts strategically in the interests of class struggle.

Re-Reading English is the manifesto for a cultural revolution. Like that other cultural revolution of which we once heard so much, its scope is, in a sense, comically limited. The State will not topple; in general, lecturers in English, even a radicalized, mobilized English, are not the stuff of which revolutionaries are made. But in the academy, and in the wider literary culture, the forces represented by this book pose a major challenge. It is, centrally, a challenge to experience: an attempt to appropriate and restrict the possibilities of experience, starting with, but inevitably not confining itself to, the experience of reading literature. Attempts like this have, perhaps, always been inherent in the criticism and teaching of literature, though often balanced by a capacity to liberate us into new, more complex experience. But the radical discourse exemplified in *Re-Reading English* seeks a greater control over experience than ever before. It does not, as its proponents naïvely imagine, break with the supposedly repressive discourses of the past; it maintains and extends them. It is a continuation of hegemony by other means.

Since this discourse is, or tries to be, rationalist and materialist, there are areas of experience, some of the most important, that must escape it. But it can, by the very manner of its articulation, block off or hinder access to its quiet domains. It can constitute a forgetting of experience, and that, prolonged over generations, would indeed be an injustice and an oppression.

This is ironic; for those who, in this book, promote this discourse, assert the priority of radical change in order to end injustice and oppression. This assertion necessarily entails a belief in experience, in a human subject who experiences. Without such a belief, injustice and oppression would not matter, except in some remote aesthetic or quasi-mathematical sense: there would be no one to suffer by it. But their discourse works to deny the human subject, to deny experience; to deny, in fact, the foundation of their radical values.

The challenge represented by *Re-Reading English* must be met. English literary culture – the dominant version of it, at any rate – rested too long on a comfortable assurance of superiority, and when it felt weak, it could always invoke F.R. Leavis to strengthen and sustain: the enemy of cultural laziness was also, ironically, its guarantee. Meanwhile, new forces, new approaches, were quietly gaining ground, and suddenly we found them everywhere, challenging, stimulating, provoking creative reappraisal, and, as in this book, uttering threats. Against those threats, reactionary ire, liberal complacency, conjurations of Leavis's ghost, are no longer any defence. We need, rather, to concentrate on the regeneration of English literary culture. In that, the writing and reading of poems, novels and plays must come first. But critics and teachers, in their necessarily subordinate roles, can help in several ways: by attending to the writing that has been going on (is still going on) while criticism has been sick of self-love; by considering the images of England produced by English literary culture; by taking account of, but not trying to appropriate, the challenges and findings of cultural studies; by critically assimilating, with a necessary recognition of their otherness, foreign literatures and modes of thought; by recognizing and encountering the complex, fascinating interpenetrations of literary and moral values; and by acknowledging and exploring the experience of reading. All the rest is criticism; but these activities will lead, irresistibly, to literature.

4 The Politicization of English

Ignore them and they'll go away: this was the initial response to proposals for radical change in English studies in higher education. They didn't go away, and other tactics were hastily adopted: blundering attacks, which proved counter-productive. Now we have reached a third stage: 'repressive tolerance' bordering on complacency. Professor John Bayley, for example, assures us that there is nothing really wrong in the state of English, and invokes – with a rather unhappy echo of a former President of the United States – the 'silent majority' of students (should English students be silent?) who remain unaffected by the agitations of a 'minority of activists' (*Times Literary Supplement*, 10 June 1983, p.587). Bayley is right, of course, to say that talk of a 'crisis' in English studies is journalistic cliché, but his promise of peace in our time rings false, and that 'minority of activists' itself smacks of journalistic cliché. There are, of course, some History Men – and Women – now active in English; but we are dealing with not a conspiracy but a complex movement of individuals, activities, and ideas, represented by at least some of the books of the 'New Accents' series, and, most recently, by Terry Eagleton's *Literary Theory* (1983); by magazines such as *Red Letters* and *Literature and History*; and by the pressure group 'Literature Teaching Politics'. Complex though this movement is, however, one main aim can, and must, be identified and challenged: the politicization of English. The intention is to appropriate the field of English studies in higher education (and elsewhere) for political purposes. Now, given the current balance of forces in higher education, such a project, in the immediate future at least, will have limited success: but the possible influence of those working for it on the whole field of English studies, and especially in those establishments of higher education where the committed are already the dominant group, should not be underestimated.

The argument for a politicized English runs like this. The notion of literature and of a canon of literary texts is an ideological construct which helps to sustain the assumptions of unjust and repressive societies, including our own. Literature, however, conceals its ideological origin and function, and presents itself as a disinterested repository of 'universal values', offers a dehistoricized image of 'Eternal Man' (woman is marginalized). The discipline of English, it is argued, developed in the nineteenth century to take over some of the ideological duties which a declining Christianity could no longer perform: promoting an illusion of national unity, concealing the class divisions of society, diverting attention from the political to the personal, strengthening bourgeois hegemony. Matthew Arnold wanted literature to replace dogma, but because of its ideological function, literature, certainly as the academic discipline of 'English', had to harden into a dogma, with a fixed canon of texts, a set of unquestioned fundamentals, and a carefully restricted field of explicit activity ('close reading' and evaluation of 'the texts themselves'). It is now necessary to expose this ideological function, and abolish or sharply displace the category of literature: English is already covertly politicized, and should now be overtly so, but to different ends.

It is not quite clear what these ends are. To take some representative examples: Antony Easthope advocates 'the democratic election of everybody in power in place of work and elsewhere in the community' (*Guardian*, 16 March 1983, p.12). Well, that might put a few radical English lecturers out of a job. Terry Eagleton calls for 'a specific, living and practical democracy' rather than the 'abstract one of the ballot box' (*Literary Theory*, p.207), but it is his form of democracy which sounds abstract. And listen to this:

> To those who want literary criticism to remain innocuous...I can have nothing persuasive to say, except perhaps to suggest that for anyone who is not a white, heterosexual, Anglo-Saxon, Protestant, employed male, it is surely possible to imagine a world which would be the better for change...Foucault's work...offers...a way of analysing the play of meaning in literary texts in the interests of change. ('Problems of Literary Theory: The Problem of Meaning', p.181)

So that's it, the poststructuralist panacea: critics of the world, unite! Catherine Belsey can, of course, always be relied upon as a chic guide to the vanities of critical enlightenment, and we can turn to her also to exemplify the level of political analysis which characterizes much contemporary committed criticism. 'Reagan,' she tells us, 'is preparing to reduce us all to radioactive rubble to preserve our freedom' ('Literature, History, Politics', p.20). This, presumably, is when he isn't getting hot under the collar about that bonfire burning in his own backyard. Such references – to nuclear weapons, unemployment, strikes, economic crisis, class struggle – are the radical critic's moral guarantee, her/his way of saying that, while your average English lecturer closes the common-room door on politics and huddles over the feeble stove of humane values, s/he's where the action is – in imagination at least, breaking into the airbase, throwing flour at the Prime Minister, even, when the fancy takes her/him, fighting in the odd guerilla war or two. To 'confront' politics and history in this way means, all too often, taking for reality a modern morality play (villains: American capitalism, late monopoly capitalism; heroes: guerilla fighters, the workers, etc.) and condemning as apathetic and insensitive those who reject this package-deal of virtues and vices and who feel, in any case, that scattering political clichés in literary essays, while it may produce a vivid glow of self-righteousness in the critic, won't help workers or guerillas one jot or tittle.

In a sense, however, the pressure to politicize English can be seen as a development of a traditional aspect of the discipline: its social mission. Surely the aim of English studies – sometimes coinciding with, though not necessarily reducible to, its ideological function – was always to make a better world, or at least a better society in England: hasn't it failed through not being political enough? Now it is true that the social reach of English in the past certainly seems to have exceeded its grasp, and any positive results it may have achieved are difficult, if not impossible, to identify and quantify. But the radical critique of the supposed ineffectualness of traditional English seems, in a sense, complicit with the capitalist-utilitarian demand that humanities subjects should show tangible results; the link between the popularization of this critique and economic pressure on higher education departments to justify themselves in cost-benefit terms is hardly coincidental. Also significant is the currency of notions of 'critical production', of 'productive' ways of reading texts: notions not a world away from those ideas of 'higher productivity' close to Mrs Thatcher's heart. Was traditional English so 'unproductive', so lacking in influence? The example of *Scrutiny* (which has now, rather strangely perhaps, come to represent 'traditional' English) suggests otherwise. It is true that many of its wider social aims went unrealized; but there is no doubt – even acknowledging the difficulty of quantification – that its influence was extraordinary (though not, necessarily, wholly to the good). And it is arguable that its influence was due, in part, to its refusal to commit itself to an explicit political ideology, even in the 1930s when, as now, the pressure to do so was very strong. Much of the 'committed' criticism of the 1930s was by comparison ephemeral, ineffective. There is, of course, the case put by Francis Mulhern in *The Moment of Scrutiny* (1979), that the ultimate failure of *Scrutiny*'s social programme was inevitable, given its refusal to assume a more directly political, quasi-Marxist cast; but to have done so would have thwarted some aspects of its social programme anyway. And it seems unlikely that the effects of politicized English – even if it achieved hegemony within higher education – would be any greater than that of *Scrutiny*'s upon the wider political world: indeed, they might well be less. If its current rhetoric is anything to go by, a politicized English would hardly be likely to raise the level of political debate, and its attempts to intervene in the political arena would simply be brushed aside by the powers that be: they may, in fact, welcome it as a safety-valve for energies that might be more dangerous if employed in direct political action.

The major effects of politicized English would be within the academy; but while the *content* of English studies would change – perhaps out of all recognition – the form in which that content was transmitted, the fact that something had to be taught and assessed, would remain largely the same. Most radical English lecturers would be no more inclined to give up their power and status than the most self-satisfied liberal humanist dozing in the old armchair of the Great Tradition, not only for reasons of self-interest, but also because they would need such power and status in order to impose, by various means, a politicized English upon students. This English would have its canon, of course: a canon not of novels, poems and plays, but of works of theory which would include, say, Saussure, Bakhtin, Althusser, Barthes, Lacan, Derrida, Foucault. Among these sacred texts, a consensus will emerge and be adjusted: it will be, once more, a matter of a shifting hierarchy; who loses and who wins, who's in, who's out. Indeed, this is already the case: Foucault's star is in the ascendant at present, but how long before the whirligig of fashion swings it down to earth? The scriptures of theory, like those of literature, will generate, are generating, a canon, and with these, too, a canon will form, indeed is forming: Hawkes, Belsey and Bennett are now well-established on students' reading-lists and in bibliographies; Eagleton's latest is automatically in, and Antony Easthope has now launched his claim for canonization. Literature is refracted through theory and then through commentary. Harassed students, who after all have their degrees to get as well as their teachers' revolution to make, will be forced to catch the sense of literary texts at two removes, if at all.

It is, surely, the theme for a modern *Dunciad*: mediocrity collapsing towards chaos. Yet it remains vitally important that a community of readers – in higher education, students and teachers – should, in recreative reading, experience literary texts, which in Britain primarily means the texts of English literature. This is not to deny that English, as a discipline, should look into its own history, examine its own grounds and methods, take advantage of the wide range of interpretative strategies, of theoretical perspectives, of philosophical enquiries available to literary studies – a range far wider, in fact, than that represented by the politicized canon of theory. Nor is it to assert that English is 'politically neutral': like any academic discipline, it occurs in, and is informed by, a specific political situation. But the *extent* to which it is political varies: some now seek to politicize it with a totalitarian thoroughness. Certainly the study of English should, and always will unless artifically constricted, lead out into cultural, social and political considerations, but it can only contribute positively to those if it remains a distinctive discipline, centred in the recreative reading of English literary texts.

These texts offer today the fullest use of the English language – of its experiential, evaluative and exploratory possibilities. This language is not an 'organic unity': it shows, in its development, tensions, splits, contradictions; but its fruitful fusions and broad, creative coalescences make it a genuinely communal achievement of human experience and responsibility. This achievement is now being lost. It is no regressive nostalgia to remark the impoverishment of modern English, as represented in the newspapers, on the radio, and – especially – on television, which has become the chief shaping influence on the language. And the rapid development of microcomputer and video technology is currently effecting a shift away from the spoken and written word more decisive than that produced by television. This impoverishment of language is an impoverishment of the possibilities of experience, and not only for a few. Literary texts, read recreatively, keep the common creation of the English language alive in its most complex forms, and potentially available for culture and society.

Literary texts are not simply 'windows on the world', giving direct access to an external reality; they are not the direct, unmediated reports of 'speaking subjects', though the work of creative individuals ('authors') situated in, but not wholly determined by, specific historical contexts, is essential. Such texts constitute explorations of the interrelationships in the human world, between language and reality, truth and illusion, value and meaning (which are not, as literature itself shows us, clear-cut binary distinctions). If literary texts endure, they do so because they attain a certain level (never rigidly fixed) of complexity in their explorations: a complexity not attainable by works in other discursive modes, for example philosophy, except in so far as they become literature. And literary works are valued according to the degree of their complexity, though criteria of complexity change, to some extent, with historical circumstances, and thus the canon – never static – changes. Such complexity is not, necessarily, that of 'organic form', of a rich, unified plenitude; it may be complexity of a deconstructive or polysemous kind. Arguably, in fact, the texts which seem to form the best 'organic wholes' are also among the most deconstructable or polysemous (*Middlemarch*, for example). But one cannot begin from deconstructive or polysemous readings: these operations are dependent on an awareness of the constructive, semantically unifying forces in the text, and of the differences between those and its deconstructive or polysemous potential. Even if the aim is to turn students into effective deconstructors or 'producers' of polysemy, it is necessary to 'construct' them, as 'competent reading subjects', first; to teach – to encourage students to learn, practise, experience, enjoy – recreative reading: reading which assumes that the text has an overall meaning that can be experienced but not paraphrased, and endeavours to recreate this by disciplined, sensitive responsiveness both to the text's local particulars and to its constructive and unifying possibilities (which may operate at deep levels). This remains the primary reading activity, without which deconstruction, or polysemous 'production', would not be possible. Those texts, especially modernist and postmodernist ones, which appear to be already deconstructed, polysemous, in fact continue to depend for their distinctive identity and activity on assumptions of coherence and semantic unity from which they depart. The constructive, unifying strategy of recreative reading is a necessary preliminary to identifying such texts, and, even if a deconstructive or polysemous approach is then adopted, must remain present as a 'background' against which the textual features that concern such approaches are foregrounded. With many texts, however, recreative reading is the best way of letting them yield up what they can offer.

The function of literature in relation to politics is to bring to bear on our political thought and action considerations of human reality and value. It does this not, primarily, by realistic representation, and certainly not by offering static notions of 'human nature' and 'universal values', but by complex explorations of the interrelationships – experiential, evaluative, linguistic, semantic – within which we live our lives, interrelationships that enable us to arrive at valid truth and value judgements upon political and other matters, but also make such judgements very difficult to reach and implement. The study of literature does not, in itself, endorse bourgeois conformity: it has always provoked dissent, of many kinds, from the status quo; it offers no easy answers. Literary texts both press upon us considerations of human reality and value, and show why they may not, in perception, thought and action, prevail: in this, they disrupt theoretical simplifications. Inevitably those, in English departments and elsewhere, who have fled a disturbing reality into such simplifications experience such literature as a scandal, an outrage, to be suppressed, extirpated. No need, of course, to burn books; now, there are subtler methods.

5 Rotten Reconstruction

A correspondent in the *Times Higher Education Supplement* recently urged more effective resistance to the bid by a radical caucus to dictate the future of literature studies in England (*THES*, 25 February 1983, p.31). *Reconstructing Literature* (1983) is clearly – despite the feeble equivocations of its editor, Laurence Lerner – an attempt at resistance, but it is hardly effective: on the contrary, it plays into the hands of the opposition. That 'seminar of radical students' invoked by Lerner in his Introduction (p.17) could spend an enjoyable two hours demolishing this book one imagines; they may feel, however, that they have better things to do.

Lerner, quoting a correspondent's deprecation of the 'dismissive contempt' of new ideas in literature studies in England, says: 'Well, we [in this volume] can all I hope claim to have avoided *that*' (p.9). But *that* is precisely what has not been avoided: all too often, *Reconstructing Literature* adopts a patronizing, condescending tone. This is most evident in Cedric Watts's contributions: that he appears twice in this collection suggests the difficulty Lerner must have had in recruiting top-rank contributors. Watts is like a middle-order, minor counties batsman who has suddenly, astonishingly, been called up to play for England: the effect, inevitably, is comic and pitiful by turns. If he had simply tried to keep his wicket, we might forgive and forget: but he attempts, in his first essay, to hit sixes off every ball. Now his main opponent is Barthes, and Barthes is not only a whole bowling attack in himself, but also has the disconcerting habit of changing the rules of the game, or indeed walking off the field – the French have never appreciated cricket.

Most of Watts's valid points have already been made by competent reviewers. It is, indeed, wrong to say that there is no extra-linguistic reality, that we should totally ignore the author, that the signifier can easily float free of the signified or referent: but it is also wrong to pretend that these issues are irrelevant to literary studies, or solvable by hasty, impatient appeals to 'commonsense'. Take, for instance, Watts's statement: 'authors patently do exist as flesh-and-blood people writing tangible works' (p.27). The matter, patently, is more complex. Most of the authors studied on literature courses are dead, and even when we read a work by a living author, that author no longer exists as a flesh-and-blood person writing that particular work. And in what sense is a work – as distinct from a manuscript or book – tangible?

Watts blunders badly when he attributes to Barthes the notion that a text means whatever its reader chooses. All Barthes's work can be seen as an exploration of the constraints on meaning, and while Watts's reading of Barthes has obviously been sketchy, an elementary primer should have alerted him to the dictum in *Critique et Vérité* (1966): 'You can't make meaning just anyhow (if you don't believe me, try)' (p.65). Watts, of course, like a vulgar Barthesian, does try: he takes Barthes's argument that a text's meaning cannot be guaranteed by its author as an argument that a text can mean whatever one likes, thus proving Barthes' point: it can't be done. Finally, Watts hits his own wicket when he follows his attack on the idea that literary works consist of binary oppositions with a claim that *The Winter's Tale* creates a world 'which blends the base and the lyrical, the mundane and the miraculous, the immediate and the mythical' (p.34). A touch of the binaries here!

There's no holding this man, though: when he comes in for his second innings, he takes on Lévi-Strauss. Against Lévi-Strauss's formulation of the meaning of the Oedipus myth – that '[t]he overrating of blood relations is to the underrating of blood relations as the attempt to escape autochthony is to the impossibility to succeed in it' (quoted, p.110) – Watts offers an older, staler form of reductionism: this, for example, is his comment on the moment when, in a production of *King Oedipus*, the eyeless King appeared on the palace steps: 'The image appeared to reflect man, striving yet erring, heroic yet blundering, thinking he can master the world yet capable of blundering into destruction; it appeared to sum up many appalling aspects of human history' (p.116).

Oh dear: it's 'Eternal Man' again: the tired clichés of a bankrupt academicism. We may note not only the consoling reduction of the real sufferings of human history to an academic spectacle, but also, once more, the slide towards binary oppositions. Watts' response to Sophocles as to Shakespeare seems indeed to demonstrate one of Lévi-Strauss's basic claims: that the function of myth is to reconcile the intolerable contradictions of reality.

John Holloway, in his contribution, praises the virtues of intellectual caution and humility – indeed, at moments, the shade of Uriah Heep hovers near – but unfortunately he does not display these qualities when dealing with recent French thinkers. He pretends to by confessing that he finds such thinkers 'obscure' (p.62). Barthes exposed this tactic long ago in *Mythologies* (1957): 'one believes oneself to have such sureness of intelligence that acknowledging an inability to understand calls in question the clarity of the author and not that of one's own mind' (1973 edn, p.34). And the evasive circumlocutions of Holloway's own style sometimes read like an attempt to create an impression of fastidious thought made by a pedantic buffoon – more matter with less art! But Holloway's discussion of Saussure, when he gets down to it, is subtle and interesting. He cites Saussure's distinction between signification and value: for example, 'sheep' and '*mouton*' have the same signification in English and French, but their value is different; we do not have, in English, 'sheep stew'. He also instances Saussure's claim that the value of *some* terms is determined by their relation to other terms in a given group – thus the value of sheep is determined by its difference from 'mutton'. In Holloway's view, however, Saussure goes on to imply that the values of *all* terms are determined by their relation to other terms and that values, in effect, create significations. Thus the distinction between signification and value is blurred. Holloway asks whether any term can be defined by the fact that it is not another term – 'Can that process of "negative definition" be maintained indefinitely, round and round as it were, so as to cover, in the end, the language as a whole?' (p.75) – and wonders if there might be some basic distinction between the system of language sounds – which is, indeed, a system of phonemic differences – and the system of language words or terms. This is fruitful matter for debate.

Gabriel Josipovici argues that writing fiction involves a basic trust in the meaningfulness of time, in the act of writing, which Barthes lacks: thus he is 'the most intelligent critic of his generation' (p.81), but – this is the implication – no more. Characteristically, Josipovici's essay is interesting but disorganized, and he makes some curious statements: for example, that Barthes was 'a great showman' (p.102), while Proust 'seems never to have felt the need to impress' (p.104), and that 'Barthes and Derrida live out their lives in the classroom; Proust and Auden do not' (p.103). But Auden, arguably, spent his life showing off to the equivalent of a classroom of clever schoolboys, and Proust's withdrawal, like Joyce's, was surely an oblique form of showmanship.

Roger Scruton's contribution seems – unexpectedly, perhaps – genuinely unassuming and exploratory. It tackles the question: is there any objective limit to critical interpretation? Scruton argues that we can distinguish meaning from association in such interpretation by appealing to a publicly accessible tradition carried on in a common culture. The difficulty is obvious: it is never clear what a tradition, or common culture, is; at any given time, there are likely to be several varieties on offer – all of them, in some sense, publicly accessible. Tradition cannot be, in itself, the rock on which meaning rests: it is not surprising that Scruton has to hint at a metaphysical support – 'A tradition is a *spirit*' (p.48). One might also argue that a tradition needs political support, though Scruton does not go into this, and it is unfortunate that his political affiliations – difficult though it might seem to be unaware of them from other sources – are nowhere acknowledged in this volume. The Contributors' Notes do not cite, among Scruton's works, *The Meaning of Conservatism* (1980). This looks too much like that 'suppression of ideology in bourgeois criticism' of which radical critics complain.

Robert Pattison offers a mildly amusing pastiche of a 'textualist' approach which seeks out contradictions in Trollope's *Last Chronicle of Barset* (1867). He rightly acknowledges the value of such an approach, as long as it does not become exclusive, but some of his objections are questionable – for instance, his claim that 'textualism encourages free-form philosophical discussion precariously balanced upon some often minor motif in a text' (p.156). The first question is surely: who – or what set of critical conventions – decides that a given textual feature is 'minor'? Leavis, after all, made textual features that might once have seemed minor – Keats's 'globed peonies', for example – carry the weight not only of a whole poetics but of a comprehensive critique of culture and society.

The remaining essays in this book are competent. Wayne Booth contends that Genette's *Narrative Discourse* (1980) is 'a model of how a serious criticism should deal with literary achievement' (p.135), Anthony Thorlby offers a sensitive piece of Kafka, and Lerner's own final contribution is interesting: he looks at titles as specific instructions – neither wholly extra-literary, nor wholly intrinsic – on how to read poems.

As a whole, however, *Reconstructing Literature* shows only too clearly why the radicals have the advantage at present. They have made literary studies *matter* as they haven't done since the height of Leavis's influence – even if, ironically, they have made them matter by threatening their very existence. There is no sense in *Reconstructing*

Literature of why, or in what ways, literary studies might matter. Secondly, in general the radicals have been far readier to assimilate Continental ideas, even if sometimes they have uncritically accepted or misunderstood them; *Reconstructing Literature* is still too dismissive. Thirdly, they have taken on board the challenges and insights of feminism; it is notable that *Reconstructing Literature* not only lacks any women contributors, but also any discussion of feminism. Fourthly, despite much arrogance, the radicals, recently at least, have made some attempt to understand the needs and wishes of students, and to develop teaching methods beyond the lecture/seminar/tutorial orthodoxy. Though all but one of the contributors to this book are professional literature teachers, students are hardly mentioned, and then dismissively, as in Lerner's complaint that 'every university teacher today' (polytechnic teachers and below need not apply) is faced with 'that student who keeps reappearing to tell us that all responses are valid because there is no fixed objective meaning' (p.13). One would have thought that a student who raised such a fundamental intellectual challenge was to be welcomed: but the challenge, no doubt, would be too great for Lerner.

A concern with the value of literature, with Continental ideas, with feminism, with students, with teaching methods, need not be the preserve of a radical sect. All of these concerns could, and should, feed into literary studies as a developing discipline that responds to the challenges of the present while conserving and enriching the real insights and values of the past. But *Reconstructing Literature* shows, unwittingly, the obstacles to this: it demonstrates that it is not literature which needs reconstructing, but some of its teachers.

6 Post-Theory

It looks as though theory, in literary studies, is here to stay. A canon of theoretical texts is forming, to replace the literary canon; there are literature lecturers who specialize in theory; courses and higher degrees in theory. There are even what might be called, on the analogy of festivals of literature, festivals of theory, in the form of conferences of literary academics. In England, of course, there is resistance; pockets of residual Leavisism; but on the whole it seems that the imperialism of theory is poised to conquer, to liberate us from that bourgeois mystification called literature. It could be, however, that the triumph of theory is illusory; that the expansion of theory is on the point of bringing about its downfall. The proliferation of theoretical options, and the increasingly obvious weakness of their claims to knowledge, is leading to a crisis, not in literary studies but in theory. This may be temporarily disguised by the institutionalization of theory in the academy; but, as far as literature is concerned, we are entering an age of post-theory.

Not, it should be stressed, of no-theory. Some of the intellectual and ethical implications of the current emphasis on theory are welcome. It is indeed valuable and proper to try and bring one's implicit assumptions into the light, make them consistent and coherent, support them by rational, explicit argument, relate them to a systematic world-view, examine them critically, challenge and question them, open them to new perspectives, new data. This rationalist, Enlightenment project is commendable, as far as it goes. There is no virtue in mystification and obscurantism, and it is certainly true that English studies, like some other areas of British culture, have had more than their fair share of these – and also of sheer mental laziness and apathy. The less salutary implications of the promotion of theory should not be forgotten, of course; theory, too, can be used to mystify, obscure, browbeat, quell challenge, close enquiry. But the positive human endeavour represented by what is now called theory can and will continue. In an age of post-theory, however, its limits will be recognized; and at those limits, we shall find literature, art.

The term 'theory' has today become a very loose one. It seems to be applied to anything from a total world-view to a few inferred assumptions. This makes it possible to claim that no statement is 'theory-free', that it is dependent, even if implicitly, on a theoretical position. You can appear to invalidate a case against theory by arguing that such a case is itself theoretically based. But this is to turn 'theory' into a transcendent tautology, to extend the term out of all usefulness. This over-extension has contributed to the illusory triumph of theory; but it will also help to precipitate its collapse. A term so wide will become meaningless. The term 'theory', one might suggest, should be reserved for coherent bodies of propositions for which it is possible to devise rigorous and consistent testing procedures. On this definition, few of the so-called theories now floating around in English studies could attain to theoretical status. It has become fashionable to say that one is using the term 'literature', in Derrida's phrase, *sous rature* ('under erasure') to indicate that it is an unsatisfactory, if temporarily convenient term. This scepticism might be more appropriately applied to the term 'theory': it is used *sous rature* in what follows.

There are, broadly speaking, two kinds of theories which now bear on literary studies. First, there is the kind specifically concerned with literature, or with an aspect of it: for example, the Russian Formalist notion of 'literariness' as linguistic defamiliarization; Bakhtin's view of the novel as 'heteroglossic', a carnival of competing voices; Todorov's poetics of narrative; German and American reader-response theories. All these theories run into problems: reader-response theory, for instance, gets into a tangle about whether the text produces the reader or the reader the text; attempts to establish the nature of literature always fall foul of exceptions that disprove the rule. Such attempts have led some critics, in fact, to the conclusion that literature does not exist; but this conclusion results from the wrong premiss: that we cannot know what we cannot theorize. But we can never theorize all we know; each assumption that we make explicit (including the assumption that it is possible and valuable to make assumptions explicit) depends on other, tacit assumptions; the attempt at a total explication of one's position would entail an infinite regress of explicating.

Theories of literature, or of particular aspects of literature, generally fail to produce conclusive results; they usually lead back, in fact, to traditional ontological and epistemological problems in philosophy. There is, however, a second kind of theory which can be brought to bear upon literature, and this is much more significant in literary studies today. Theories of this kind are not centrally concerned with literature; indeed, they may marginalize or abandon it as a category. Such theories are drawn from philosophy, psychology, sociology, anthropology, linguistics, semiology, from the whole field of the 'human sciences': they include Marxism, phenomenology, existentialism, structuralism, poststructuralism, deconstruction. It is notable, however, that literary critics have, in the main, avoided those areas of the human sciences, such as experimental psychology, which come closest to 'hard' science: their preference has been, in general, for the more poetic, suggestive, indeed 'literary' areas. This accounts, in part, for the popularity of Freud, Lacan, Foucault. But their theories are characteristic of those adopted by literary critics in that they neither offer, nor imply, any rigorous testing procedures. It is difficult to see how one could test Freud or Lacan; and while Foucault undoubtedly used empirical evidence, it is, by his own epistemology, perfectly open to interpretations other than those which he put upon it.

Deconstruction and poststructuralism represent a culmination of theory which also heralds its collapse. Deconstruction, maintaining that the pervasive play of rhetoric turns all discourse against itself, undermining its apparent logic, discloses the ineluctable treachery of its own discourse: paradoxically, if its own statements stand, its own statements cannot stand. Poststructuralism and deconstruction developed in France in the late 1960s and early 1970s, and their effect, on the intellectual plane, is rather like that of other, less esoteric aspects of those times: pop music, drugs, 'permissiveness'. They offer an euphoric sense of liberation, revolution, renovation, with the added bonus of apparent intellectual legitimacy. When poststructuralism and deconstruction spread, through translation and commentary, into England in the later 1970s, they provided substitute gratifications for those who had renounced, or missed out on, 1960s excitements. But their promise of revolution had already been belied: in France, for example, those most prominently associated with the magazine *Tel Quel* had moved towards liberal humanism or neo-conservatism. In England, they have been allied to that older promise of revolution offered by the Left: in fact, to a set of sedimented political prejudices and quasi-Marxist clichés. Theory has collapsed into politics and into a disguised, unformulated ethics. The supposedly rigorous questioning which English politicized poststructuralists direct at other ideologies stops when it comes to their own; they still, *pace* the shifting signifier, hold some truths to be self-evident.

Most of the theories now active in literary studies should be redefined in three ways: as hermeneutic devices, as myths, and as art-works (often of a rudimentary kind). As hermeneutic devices, they help us to interpret texts: they make it possible to read familiar or neglected texts – for example, *Middlemarch* (1871-2) or Swinburne's *Tristram of Lyonesse* (1882) – in ways which alert us to, or seem to account for, features previously unexplained or overlooked. As myths – and one has in mind here that kind of theory which offers or implies a total world-view, even if it rejects the concept of totality – they belong to those attempts to explain our condition which stretch from ancient religions to poststructuralism and beyond, and which we judge against our individual and collective experience. And it is questionable whether our recent myths, despite their novelty and undoubted power, are necessarily superior to the myths of the past – though one might draw some interesting comparisons between, for instance, deconstruction and Nagarjunan Buddhism, which dissolves a metaphysics of presence into a metaphysics of absence, the Void. As art-works, theories offer the rhetorical, structural and imaginative experiences that we find, at best, in art. It is interesting to note, in some of the French pioneers of poststructuralism and deconstruction, a constructive turn in their own texts towards art: the later writings of Barthes and Derrida, with their 'poetic', discontinuous qualities, show not theory taking over from art, but art taking over theory. Of course, some theories can have greater aesthetic quality than some purported art-works; and our current thirst for literary and paraliterary theory can be related to a comparative weakness in contemporary literature (as well as, perhaps, a failure to pay full attention to contemporary literature). Possibly, however, today's theory will help to provide the frameworks, the reference points, the mythology, for the literature of the future as classical and Christian mythology did for the literature and other arts of the past.

These remarks, it may be said, themselves imply theories – of interpretation, of myth, of art – that need substantial elaboration and thought. Certainly it would be interesting to investigate them further; one might even think about whether testing procedures could be devised for them which would entitle them to proper theoretical status. One might also consider their educational implications, though these would lack the false clarities that teaching theory provides. But they are offered here as provocations, suggestions, hermeneutic and heuristic hints, 'speculative instruments': post-theoretical promptings.

7 Euphoria, Ltd

When Paris students took to the streets in 1968, Claude Lévi-Strauss, the grand master of structural anthropology, was reported to have said with horror: 'What happens if they touch the libraries?' In 'The Death of the Author', published in the same year, Roland Barthes, no street-fighting man, offered a way of shattering the libraries, the sacred texts of Eternal Truth, without upsetting a single shelf:

> literature (it would be better from now on to say *writing*), by refusing to assign a 'secret', an ultimate meaning, to the text (and to the world as text), liberates what may be called an anti-theological activity, an activity that is truly revolutionary since to refuse to fix meaning is, in the end, to refuse God and his hypostases – reason, science, law. (*Image-Music-Text*, 1977, p.147)

The starting-point of Barthes's essay is by now well-known: an attack on the concept of the 'author' as the source of the text and the guarantee of its meaning. To write is to function as the node of a range of discourses that one does not control or unify; the 'author' is not the cause, but an effect of the text – or rather, of a particular way of reading, of structuring the text; he does not determine or limit its significance. And this is not to say, with the New Critics, that the text is a comfortable liberal plenitude where contraries and ambiguities co-exist in a tense, but ultimately harmonious, equilibrium; it is a site of struggle: 'a multi-dimensional space in which a variety of writings, none of them original, blend and clash'. (*Image-Music-Text*, p.146). It is dispersed, decentred, fragmented, fissured, incorrigibly plural.

The implications of Barthes's essay go far beyond literature, however. They are total; and in that, characteristic of poststructuralism at its most euphoric. All is supposedly shaken: literature, religion, reason, science, law, the individual subject. Barthes, it seems, has rewritten Dostoevsky: if the author does not exist, then everything is permitted; and this is cause not for terror but for joy. It is the total claims of poststructuralism that account for the passionate intensity of its enthusiasts and enemies, but also for its inability to sustain its liberating promise. By calling all into question, it calls itself into question, giving itself no ground upon which to base its own challenges and to develop constructive possibilities. It is hardly surprising that, even by 1971, only three years after 'The Death of the Author', Barthes's rhetoric can take on an autumnal tone:

> In fact, today, there is no language site outside bourgeois ideology: our language comes from it, returns to it, remains closed up in it. The only possible rejoinder is neither confrontation nor destruction, but only theft: fragment the old text of culture, science, literature, and change its features according to formulae of disguise, as one disguises stolen goods. (*Sade-Fourier-Loyola*, 1976 edn, p.10)

The optimistic claim of a 'truly revolutionary activity' has been replaced by a pessimistic total claim: that bourgeois ideology is, for the moment at least, inescapable. The project of shattering the library of Western culture has diminished to a campaign of petty pilfering. We are back inside the whale.

Deconstruction was always more cautious. Consider what might stand as a classic deconstructionist statement (if such a thing is possible) – Jacques Derrida's contrast, in 'Structure, Sign and Play in the Human Sciences' (1966) between two kinds, or 'interpretations', of 'interpretation':

> The one seeks to decipher, dreams of deciphering a truth or an origin which escapes play and the order of the sign, and which lives the necessity of interpretation as an exile. The other, which is no longer turned toward the origin, affirms play and tries to pass beyond man and humanism, the name of man being the name of that being who, throughout the history of metaphysics or of ontotheology – in other words, throughout his entire history – has dreamed of full presence, the reassuring foundation, the origin and end of play. (*Writing and Difference*, 1978, p.292)

Derrida's vocabulary – which has been enormously influential – obviously loads the argument. On the one side are the dreamers, who dwell in illusion and seek reassurance; on the other, the deconstructionists, who affirm, who play, who seek to transcend ('pass beyond'). And, like Barthes in 'The Death of the Author', Derrida generates excitement by total claims, encapsulated in the phrase 'throughout his entire history' – a characteristic Derridean locution which gives the exciting sense that we are awakening from a dream as old as man, and that we must choose the side of clarity. But, again characteristically, he moves on almost at once to apparent retraction and qualification: though he has indicated which kind of interretation we should prefer, he says that he does 'not believe that today there is any question of *choosing*' between the two (*Writing and Difference*, p.293). By a convenient paradox, however, this serves to add weight to his earlier loading of the case in favour of the view that there can be no truth or origin or foundation that offers ground on which to choose: his denial of the question of choosing in effect makes a choice. But it also provides an exemption clause: we can, if we wish, use the first, less favoured kind of interpretation when appropriate.

This combination of total claims with retractions and qualifications that both confirm these claims and provide an exemption clause is developed in Derrida's most extended iteration of his position, *Of Grammatology* (1967). This seeks to broach 'the deconstruction of *the greatest totality* – the concept of the *epistémè* and logocentric metaphysics – within which are produced, without ever posing the radical question of writing, all the Western methods of analysis, explication, reading, or interpretation' (1976 edn, p.46). But it is careful to stress that 'the movements of deconstruction do not destroy structures from the outside. They are not possible and effective, nor can they take accurate aim, except by inhabiting those structures. Inhabiting them *in a certain way*, because one always inhabits, and all the more when one does not suspect it' (p.24). So although we can begin to deconstruct 'the greatest totality', we can and must only work against it from within; this necessity confirms the existence and scale of the totality, justifies our tactical deployment of logocentric techniques, and partly excuses our unwitting logocentric lapses, indeed turning these into further proofs of the totality's pervasiveness.

Of Grammatology takes matters further, however; for even if we could ever escape logocentric metaphysics – even if we do escape them, momentarily, at the extreme of deconstructive rigour – it is only to become dizzily aware of a greater, indeed the truly greatest, totality: the arche-writing, which encompasses both speech and writing in the more usual sense; the play of differing/deferring that Derrida terms *différance*; the constant movement of the trace, the endless flicker of absence/presence. We can identify three typical moves in Derrida's argument (though these are not necessarily made in linear order): he constructs, by simplification and abstraction, a totality – 'logocentric metaphysics'; contends that we cannot simply break with, and must work within, that totality (contentions which serve to provide circular confirmations of that totality, and an exemption clause for deliberate or inadvertent logocentric behaviour by the deconstructionist); and finally gestures towards the truly total totality – the arche-writing – that lies beyond and within logocentrism. In *Of Grammatology*, even before the euphoria of 1968, Derrida has already enmeshed himself in his own trap: in that, he anticipates the whole history of deconstruction.

The cases of Derrida and Barthes are representative. It is significant that, as the 1970s proceed, both move, in their respective ways, into a more fragmented mode of writing that more obviously betrays literary longings – for example, Barthes in *Roland Barthes* (1974), *A Lover's Discourse* (1977) and *Camera Lucida* (1980); Derrida in *Glas* (1974) and *Signsponge* (1975). It is also significant, in a rather different sense, that they increasingly achieve academic respectability. Their itineraries have been and are being repeated by others, with varying degrees of intelligence, insight, style and sophistication, and with many local variations; but always, finally, with a breakdown of the original projects. Poststructuralism and deconstruction are, in a way, inevitably short-lived. Initially they create a sense of euphoria and then, unable to sustain themselves or to develop constructively, they fall back into the old modes they purportedly challenge, and into the practice of a sceptical method that, while it provides a powerful weapon against opponents, and while it may yield specific moments of interest, ineluctably entails self-contradiction, and can too easily become predictable and repetitive. What follows seeks to suggest, in a necessarily broad and provisional manner, the limitations of poststructuralism and deconstruction, and their adverse effects upon literary criticism.

Poststructuralism and deconstruction claim to be anti-theological; but their appeal resembles that of religion. The rhetoric seems to dissolve what it characterizes as false, consoling appearances, and to show the world, and one's 'self', as they really are, or are not. The poststructuralist vision – especially in those politicized versions influenced by the earlier Barthes, by Lacan, by Althusser, by Foucault – is lurid: the world, the illusory 'I', is revealed as oppressed, controlled, libidinous, contradictory, fallen. This vision may mix uneasily with Marxism to hold out some hope of salvation.

Deconstruction shelves salvation, but it does offer a strenuous ascesis, a constant mortification of what Derrida calls 'the exigent, powerful, systematic, and irrepressible desire' for a transcendent signified (*Of Grammatology*, p.49). It discloses, not the presence of God, but absence; to be sure, a sophisticated notion of absence, as the constant play of differing/deferring; but the inversion remains within a theological opposition. This might seem deconstructively inevitable. To try, like the Enlightenment or Marx, to achieve at a stroke a total break with theological modes, may merely be to reinstate God in a new guise: as reason, say, or the relations of production. The first, necessary stage in any deconstructive operation is to reverse the hierarchy: in this case, presence/absence. But is this the relevant hierarchy? Derrida's God, like Barthes's, is the God of totality; he has said: 'The motif of homogeneity [is] the theological motif *par excellence*' (*Positions*, 1981, pp.63-4) If one did want to deconstruct this God, the relevant hierarchy might be: totality/non-totality. But Derrida stays within the first term of this hierarchy; he remains a monotheist. He sees absence, the flickering play of the trace, everywhere: his idea of *différance* dissolves differences; he finds all appearances both illusory and inescapable. He is, in his way, as totalisingly theological as those he would oppose.

The results of importing totalisingly theological notions into literary criticism are likely to be similar, however secular those notions purport to be. Literary texts that do not conform to them are rejected or deprecated, or – and this is the more sophisticated approach – reinterpreted in such a way as to show that they covertly confirm or anticipate the faith: an allegorical or typological approach. Thus the 1970s saw poststructuralist attacks on the 'classic realist' texts of a Balzac or George Eliot, which were seen as offering a rigid hierarchy of discourses, attempting an imaginary resolution of contradictions, and providing a falsely secure subject-position for the reader. In the 1980s, this gave way to an approach which seeks to show how those 'classic realist' texts are exactly exactly what poststructuralism and deconstruction would lead us to expect them to be: split, dispersed, plural, subverting their proferred hierarchies. Of course, rejection and/or reinterpretation of texts in the light of explicit or implied world-views will characterize, to some extent, any kind of critical approach, not only those permeated by religious or quasi-religious notions (or perhaps one could argue that all critical approaches will inevitably be permeated by quasi-religious notions). But there are different degrees of flexibility, and the totalising tendencies of poststructuralism and deconstruction lead, once their initial innovative impact has worn off, towards rigidity. In a sense, we know what a poststructuralist or deconstructionist reading will say, though it may be interesting to see the details worked out, and to observe the points at which the criticism escapes the ostensible theoretical schema.

Poststructuralism and deconstruction exemplify a failed rebellion which is also a revolt against reason (in this respect, their French provenance is clearly relevant). For all their attempts to exorcise it, the ghost of Cartesian reason – of a mind split from a body, from emotions and instincts – still haunts them. Again, one might say, this is inevitable: all breaks are 'reinscribed in an old cloth' (*Positions*, p.24). But the persistence of the Cartesian split has dubious consequences for literary criticism. These are indicated in a comment of Derrida's: 'I believe that the risk of sterility and of sterilisation has always been the price of lucidity' (*The Structuralist Controversy*, 1970, p.271). Poststructuralism and deconstruction depend upon the intellect withdrawing from and analysing experience, as this comment by Christopher Norris inadvertently suggests: 'The truth is that deconstructionist theory can only be as useful and enlightening as the mind that puts it to work' (*Deconstruction: Theory and Practice*, 1982, p.133). It is indeed a 'mind', split from a body, from emotions and instincts, that goes to work in poststructuralism and deconstruction. They conceive of literary texts, in effect, as deviations from a model of rational, non-contradictory thought, even when such deviation is seen as analogous to similar but concealed deviation in rational thought itself. Supposed aporiae or 'blind spots', gaps, silences, contradictions, are eagerly sought out, industriously 'produced', but those very notions – of aporiae, gaps, silences, contradictions – are rationalist ones. Though poststructuralism and deconstruction have challenged, in theory, the Cartesian ego, the 'I that thinks', they have set up a new 'I' – or at least, offered a superior subject-position – which watches, dazzled and euphoric, the whirls and turns of the text and of that other 'I' which naïvely believes itself to be unified and substantial. As Jonathan Culler points out, 'the effect of deconstructive analyses, as numerous readers can attest, is knowledge and feelings of mastery' (*On Deconstruction*, p.225)

The point here is not to denigrate rational thought, but to recognize its limits; and it is at those limits, perhaps, that art begins. Poststructuralism and deconstruction in fact succeed in denigrating both rationality and art; they employ notions from rational thought, but deny those notions any grounds, and evade the responsibilities of rationality at key moments; they apply those notions to art and to literature, without considering that they might be inappropriate, that other modes of understanding might be required. Literature, or any other art-form, is not a magic mirror in which divisions are dissolved – though the potential healing and unifying power of art should not be scorned in obeisance to some ideological puritanism. Literature can and does arouse emotional and instinctive responses ('felt in the blood, and felt along the heart') that poststructuralism and deconstruction tend to repress, especially when those responses are stirred by such suspect phenomena as mimesis. Recently, some attempts have been made to rehabilitate proscribed emotions; in particular, Barthes's later work tries to find ways of talking about such taboo topics as pleasure (and not only *jouissance*), love, tenderness. Certain feminist approaches that have drawn upon poststructuralism and deconstruction have tried to allow for emotional responses and have pointed out, with some justice, that traditional modes of criticism which have stressed 'spontaneity' have in fact ruled out particular reactions – for instance, women's uneasiness or anger at sexist gender representations – as, say, immature and self-indulgent. One thinks of F.R. Leavis's concern for 'emotional hygiene' (*The Living Principle*, p.75). But discriminating among feelings in terms, for example, of 'emotional quality' is different from repressing feeling as philosophically and ideologically illegitimate: the perpetuation of the Cartesian mind/body split in poststructuralism and deconstruction contributes to such repression.

Poststructuralism and deconstruction also abuse the authority of science. The 'scientific' project may seem to belong to an earlier phase of theory; for example, Barthes speaks of the 'petit délire scientifique' (*Roland Barthes*, p.148) of his structuralist period. But the appeal to the prestige of science persists. It is epitomized in the image, much favoured by Althusser and Lacan, and avidly adopted by some later enthusiasts, of the 'Copernican revolution'. The 'decentring of the ego', of the conscious, Cartesian 'I that thinks' begun by Marx and Freud and supposedly developed in structuralism and its successors, is compared with Copernicus's 'decentring' of the earth from the solar system. The image implies an unequivocal breakthrough, which only ignorance and reactionary prejudice can deny. It depends for its effect on the echoes of an almost Victorian faith in science as an authoritative mode of knowledge by which we move steadily, if sometimes uncomfortably, towards greater enlightenment.

The scientific pretensions of poststructuralism and deconstruction are in fact very dubious. Of course it has now become notoriously difficult to define science; but in a definition derived from, say, Karl Popper, it is not easy to see how the claims of poststructuralism and deconstruction could be tested in ways that would expose them to possible falsification; while by the now influential model of science suggested by Thomas Kuhn, it is questionable whether enough anomalies could ever accumulate, or whether a sufficiently satisfactory solution to a set of problems could ever emerge, to bring about a genuine 'paradigm shift'. (The use of this latter term as a loose metaphor for current realignments in literary criticism itself demonstrates the persistent desire for quasi-scientific authority.) As 'sciences', poststructuralism and deconstruction suffer a similar problem of validation to psychoanalysis, with which they clearly have close links: it is debatable whether they could ever be proved wrong, since apparently contradictory evidence can always be reinterpreted, with sufficient ingenuity, as concealed confirmation. It is possible to take a wholly relativist view of science, to see the concept of what constitutes a scientific theory, and the procedures by which that theory is supposedly tested, as specific to a particular social and cultural situation, and without universal validity; this view would, in fact, accord with poststructuralist and deconstructionist scepticism; but it would also, by subverting the authority of science, undermine their appeal to that authority.

If poststructuralism and deconstruction can hardly count as scientific, their rhetorical invocation of science none the less contributes to their influence, and to their cramping effect upon literary criticism. It implies that they represent the latest and best in knowledge; it confers upon the critic who employs them an easy sense of superiority over literary texts. Those texts can never surprise him, never teach him anything he does not already know. Assured progress has been made in the human as in the natural sciences, and our knowledge of humanity, as of the physical world, has unequivocally increased; Barthes, or the discourses that constitute him, must know more than Balzac, Derrida than Dickens. Thus Catherine Belsey, who makes much use of the 'Copernican revolution' image, asserts: 'A form of criticism which refuses to reproduce the pseudo-knowledge offered by the text provides a real knowledge of the work of literature' (*Critical Practice*, 1980, p.129). The uncomfortable possibility that the literature of the past embodies any kind of human wisdom (and not the wisdom of its 'authors' only) is denied. This is the recurrent arrogance of the present – a vulgar scientism, a willed or inadvertent failure of historical memory.

It is true that it is now increasingly allowed that past literary texts (though not their 'authors') may have dimly anticipated the findings of today's luminaries; but 'knowledge' is in the possession of the enlightened critic (or of the discourses that circulate through him), and the appeal to the prestige of science lends this 'knowledge' a spurious authority. To some extent, of course, we will always read past texts in the context of our own time, of currently dominant ideas, and will reject or reinterpret them according to our present preoccupations. Moreover, to discriminate among and within texts is inevitably to assume that, in certain respects, one 'knows better' than those texts. But to acknowledge that we may, in some cases, indeed 'know better' than the past is not to make the assumption, which the 'Copernican revolution' sort of image reinforces, that we unequivocally and indubitably do so.

Though poststructuralism and deconstruction claim to subvert the law, they have, at least as far as literary criticism is concerned, established a new body of binding rules and promoted the careful policing of critical discourse. D.H. Lawrence once protested in a poem: 'They say I wrote a naughty book/With perfectly awful things in it,/putting in all the impossible words/like b--- and f--- and sh--.' (*Complete Poems*, 1972, p.491). Today, in the field of criticism, we have another set of 'impossible words'; these are conveniently gathered in this passage from Raman Selden's *A Reader's Guide to Contemporary Literary Theory* (1985):

> readers may believe that theories and concepts will only deaden the spontaneity of their response to literary works. They may forget that 'spontaneous' discourse about literature is unconsciously dependent on the theorising of older generations. Their talk of 'feeling', 'imagination', 'genius', 'sincerity', and 'reality' is full of dead theory which is sanctified by time and has become part of the language of common sense. (p.3)

'Realism'; 'sincerity'; 'spontaneity'; 'feeling'; 'imagination'; 'genius'; 'reality': these are the taboo terms now. Selden talks of 'dead theory'; but he leads us into the dead land, where lips that would kiss form prayers to the broken tablets of poststructuralist and deconstructionist law – law which is more powerful, more pervasive, by its fragmentation and dispersal. In the courts of the shifting signifier, there are no judges, no advocates, no rights of appeal: reason and science may be used against you, but cannot be called in support of your own case; and subjective testimony, of the wrong sort, can instantly be discredited.

Poststructuralism and deconstruction have focused particularly on attacking the concept of the individual human subject: the notion of the 'decentring of the ego' as a 'Copernican revolution' exemplifies this, while Barthes's assault on the notion of the 'author' can be situated within a much broader challenge to the idea of the 'individual'. This clearly has major implications for literary criticism, which has often worked in terms of literary texts as expressions of individual authors, as evocations and explorations of individual states of mind, as presenting individual characters, as relating to individual readers. In a complex analysis that draws on Marxist, psychoanalytic, linguistic and semiotic perspectives, the idea of the unified, centred, substantial self (hardly dominant, in fact, in twentieth-century literature and culture) is seen as an illusion: the results of the child's misrecognition of himself as an imaginary unity in the 'mirror stage' and of his insertion into language and the symbolic order; of the suppression of the difference between the 'I' of which one speaks and the 'I' that speaks, the subject of the enounced and the subject of the enunciation; of the reproductive mechanisms of bourgeois society that construct obedient subjects who naïvely believe that they 'freely' consent to their unperceived subjection.

The concept of the constructed subject has, paradoxically, a strong subjective appeal. Like Calvinism, it ensures that you have at least recognized that most people are damned, even if you cannot be sure of your own salvation. It interpellates you, hails you into a subject-position of privileged knowledge, even if it is the knowledge that the 'I' that thinks it knows is itself no more than a temporary subject-position. Consider this passage, from Althusser's highly influential 'Ideology and Ideological State Apparatuses'; he identifies an 'ideology of the School' that is

> universally reigning because it is one of the essential forms of the ruling bourgeois ideology: an ideology which represents the school as a neutral environment purged of ideology . . . where teachers respectful of the 'conscience' and 'freedom' of the children who are entrusted to them (in complete confidence) by their 'parents' (who are free, too, i.e. the owners of their children) open up for them the path to the freedom, morality and responsibility of adults by their own example, by knowledge, literature and their 'liberating' virtues.
>
> I ask the pardon of those teachers who, in dreadful conditions, attempt to turn the few weapons they can find in the history and learning they 'teach' against the ideology, the system and the

> practices in which they are trapped. They are a kind of hero. But they are rare and how many (the majority) do not even begin to suspect the 'work' the system (which is bigger than they are and crushes them) forces them to do, or, worse, put all their heart and ingenuity into performing it with the most advanced awareness (the famous new methods!) So little do they suspect it that their own devotion contributes to the maintenance and nourishment of this ideological representation of the School... (*Lenin and Philosophy*, 1977, p.148)

How many, reading this, must have felt themselves called, must have seen themselves among those rare birds who can perceive those realities to which others, the dull majority, are blind. If the subject is put in question in Althusser's essay, analysed as a means of ideological reproduction, the ego – in the ethical sense of the term – is dangerously inflated, granted a licence to scorn any attempt at disinterestedness and to impart its own prejudices and idiosyncrasies. It is also provided with a powerful rhetorical weapon. The concept of the constructed subject permits the well-known operation whereby dissent is reinterpreted as unwitting confirmation. If 'I' take the view – or am hailed into the subject-position – that holds individual subjects to be linguistic and ideological constructions, and you deny this, 'your' denial, however it is argued, can be taken as further evidence of the ideological construction to which you are blind and which in fact causes you to want to deny it and to believe that you can freely do so. It is as if one were to say, to a person putting an argument against Christianity: It is the Devil speaking in you. It is an appeal to an agency or process beyond your conscious cognizance and control. You can only 'know' it by accepting the belief system within which it is held to be true.

The notion of the constructed subject is offered as demystifying. To a degree this is justified, in so far as it helps to challenge the idea of the 'autonomous individual' abstracted from specific historical, political, social and cultural circumstances. But it can too easily become a new form of mystification, or, more precisely, the revival, in a fresh guise, of an old one: the denial of another's experience (experience itself being seen as an ideological production). In this respect, it contributes to a kind of solipsism; it is a means of trying to eliminate, or diminish the impact of, other persons; in denying the experiencing 'I', in collapsing the 'I' of the other into ideology, one tries to exorcise that other who may dissent, oppose, resist; one engages in a sort of 'magical thinking', an illusory dissolution of obstacles.

The concept of the constructed subject also offers a new, strange refreshing sense of oneself. It is often presented as unnerving, perhaps repellent (thus implying that it needs a certain courage and honesty to accept it); but there is another aspect to the matter, indicated in one of Wittgenstein's comments on Freud, in a letter to Norman Malcolm: 'He always stresses what great forces in the mind, what strong prejudices work against the idea of psycho-analysis. But he never says what an enormous charm that idea has for people' (*Ludwig Wittgenstein: A Memoir*, 1984, pp.100-1). The idea of the constructed subject (which owes obvious and acknowledged debts to Freud) also has an enormous charm. If it discloses your subjection, it also enables you to see yourself in a different way, and thus, in a sense, enhances your freedom. If it evacuates you, it also makes you much more interesting. And perhaps it lifts a burden too. Sartre says in *Words*: 'you can get rid of a neurosis but you are never cured of yourself' (p.157). But the notion of the constructed subject gives you a cure for yourself, or at least lets you put your 'self' into process in an exciting way. It remains a form of romanticism, and returns into a kind of narcissism; the eye gazes, not into a still pond, but into a vortex in which its image endlessly, thrillingly, breaks and reforms. 'The mind, a single nowhere, swoons to feel/Its multilocal multiplicity.' ('Paul Valéry', *Poems of G.S. Fraser*, 1981, p.98).

It is claimed that the concept of the constructed subject is a radical one, subverting the notion of the 'individual' that is, supposedly, the keystone of bourgeois ideology. But it could be seen, perhaps more convincingly, as a mode of conformity to the dominant demands of our time. It is true that some conservative political rhetoric still appeals to the 'individual'; but the very explicitness of such appeals might make us question whether the idea of the individual is any longer hegemonic, any longer part of what is taken for granted. It is arguable that one of the major needs of modern societies – whatever their ostensible political creed – is in fact for subjects that can constantly be constructed or manipulated to consume new goods, take up new working practices, subserve new technology. The post-structuralist idea of the free-flowing subject is close to the ideal modern worker or manager, always able to assume new subject-positions in accordance with productive requirements. The notion of the mobile subject is the poststructuralist and deconstructionist equivalent of 'On yer bike'.

This is not, of course, to deny that it is of immense interest and value to explore the ways in which subjectivity is considered in and across a range of discourses – theological, philosophical, psychological, medical, juridical and, indeed, literary; in fact, it could be argued that literature has always been engaged in such explorations, and with considerably more subtlety, sensitivity and complexity than poststructuralism and deconstruction. Poststructuralism and deconstruction do not offer an adequate theory of the subject; they simply eliminate it, and then become incoherent or self-subverting when they wish to distinguish, descriptively and/or evaluatively, among forms of subjectivity, and when they wish to allow for experience and volition. Rightly rejecting the notion of the absolutely sovereign individual, they shift to a belief in language and ideology as sovereign; *pace* Foucault, they have still not cut off the king's head.

Only apoplectic reaction would deny that poststructuralism and deconstruction have had some stimulating effects upon literary criticism. Their ontological and epistemological challenges have raised important issues for critical theory and practice – for instance: What is an 'author', a 'reader', a 'text'? How do we 'know' the text? Does the text 'know' us? How does 'text' relate to 'world'? They have helped to contest the tyranny of interpretations fixed by an appeal to authority rather than by argument (as well as valuably questioning such distinctions as 'authority/argument'). They have widened our sense of the possibilities of meaning in texts. They have drawn attention to aspects of texts previously ignored, neglected, or deprecated in the drive to discover a univocal message, an organic unity. They have enabled us to see classic texts in different ways – that ponderous monument known as 'the nineteenth-century novel' can now never be quite the same again, thankfully – and to approach 'difficult' twentieth-century work, from the great texts of Modernism to current 'experimental' writing, with potentially more rewarding reading strategies.

But they have also had restrictive effects, and, with their assimilation and the loss of their innovative force, these are increasing. These effects are not accidental, not the result of misinterpretation and misapplication; they are inherent in theories that make total claims which destroy their own grounds and any basis for constructive development. In poststructuralism and deconstruction, religion, reason, science, law, the individual subject, all those demons supposedly driven out by Barthes, made deconstructible by Derrida, return, in negative form, to oppress literature.

8 Sartre/Barthes

The deaths of Sartre and Barthes within weeks of each other in 1980 removed two men who had come to represent major stages in French intellectual culture: Sartre, existentialism and a 'humanized' Marxism; Barthes, structuralism and poststructuralism. Inevitable irony curved round their fame. Sartre had savaged the myth of the 'genius', the 'author with a destiny', and attacked the 'star system' in which he glittered brightly; he had sought to dissolve himself back, conceptually at least, into the human collective, to become 'a whole man, made of all men, worth all of them, and any one of them worth him' (*Words*, p.158). Barthes had pronounced the 'author' dead, as cultural institution and as source and semantic guarantor of a text; had worked to disperse the supposedly unified individual subject into a plurality of constitutive discourses; had laid bare the ways in which that monster, bourgeois mythology, turned a constructed culture into a mystifying 'nature'. But both had been 'recuperated' by that mythology as 'authors', as 'geniuses', as – to borrow Giscard d'Estaing's stultifying obituary comment on Sartre – 'great luminaries of our time'. Such eulogies shed no light. But the fact remains that, among a range of remarkable writers and thinkers – Camus, de Beauvoir, Lacan, Althusser, Derrida, Kristeva, Foucault – Sartre and Barthes stood out, and this cannot be explained away as due merely to the machinations of bourgeois – or radical – mythology. It is due primarily to their ability to focus and dramatize, as no others could, a host of pressing literary, aesthetic, philosophical, political and ethical issues. This essay considers some aspects of their work which seem to bear most pressingly on current debates.

Writing, reading

Sartre and Barthes, if not 'authors', were certainly writers, concerned throughout their lives with the practice of writing in a way that resists easy classifications into 'novelist', 'critic', 'philosopher', and so on. Sartre has made clear in essays, in interviews, and above all in *Words* (1963), his early sense of his 'destiny' as a writer, and if in later life he tried increasingly to flee that fate, he mainly did so, paradoxically, through writing: 'I still write. What else can I do?' (*Words*, p.157). Barthes can be seen – too conveniently, no doubt – as moving *towards* his destiny as a writer. There is the literary and cultural criticism and theory – for example, *Writing Degree Zero* (1953), *Mythologies* (1957), *On Racine* (1963); the remarkable 'break' of *S/Z* (1970), in which the critical meta-text explodes the supposedly primary text of Balzac's *Sarrasine*; and then the more 'creative' mode of, for instance, *A Lover's Discourse* (1977) and *Camera Lucida* (1980). Barthes never wrote a novel, and, when pressed on the matter in later life, usually denied that he intended to do so. As Jonathan Culler points out, however, he devoted several courses at the Collège de France to 'Preparation for the Novel' and showed an interest in novelist's appurtenances – Balzac's dressing-gown, Flaubert's notebooks, Proust's cork-lined room (*Barthes*, 1983, pp.21, 119). His challenge to the division between 'criticism' and 'literature', increasingly enacted in his own writing, might be seen, despite its radical mask, as a bid for the status of writer, indeed, dare one say it, of author. As his first book, *Writing Degree Zero*, said: 'the intellectual is still only an incompletely transformed writer' (1968 edn, p.28).

It seems easier to sort Sartre's work into traditional genres – novel, play, short story, essay, treatise – though once we look closer, fiction flows into philosophy, drama into the essay. As a novelist, Sartre's most satisfying work remains his first, *Nausea* (1938). It is hard to think of a better 'philosophical' novel, though clearly the categories and methods of Sartrean philosophy owe much to the novel as a mode of writing. *Nausea* takes a traditional realist mode – the personal journal – and employs it to explore a postmodernist sense of absurdity, for example by its challenge to causal rationality (especially as manifested in the sense of order and necessary sequence produced by the conventional novel) and by its interweaving of surrealist elements: the Magrittesque portrayal of the Bouville bourgeoisie out for their Sunday stroll, the Dali-like viscosity of the chestnut-tree root in the park. The traditional form of *Nausea* both contradicts, and enhances by contrast, the sense of absurdity; a characteristically Sartrean tension is set up between the achingly lucid mind and an overwhelming sensuousness and immediacy that threatens to melt down rational meaning. From the banal itinerary of a lone researcher's life – the library, the café, the art gallery – Sartre creates dramatic situations, though much of the drama is within Roquentin's consciousness. His visit to the art gallery, for instance, is superbly controlled in its rhythm and timing, in its build-up to the scathing denunciation – which is also part of a precise philosophical analysis within the novel – of the 'bastards' who try to give a sense of necessity to their ineluctably contingent existence.

The *Roads to [or of] Freedom* trilogy (1945-9) is a less certain achievement. The first volume remains admirable in its particularization, through a range of characters, of a historical moment, and its comic aspect has perhaps been insufficiently noted. Subsequent volumes have undoubted *longueurs* (though these have a certain mimetic justification in view of the atmosphere of tension and inaction, punctuated by sudden bursts of movement, that Sartre wishes to convey). But there are some remarkable moments: the account of the exodus from Paris at the beginning of the third volume, *Iron in the Soul* (1949), stands in the major tradition of the historical novel, with Scott and Tolstoy. The ironic liberation attained by Mathieu later on in the novel, as he fires his last rounds from a church tower at the advancing Germans, is unforgettable:

> "Christ!" he said out loud. "No one shall say we didn't hold out for fifteen minutes!"
>
> He made his way to the parapet and stood there firing. This was revenge on a big scale. Each one of his shots avenged some ancient scruple. One for Lola whom I dared not rob; one for Marcelle whom I ought to have left in the lurch; one for Odette whom I didn't want to kiss [*baiser*]. This for the books I never dared to write, this for the journeys I never made, this for everybody in general whom I wanted to hate and tried to understand. He fired, and the tables of the Law crashed about him – Thou Shalt Love Thy Neighbour as Thyself – bang! in that bugger's face – Thou Shalt Not Kill! – bang! at that scarecrow opposite. He was firing on his fellow men, on Virtue, on the whole world. Liberty is Terror. The Mairie was ablaze, his head was ablaze. Bullets were whining round him free as the air. The world is going up in smoke, and me with it. He fired: he looked at his watch: fourteen minutes and thirty seconds. Nothing more to ask of Fate now except one half-minute. Just time enough to fire at that smart officer, at all the Beauty of the Earth, at the street, at the flowers, at the gardens, at everything he had loved. Beauty dived downwards like some obscene bird. But Mathieu went on firing. He fired. He was cleansed. He was all powerful. He was free. (1950 edn, p.245)

Roads to Freedom is of course unfinished, though Sartre continued to work on it into the 1950s, and previously unpublished sections have appeared posthumously in the Pléiade volume *Oeuvres Romanesques* (1981). Its incompletion is surely appropriate, however, in a century when it has seemed much more difficult to make sense of the world within the traditional framework of the novel and of historical narrative.

In his plays, as in *Nausea*, Sartre combined a sense of formal and rational order with a strong pull towards the breakdown of structure and meaning. In a sense, his drama is very Shavian, very much a theatre of ideas; in an interview of 1961, a French mispronunciation by his questioner, Kenneth Tynan ('le droit', the law, for 'la droite', the political right) provoked, before Tynan could correct himself, this response:

> The law *is* theatre. For at the roots of theatre there is not merely a religious ceremony, there is also eloquence. Consider the characters of Sophocles, of Euripides, even of Aeschylus – they are all lawyers... They come forward with a cause to defend. Others take the opposite side and plead against them. At the end, there is a catastrophe in which everyone is judged, and matters return to normal. The stage is the courtroom in which the case is tried. (*Sartre on Theater*, 1976, pp.126-7)

But Sartre's stage courtroom – in this, of course, like a real courtroom – brings with it, bending against its framework of rational debate aimed at reaching truth and finding proper grounds for action, a pressure of absurdity, of claustrophobic enclosure, of inarticulable terror, that calls to mind Beckett and Pinter. This tension between order and chaos is at its most concentrated in that *tour de force, No Exit* (1945), but in other plays – for instance, *The Devil and the Good Lord* (1951), *The Condemned of Altona* (1960) – it is linked, without loss of intensity, to wide-ranging historical and political issues.

Sartre's studies of Baudelaire, of Genet, of Flaubert, can be seen, as Michael Scriven has proposed in *Sartre's Existential Biographies* (1984), as alternatives to the traditional 'bourgeois' novel. Sartre said of *The Family Idiot* (1971-2; 1988) that he wanted it to be read as a novel, but as a *true* novel (*Situations X* , 1976, p.94). It could also be suggested that these studies – especially the Flaubert, when we have, at least provisionally, come to terms with it – may help to reinstate, in a much more sophisticated form, that traditional and today very dubious mode of the 'critical biography'. In its 'progressive-regressive, analytic-synthetic method', which moves between family situation and broad historical context, and from the objective significations of an individual's work back to an attempt to reconstitute that individual's original project, *The Family Idiot*, in particular, offers approaches that can be employed – and, where necessary, adapted – in the investigation of other writers and their work. It would be especially interesting to do this for some revered English authors who have mainly been seen, within native critical perspectives, in 'spiritual' terms – for instance, Coleridge, Wordsworth, Dickens, George Eliot, D.H. Lawrence. And, of course, for Sartre himself. But it could be argued that Sartre's 'critical biographies' are themselves partly autobiographical; as Genet said: 'I don't think he's written a book about me. His book called *St Genet* was really about himself' (*PN Review* 32, p.51).

Sartre did, however, write an autobiography, though it covered only the first ten years of his life. *Words* is, as he acknowledged, a farewell to literature, an exposure of literary practice as neurosis, a choice of the imaginary, that is notably 'literary', very well-written. Though it appears ruthlessly to take stock and set in order, its epistemological status is challenged precisely by that stocktaking; Sartre is caught in the paradox of the Cretan liar. What he writes at one point in *Words* might apply to the book as a whole: 'What I have just written is false. True. Neither true nor false, like all that is written about madmen or about men' (p.45). Barthes's autobiography – if that is the term for it – is also self-subverting. In the *écrivains de toujours* series – which is not normally written by the writer himself – it warns us that 'all this must be considered as if spoken by a character in a novel – or rather by several' (1977 edn, p.119). Since this warning itself could be considered as if it were issued by a character in a novel, we are once again in a Cretan-liar situation. Whereas Sartre, in *Words*, characteristically adopts a totalizing approach, *Roland Barthes* – also characteristically, at this stage of its subject's career – works through dispersal; it is a montage of penetrating, idiosyncratic, whimsical, amusing, fertile fragments. And thereby closer to the 'truth'? Not necessarily; as one fragment of *Roland Barthes* reminds us, the fragment is, finally, also a form of rhetoric (p.95).

Sartre and Barthes were both wary of poetry. For Sartre, poetry was language absolved from its communicative function; as he says in *What is Literature* (1948): 'Poets are men who refuse to *utilize* language' (1967 edn, p.5). The notion of poetry endorsed in *What is Literature* bears some likeness to I.A. Richards's view that the 'emotive' language of poetry gives us 'pseudo-statements' which are non-referential and not subject to verification. But in contrast to Richards, Sartre certainly did not feel that poetry 'is capable of saving us' (*Science and Poetry*, 1926, p.82). Barthes's *Writing Degree Zero* puts forward a similar view of poetry's autonomy: 'the Word in poetry can never be untrue, because it is a whole' (p.40). The conclusion to Barthes's *Mythologies* links poetry with mystification: to poeticize is to posit a reality that is ultimately impenetrable and irreducible, that escapes the lucidity of the mythologist. But for Barthes, increasingly, prose too is mystifying, as indeed is language of any kind; it is totalitarian, wholly enclosing and constructing us; there is no place for us outside bourgeois language, and no other language. Only fissures, faults, sudden failures of meaning, offer a momentary escape. This escape is most eloquently evoked – inevitably, paradoxically, through words – in Barthes's account, in *Empire of Signs* (1970), of that 'fictive nation' called Japan – an imaginary country, a Westerner's Orient, composed of Barthes's acute observations on an actual journey and his own longings. Writing is, in its way, a *satori* 'which causes knowledge, or the subject, to vacillate: it creates *an emptiness of language*'. And 'all of Zen, of which the haiku is merely the literary branch... appears as an enormous praxis destined to *halt language*' (1972 edn, pp.3, 4, 74).

For Sartre, language formed part of the 'pratico-inert', the network of objects and practices which human beings fashion in interaction with the material environment, but which then weighs upon them and can thwart their needs and intentions. Men make their own discourse, but they do not make it just as they please, and their own words may turn against them like swords. To that extent, for Sartre as for Barthes, language is oppressive. But Sartre's view of language is more optimistic: since language is shaped by human beings, it can be worked on and reshaped by them. Language, at least in prose, can function as a means of communication; the writer can, and should, call a cat a cat. Sartre always maintained the distinction – of a kind much challenged, of late, by deconstruction – between the language of his philosophical works, which he saw as direct and unrhetorical, and the 'literary' language of his fictions and autobiography, though he recognized that, in practice, the division could never be complete. Barthes's later work sought, impossibly, to escape, in language, a language seen as irremediably mendacious, through the constant self-subversion of propositions. Sartre held that valid proposition was still possible.

Sartre's analysis of reading is likely to seem remarkably balanced today, granting due weight to both reader and text. *What is Literature?* defines reading as a fusion of perception and creation. The value of a literary work is its appeal to the reader's freedom; it presents, but does not overwhelm; it proposes, rather than imposes, a task which the reader is free to choose, or refuse, to carry out. The reader freely gives his imaginative assent, his belief, to the work, and can revoke it at any time: reading is a 'free dream' (p.35). The literary object is realized *through*, but never given *in*, language: the reader projects and constructs, beyond the words but guided by them, a synthetic form. Reading is 'directed creation' (p.31).

In his earlier work, Barthes is drawn to the classical structuralist project as it bears on texts – literary, biblical, popular: the Casaubon-like quest for a Key to all Narratives. But in *S/Z*, Casaubon becomes a poststructuralist, Will Ladislaw, who combines an elfin unconcern for established authorities with a formidable cultural and methodological apparatus. *S/Z* distinguishes between the 'readerly' and 'writerly' text: the former seeks to impose on the reader a hierarchy of discourse and a unitary meaning; the latter acknowledges its plurality and instability, allowing the reader to 'rewrite' it. The reader should not submit to the readerly text; he should assault it, fragment it; thus revealing, perhaps, that it is writerly after all.

To interpret a text is not to give it a fixed, closed meaning, but to bring out the plurality which, in fact, constitutes it. A text is not a structure of signifieds, but a galaxy of signifiers. Opening it out is not a matter of making it mean anything one likes; it involves a very sophisticated, constantly expanding awareness of the range of interpretative codes, of connotative possibilities, invoked by a text and available to a reader. This is where both structuralist skills and individual sensitivity are required. But for Barthes, the reader is not a free, sovereign subject: the 'I' that comes to the plural text is already, itself, a plurality of other texts, of codes whose origin has been lost.

The later Barthes is in quieter mood; now he concentrates on hedonism, on the plural yet distinctive subject's enjoyment of reading. The division between a culturally reassuring *plaisir* and the joyous coming of *jouissance* is both invoked and blurred. Though this Barthes breaks codes, he also wants to retain them. *Le plaisir du texte* comes not from the disappearance of order and structure but from its gaps and slippages. 'Neither culture nor its destruction is erotic; it is the fault between them which becomes so' (*The pleasure of the text*, 1976 edn, p.7, translation modified).

It was Barthes's lack of respect for the classic, readerly text, his iconoclasm and irreverence, his inversion of such shibboleths as 'organic unity', his interest in pleasure, that made him seem so liberating in the 1970s to some English critics reared in a senescent Leavisism. Previously, most dissent from Leavis had continued to argue largely in his terms; now, it seemed, the hold of the Great Tradition was broken, in a breathtaking way: the sense of light and air was intoxicating. Moreover, in times which, compared to the 1970s, seemed much more quiescent politically, Barthes seemed to offer a way in which the revolution might still be pursued within the safety of the study and seminar room. Breaking the text, putting the signifier into play, could contribute to the millennium; the death of the subject would hasten the end of subjection.

The subject and nature

Against surrealism, determinist Marxism, organicist sociology, structuralism, and poststructuralism, Sartre maintained, though with modifications, the concept of the individual human subject: not as a pre-given essence – a notion that would in itself, in Sartrean terms, displace or replace the subject by spiritual, psychological, or biological forces – but as a freely choosing, actively self-constructing existence. His remark on the fallacy inherent in the liberating project of surrealism could today be applied to that of poststructuralism: 'there's no one to liberate' (*Situations II*, 1948, p.323). In *The Problem of Method* (1960), he pointed out the inability of determinist Marxism to account for the particularity of an individual life: 'Valéry is a petit bourgeois intellectual, no doubt about it. But not every petit bourgeois intellectual is Valéry' (1963 edn, p.56). He also noted that when the individual subject is abolished or ignored, it tends to reappear through the personification of broader forces: 'bureaucracy becomes a person with his enterprises, his projects, etc; he has attacked the Hungarian democracy (another person) because he could not tolerate...and with the intention of...etc.' (p.162). Such personification is evident today in the poststructuralist analysis of certain modes of discourse as oppressive; why, after all, should modes of discourse want to oppress – and who, in any case, would they be oppressing? The *Critique of Dialectical Reason* was concerned, among other things, to rebut the idea that human groups can be understood as hyper-organisms. Though they may certainly appear as such, they are intelligible only in terms of the projects and actions of individuals. And Foucault's 'archaeology of consciousness', Sartre commented, might better be termed 'geology' ('Jean-Paul Sartre répond', p.87)

Sartre's insistence on retaining the individual subject was not simply a humanist faith, but a recognition of the concept's explanatory and ethical function. Without the subject, there is a tendency to explain events by forces that are, strangely, both personified and metaphysical. The unconscious, history, structure, discourse, desire, become human, like Greek gods all-too-human, but also embodying awesome, supernatural powers. Of course the concept of the individual, if abstracted from social and political conditions, can become metaphysical and mystifying; but it can also be used against metaphysics and mystification, including the materialist kind. And the abolition of the subject may function oppressively; if you are only a product of history, or an effect of language, then 'your' experiences, feelings and wishes need not, if politically inconvenient, be taken seriously.

His increasing awareness of political and social constraints modified Sartre's assertion of the individual's freedom. In 1969, looking back on his statement of twenty-five years before that 'whatever the circumstances, and wherever the site, a man is always free to choose to be a traitor or not', he exclaimed: 'It's incredible, I actually believed that!' ('Itinerary of a Thought', p.44). But while material exigences might be barely resistible, free praxis was still necessary to yield to them. As the *Critique* had argued, the worker condemned to a lifetime of labour still, through his actions in given conditions, had to carry out his sentence.

Barthes took up, or was taken up by, the standard poststructuralist position: that the subject is an effect of language. But his later work became more and more subjective, concerned with personal experience, even though that experience was enacted through a *bricolage* of discursive fragments. At the outset of his Flaubert, Sartre said that there was no guarantee that a man was not a multiplicity; (1981 edn, p.ix) but *The Family Idiot* worked massively to demonstrate otherwise. Barthes discovered or dramatized himself as Legion, but out of this a distinctive consciousness emerged: alert, ironic, wearing its learning lightly; increasingly languid, at the end a little weary. Sartre wrote in *Words*: 'you can get rid of a neurosis but you are never cured of yourself' (p.157); Barthes's shattered fragments of discourse still served as mirrors.

Sartre's concept of the freely choosing, self-making subject carried with it a rejection of the notion of a fixed 'human nature' – although one could say that, for him, freedom was a kind of human nature, an ontological given. Barthes also attacked the notion of 'human nature', most memorably in *Mythologies*; for instance, in his account of the way in which the exhibition *The Family of Man* presented photographs that purported to show 'universal' experiences of birth, death, family life, etc. from various parts of the world, and thus denied social, cultural and economic differences (pp.100-2). *Mythologies* identifies the notion of 'nature' as the cornerstone of a bourgeois ideology which disguises states of affairs that are culturally produced and historically variable as natural and immutable.

Since *Mythologies* – though not, of course, simply as a result of it – this has become a very popular notion: close, indeed, to *doxa*. The basic operation in radically-inclined cultural studies today is to show that what is supposedly 'natural' (in relation, for example, to the behaviour of women) is, in fact, cultural and changeable. But if the transformation of 'culture' into 'nature' can be mystifying, the reverse process, dissolving 'nature' into 'culture', can, in certain circumstances, seem very much like 'magical thinking' of the kind analysed by Sartre in *Sketch for a Theory of the Emotions* (1937). The real intractability of the world is reduced to culturally produced signifying systems, which can be, in imagination, quickly dismantled. Of course we can never find a 'nature' outside culture, but this does not mean that the attempt to locate and define the natural within culture is invalid. Moreover, while the concept of 'nature', like that of the individual subject, can certainly be used oppressively, it need not necessarily be so; it may prompt recognition of material realities that must be taken into consideration in the attempt to gain greater freedom; it may serve to help resistance to 'technological determinism', the idea that particular technological developments make certain consequences inevitable. The abolition of 'nature' may have a further consequence: it may seem to rid the world of substance, lead to existential impoverishment. Barthes's conclusion to *Mythologies* recognized this: the demystifier 'constantly runs the risk of causing the reality which he purports to protect, to disappear' (p.158). His later interest in 'an emptiness of language' appears to figure a desire for an extra-cultural, 'natural' condition, a pure signified without signifier; and as Jonathan Culler suggest, Barthes's stress on the body in his last works seems to imply a return to an idea of a grounding natural reality (*Barthes*, p.120). Barthes tried to drive out nature, not with a pitchfork but with a range of precision tools; however, it kept coming back.

Politics and ethics

For the post-war Sartre, politics, notoriously, became of great importance; his political activity became his most public dimension. Anarchistic and comparatively ignorant of politics in the 1930s, after the war he determined to throw himself into the 'rough-and-tumble' of politics – or, more precisely, of the kind of rhetorical-political activity characteristic of intellectuals in peace-time, especially in France: editing magazines, writing essays and pamphlets, signing petitions. Such activity was not without hazard – during the Algerian war, the OAS twice tried to blow Sartre up – but it remained within a traditional framework. In the 1960s and early 1970s some of Sartre's political actions became more public and dramatic. In 1967, he presided over the Russell Tribunal in Stockholm which charged the USA with war crimes in Vietnam, and in 1968, as Simone de Beauvoir recalls, he spoke at the Sorbonne in support of the 'wild democracy' created by the rebelling students (*All Said and Done*, 1974, p.427). Certain celebrated gestures had a comic side: the distribution in the street of a banned Maoist newspaper, which led to a three-hour detention; a speech delivered from a barrel outside the Renault works at Billancourt. It is difficult to imagine Barthes doing such things. Absurd though some of these actions were, they formed part of his attempt to redefine the role of the intellectual. He argued that the traditional, petition-signing *intellectuel de gauche* he had been for most of his life should be replaced by the activist *intellectuel gauchiste*, ready to put his body as well as his mind on the line, who sought to engage himself more directly in political struggle, for example by taking a factory job alongside the workers. Of course it was easy for Sartre, by then in his late sixties, to advocate this; as he acknowledged, if he had gone and knocked at a factory door asking to be taken on as a semiskilled worker, 'it would have been a farce, if only because I was already far beyond the retirement age' (*Sartre in the Seventies*, p.54). The notion of the activist intellectual did not last. Foucault's concept of the 'specific intellectual' which allowed intellectuals to fight their political battles on their 'institutional sites' – i.e., to keep their jobs – proved, understandably, more popular.

In his immediate responses to political events, especially revolutionary initiatives, Sartre often seems to have indulged in euphoric 'magical thinking'; this led to the series of disillusionments summed up by Simone de Beauvoir in *All Said and Done*: Russia, Algeria, Cuba, Czechoslovakia, Paris 1968 (of course, Sartre was hardly alone in his successive enthusiasms and disappointments). Sartre's delight in rhetoric contributed, no doubt, to a 'magical' effect. It is most notable in his Preface to Frantz Fanon's *The Wretched of the Earth* (1961) – a Preface which stands in a curious contradictory relationship to Fanon's text, offering the white intellectual's seal of approval even as it denies white discourse any relevance to that of the blacks. The historical context of the Preface should be recalled, the France of the Algerian war, which partly accounts for Sartre's vivid picture of a nation threatened by fascism and civil war: 'you will have to fight, or rot in concentration camps' (1967 edn, p.26). But it hardly justifies the revolutionary optimism with which Sartre affirms that he is sure that 'we' will soon join the ranks of those who, through revolution, will make the history of mankind.

Sartre's major contribution to political philosophy, however, is the *Critique of Dialectical Reason* (1960). Only the first volume was published in Sartre's lifetime, and it is on this that we will focus. It is a difficult book; Sartre wrote it very quickly, constantly chewing amphetamines, and while he later justified the style as enacting, in the length and complexity of its sentences and paragraphs, the process of dialectical thought, he also acknowledged that the book could have been better written (*Situations X*, p.75). The English translator and editor, who have shortened sentences and added sub-headings, have made it more accessible.

In the *Critique*, Sartre sees all human history as characterized, up to now, by scarcity – most fundamentally of food, but also of people (labour, consumers) and of other resources – for instance, time. Scarcity – which need not be directly present, but can function as a feared possibility – is the source of violence; in an environment of scarcity, men see those who compete with them for scant resources as counter-men who, precisely because they share human needs and capacities, threaten man's very existence. As Sartre famously puts it:

> Nothing – not even wild beasts or microbes – could be more terrifying for man than a species which is intelligent, carnivorous and cruel, and which can understand and outwit human intelligence, and whose aim is precisely the destruction of man. This, however, is obviously our own species as perceived in others by each of its members in the context of scarcity. (1982 edn, p.132)

In the battle against scarcity, men use the inertia of matter – in the form of tools and their own bodies – to work on matter, but the results of their actions, inscribed upon material objects and material practices, bears down on them and can turn against them to frustrate their ends. This network of humanly shaped material objects and practices Sartre calls, as mentioned above, the 'practico-inert'. Traditionally in China, the peasants tore up trees and shrubs to clear space for crops; but this positive action – the elimination of an obstacle to production – turned into a negative consequence, a lack of protection, since the trees and shrubs had functioned not only to obstruct cultivation but also to retain the loess of the mountains and peneplains; no longer retained, this congested and swelled the rivers, resulting in catastrophic floods. As the *Critique* says: 'Man has to struggle not only against nature, and against the social environment which has produced him, and against other men, but also against his own action as it becomes other' (p.124).

One means by which individual and social behaviour is regulated in an environment of scarcity is through the *series*. Sartre gives an everyday example: the bus queue. Each individual wants a seat, or at least a standing place; there may not be enough seats for all; each individual is the other to the other; each may be one-too-many. The queue controls competition, but it also isolates each individual, turns him against his neighbours; the possibility of a common action is eliminated. Similarly, individuals join a 'queue' for jobs, houses, etc., in which they are in competition with other individuals; the possibility of bonding together with those individuals to demand more jobs, better houses, is likely to seem remote; the attempt to do so may simply mean that one loses one's place in the queue. But at certain historical moments the series can fuse into a group, which acts collectively (though it never ceases to be composed of, and comprehensible in terms of, individuals) against a common threat. Once the heat of immediate action has cooled, however, the group is threatened with the danger of a collapse back into seriality. It must be perpetuated by an explicit or implicit *pledge*: each member swears an oath of loyalty to the group; if he breaks it, every other member has the right to exercise sanctions against him – ultimately, to kill him. Thus group solidarity is maintained by terror. Yet if the group persists, it is threatened in another way: by the specialization of functions that its growing tasks impose upon it; it becomes an organization, then an institution, and this may prepare the ground for a dictator, a Stalin (of course, organizations and institutions can also arise directly from serial formations). The 'dictatorship of the proletariat', Sartre claims, is an impossibility: 'historical experience has shown quite undeniably that the first moment in the construction of socialist society – to consider it at the still abstract level of power – could only be the indissoluble aggregation of bureaucracy, of Terror and of the cult of personality' (*Critique*, p.662).

Sartre suggests that this first stage, at least in the Soviet Union, may be approaching its end; but he has clearly got into difficulties. Thus, a paradox: the *Critique*, despite Sartre's radical commitment, seems to hold out scant revolutionary hope. Shortly after finishing the first volume, Sartre went to Cuba, then in a state of post-revolutionary euphoria, and wrote a series of enthusiastic articles for *France Soir* – 'Cuba, si!' He later claimed that he had also told the Cubans: 'your time of terror is still ahead of you' (*Sartre by himself*, p.94). Whether or not he actually said this, such a prediction could certainly have been made on the basis of the *Critique*. Indeed, the *Critique* could be seen as a profoundly conservative, pessimistic work in some respects; it has an Old Testament quality in its vision of men compelled to labour and violence, to wrest bread from the grudging earth by the sweat of their brow, to turn like Cain against their brothers, to see their acts stolen from them and returned to them as oppressive fatalities. In *The Mask of Politics* Maurice Cranston has suggested that the Sartre of the *Critique* can be compared, in some respects, to Hobbes and Machiavelli (pp.108-10) and, understandably, the *Critique* has made some Marxists uneasy. For instance, Ronald Aronson, in *Jean-Paul Sartre – Philosophy in the World* (1980), takes issues with the *Critique*'s stress on scarcity as an ineluctable fact of human history (at least up to now), and suggests that scarcity was to some extent created by a human decision, in specific historical circumstances, to struggle against their environment rather than to accept its limits: for example, hunter-gatherers might minimize their needs and have more than enough to go round. 'Sartre fails to explore the historical choice which *makes there be* scarcity in the first place' (p.255). It is open to question as to how much of a 'choice' this is; but Aronson is right to question Sartre's tendency to convert scarcity into an absolute, and his neglect of the co-operative efforts that human beings, even if socially divided, must necessarily make to survive.

The stress on scarcity and violence give the abstract analysis of the *Critique* a powerfully dramatic, even melodramatic, tone. Sartre's references to violence in his political writings have attracted much attention. This is partly because such references seem exciting and easy to understand; but it is undoubtedly true that Sartre's relish for violence, at least on paper, has been excessive, an indulgence in what Camus called 'la violence confortable' (*Essais*, 1965, p.356). The *Wretched of the Earth* Preface unreservedly endorses Fanon's romantic notion of violence as cleansing: 'violence, like Achilles' lance, can heal the wounds that it has inflicted' – as the simile emphasizes, a distinctly 'magical' piece of thinking (p.25). But no political philosophy, even if (or especially if) it asserts absolute pacifism, can escape the question of violence; and, short of total pacifism, it must imply, or make explicit, criteria for determining what constitutes the legitimate and illegitimate use of violence (or 'force'). It is not difficult, in the contexts in which Sartre has advocated violence – such as the Algerian and Vietnam wars – to grasp his criteria for legitimacy, though one may certainly dissent from them. But it is primarily the criteria that must be challenged, not 'violence' as an abstraction.

Barthes, despite the subversive force of some of his maxims and suggestions, was never the most militant of writers; as he grew older, in contrast to Sartre, he increasingly withdrew from politics. For instance, the conclusions to some of the pieces in *Mythologies* – which were originally written for *Les Lettres Nouvelles* in the 1950s – have a polemic political edge that distantly echoes Sartre; but *Roland Barthes* ambiguously calls these conclusions *clausules* with 'a triple function: rhetorical (the scene ends decoratively), signaletic (thematic analyses are recuperated, *in extremis*, by a project of commitment), and economic (the effort is to replace political dissertation by a lighter ellipsis…)' (p.55). This is characteristic of the later Barthes's distancing of himself from conventionally politicized discourse, the arrogant *doxa* of the Militant. He moves from politics to ethics. As to violence, he says in *Roland Barthes*, addressing himself as *vous*, 'you would be somewhat Buddhist!' (p.143 – translation modified). *Roland Barthes* observes that violence always organizes itself 'into a *scene*: the most transitive of behaviour (to eliminate, to kill, to wound, to humble) was also the most theatrical'. In this perspective, violence is not – as Sartre would have it in the Fanon Preface – cleansing and liberating, but an unwitting repetition, a re-enactment of stereotypes (a possibility that Sartre does seem to have been at least partly aware of – see the account of Mathieu's last stand, quoted above). But such a response to violence is also, as *Roland Barthes* acknowledges, 'the stock reaction of an intellectual, of a "clerk"' (p.160). And it hardly solves, though it may shed some light on, the problem of violence in politics.

The implied ethics of the later Barthes are distinctly 'personal': respect and solicitude for the particularity of individual experience on a psychological and corporeal level – though neither mind nor body are to be seen as unitary essences. It is an individualist, aesthetic ethics, with echoes of Valéry, Proust and Gide, and, from an English perspective, of the Bloomsbury group. *Roland Barthes*, however, questions the rigid division between ethics and politics:

> Is there not always something ethical in the political? Is it not Value that establishes the political, the order of reality, pure science of social reality? In the name of what does a militant decide to... militate? Though wrenched away from any ethic, any psychology, does not political praxis have a... psychological and an ethical origin?

At once, the suggestion is undercut, as a 'literally *retarded* notion, for by coupling Ethics and Politics, you are about two hundred years old' (p.127). None the less, Barthes goes on to suggest that the notion that ethics and politics are linked may still be useful; and Barthesian ethics may, as Stephen Ungar has suggested in *Roland Barthes: The Professor of Desire*, figure a politics in which 'social change begins when individual value is shared within a collectivity such as the community of friends' (p.163). This may be seen, with some justice, as idealistic, impractical neo-liberalism: the *Tel Quel* coterie as the image of the good society. But it is also a response to the failures and distortions of militancy and commitment, which have been lived much more widely and intensely in France than in England.

Sartre, too, had a strong ethical cast. *Nausea* in its denunciation of the 'bastards', *Sketch for a Theory of the Emotions* in its analysis of 'magical thinking', *Being and Nothingness* in its exposé of 'bad faith', exemplify a rigorous ethical drive. The end of *Being and Nothingness* promised an ethics to follow, to be grounded, perhaps, in the ontological inescapability of freedom. Like other such promises, this was not kept, but as recently published notebooks show, Sartre worked hard on the problem. With his post-war political involvement, morality partly gave way to a quasi-Communist 'realism', in which acts were evaluated in terms of efficacy, not ethics; this finally led him, he felt, to a point where he 'had blocked out all ideas of morality' (*Sartre by himself*, p.78). But his original political conversion, as he described it, had an ethical base: 'In the name of those principles which it had inculcated into me, in the name of its humanism and of its "humanities", in the name of liberty, equality, fraternity, I swore to the bourgeoisie a hatred which would only die with me' (*Situations*, 1965, p.287). Throughout his career, Sartre's objection seems to have been less to 'universal values' than to the fact that such values were not universally applied. Even during his period of 'realism' many of his political statements – his denunciation of the French use of torture in Algeria, for example – rang with moral fury, although it is certainly true that, on a range of issues, he judged one side much more harshly than the other. In the later 1960s, however, he became consciously concerned to reunite ethics and politics and contest the relegation, in some Marxist thought, of morality to mere superstructure. He kept much of his revolutionary intransigence, but the Sartre who condemned the Soviet invasion of Afghanistan and campaigned to help Vietnam's boat people was closer than he might have liked to believe to the Camus he had once so magisterially reprimanded. It seems that ethics, like the subject and nature, are rather difficult to do without.

Sartre was, in a sense, the last of the great nineteenth-century thinkers; he aspired to global explanations, to system-building on a comprehensive scale. But his systems stayed incomplete; his totalizations fell short of totality. His most massive undertakings – *Roads to Freedom, Critique of Dialectical Reason*, the Flaubert – remained unfinished. And he himself said that the works of his which had the best chance of survival, and which he would like to be read in the future, were the volumes called *Situations* – collected essays, introductions, reviews, interviews: occasional pieces, immmediate responses to events (De Beauvoir, *Adieux*, p.165; *Situations, X*, p.155). Barthes, too, showed global longings, in his enthusiasm for the structuralist project, his 'petit délire scientifique'; but his later work enacts, in its fragmentary, provisional, constantly self-subverting form, a rejection of system – the alphabetical arrangement sometimes adopted a parody of order. Though theoretical terms, often, in classical structuralist style, of a binary kind ('*plaisir / jouissance*', '*studium / punctum*') are generated, they are deployed more as rhetorical devices to facilitate writing than as fixed categories. His last book, *Camera Lucida* (1980), even goes so far as to speak of

> the only sure thing that was in me...: a desperate resistance to any reductive system. For each time, having resorted to any such language [e.g. of sociology, of semiology, of psychoanalysis] to whatever degree, each time I felt it hardening and thereby tending to reduction and reprimand, I would gently leave it and seek elsewhere: I began to speak differently. (p.8)

This is not to say, however, that we should bracket out the concern of either writer with system, with analysis. It is this concern which helps them to bring, to the particular and personal, modes of discourse and investigation that serve to defamiliarize, to make us see the everyday or apparently trivial afresh: a café waiter, a bus queue, a wrestling match, a lover's dark glasses. With Sartre, the modes are those of phenomenology, of existentialism, of heuristic Marxism; with Barthes, those of linguistics, semiology, psychoanalysis, structuralism, poststructuralism. In each case, the modes are mixed, adapted, developed in distinctive ways, with new-minted terms and concepts. The importance of Sartre and Barthes is that they offer fresh ways of writing which, in their distinctive movement between the particular and the general, the analytic and the evocative, challenge traditional categories, both literary and non-literary, of understanding, exploring, constituting experience. Both writers, especially Barthes, were aware of the danger that defamiliarization could become *doxa*: and the academic assimilation of certain aspects of Barthes's work in particular, has not escaped this fate. Moreover, the notion that defamiliarization is preferable to the presentation of 'what oft was thought, but ne'er so well expressed' may be a modern piece of *doxa*. Perhaps it is the writer's function not so much to defamiliarize as to rehabilitate the familiar by trying to express or represent it as faithfully as possible – though this may, in itself, involve some defamiliarization, of a kind which produces a shock of recognition. It could be argued, however, that Sartre and Barthes sometimes achieve this too, and that this is another reason why they engage us. And even if we finally conclude that traditional modes of apprehending experience remain the best, we should certainly confront the challenges of Sartre and Barthes, and assimilate what they have to offer. For their texts enact at least one ancient truth: writing is a form of generosity.

9 From a Tight Place: Raymond Williams

Socialist, cultural analyst and theorist, literary critic, novelist: Raymond Williams combined all these roles. He was the most prominent writer in post-war England to try to develop a totalizing perspective on human activities. As Patrick Parrinder says: 'Allowing for an evident difference in stature, parallels can be drawn between his very English career and that of Sartre' (*The Failure of Theory*, p.73). Williams's relatively early death in 1988, at the age of sixty-six, was a large blow to the intellectual Left and brought a wider sense of loss. What would he have said about the collapse of communism in Eastern Europe and the USSR, about the New World Disorder, about the British Labour Party's third successsive election defeat? How would he have lived the twilight of socialism?

Williams's death produced warm and wide tributes. But in an essay collected in *Heroes and Villains*, R.W. Johnson sounded a more sceptical note. He acknowledged his agreement with Williams, and E.P. Thompson, 'on many, perhaps most, of the big political issues' (p.136), but found Williams's political writing 'repetitive, ritualised, empty and downright evasive' (p.143). Johnson is renowned for pugnacious polemic, and his judgement is doubtless 'unfair': but, the obituary moment over, it is time to take a cooler look at Williams's work. This essay will focus on six aspects of that work: his analysis of culture; his study of drama; his view of television; his novels; his exploration of 'the country and the city'; and his political thought as exemplified in *Towards 2000* (1983).

Towards a Theory of Culture

Culture and Society, Williams's best-known and most influential book, came out in 1958. In this book, he moved away from the more specifically literary concerns of his earlier work on criticism and on drama to consider the notion of culture which had developed in England from the time of the Industrial Revolution. Williams argues that this notion emerges in response to the social changes which industrialization brings. As the nineteenth century continues, it comes into conflict, for some thinkers at least, with the idea of democracy, which is seen as a threat to culture. It also becomes more and more isolated and specialized, confined to the keeping of an increasingly small, and sometimes imaginary minority – from Coleridge's clerisy, through Arnold's remnant, to Leavis's 'educated public' in the twentieth century. At certain times, moreover, the notion of culture tends to become restricted to a rarefied 'aesthetic sphere', especially towards the end of the nineteenth century. A split opens up between the idea of 'culture' and the idea of 'society'. Williams seeks to acknowledge what he feels to be the valuable elements in the notion of culture – its stress on wholeness, tending, nurturing, growth – while rejecting what he sees as its negative aspects: its mystifying organicism, its denial of social and political conflict, its confinement to a minority, and its construction, in the twentieth century, of a mythical 'mass civilization'.

In *Culture and Society*, Williams also explores some of his own positions. He rejects the notion of 'masses', contending that the term is never seen to apply to oneself or those one knows: 'There are in fact no masses; there are only ways of seeing people as masses' (1963 edn, p.289). But, as Terry Eagleton suggests in *Criticism and Ideology*, this could also be said of 'classes' – and this would create difficulties for any radical project that depended on the agency of 'the working class' (1978 edn, pp.28-9). Williams, however, attacks the idea of 'the masses' and the related notion of 'mass-communication' because he sees these as 'the real danger to democracy, not the existence of effective and powerful means of multiple transmission' (p.293). For Williams, *contra* Marshall McLuhan, the medium is not the massage.

Such ideas of the 'mass' are, Williams suggests, complicit with a 'dominative attitude to communication'; he observes that 'almost every kind of leader seems to be genuinely afraid of trusting the processes of majority discussion and decision' (p.303). We might ask here what result 'the processes of majority discussion and decision' might produce in present-day Britain in regard to such matters as capital punishment and immigration – or whether they could be trusted, in the Islamic world, to settle the fate of Salman Rushdie equitably. Williams's assumption is, presumably, that a sufficiently open and informed process of majority discussion and decision would produce the most desirable result; the problem would then be to assess what constituted a sufficiently open and informed process. Such a process might tend to be assessed in a circular way – by the efficacy with which it produced the results desired by particular parties.

Williams also tackles the issue of 'equality' and proposes the idea of 'equality of being'. This notion seems to derive from Williams's discussion of D.H. Lawrence earlier in *Culture and Society*, where he quotes, with approval, Lawrence's affirmation, in his essay 'Democracy', that 'no man shall try to determine the being of any other man, or of any other woman' (Williams's reiteration of the quote omits 'or of any other woman'). Williams contends: 'We must ask, and require the answer, of anyone with a social philosophy, whether this principle is accepted or denied. Some of the most generous social movements have come to fail because, at heart, they have denied this' (p.208).

To affirm 'equality of being' invites immediate assent: but this is precisely the problem. It wins easy assent because its meaning is vague. Perhaps to demand exact meaning is to miss the point: isn't 'equality of being', like Leavis's 'life', a necessary term, even if, or especially if, we can't define or quantify it? But notions like 'equality of being' could be and have been used to justify material inequality: we are all – for instance – equal in the sight of God. At this stage, Williams lacks an ontology of the kind we find in, say, Sartre – a concept of the human 'being' as a becoming, a freedom. Arguably, Sartre's concept is, in the end, no less vague, and, as Sartre himself found, an ontology does not necessarily, or easily, ground or generate a morality and a politics: a human being may be a freedom, but this does not entail – indeed it would seem paradoxical if it did – that a freedom should behave or be allowed to behave in certain ways. None the less, the lack of an explicit and coherent theory of being and/or becoming in *Culture and Society* relates to further problems – for instance, its notion of the 'dominative mood' (p.305). Is it really just a matter of a 'mood'? Shouldn't we ask why certain people or groups should want to dominate others, or why a 'dominative mood' should become dominant? In this area, Sartre's analyses of the dialectic of oppression are relevant; Sartre attempts to explain, in non-essentialist and materialist terms, why human beings oppress their own species.

Williams distinguishes between working-class and bourgeois attitudes in terms of alternative notions of social relationship – one communal, one individualist. He sees the communal notion as the essential working-class idea. This attempt to identify an 'essential' working-class idea is particularly problematic. His account of Arnold in *Culture and Society* argues that 'the worst harm done by the "stock notion" of class, a notion receiving constant assent from the material structure of society, was that it offered category feelings about human behaviour, based on a massing and simplifying of actual individuals, as an easy substitute for the difficulties of personal and immediate judgement' (p.126). Very good: but compare this statement from the conclusion to *Culture and Society*: 'The great majority of English working people want only the middle-class material standard and for the rest want to go on being themselves' (p.311). For 'great majority' substitute 'mass': for here we have, surely, 'a massing and simplifying of actual individuals' that substitutes, easily and comfortingly, 'for the difficulties of personal and immediate judgement'. This is Williams as Arnold inverted: he is simply turning upside-down the crude notion he purports to attack – that most working-class people are desperately anxious to become middle-class. He goes further:

> When we speak, for instance, of a working-class idea, we do not mean that all working people possess it, or even approve of it. We mean, rather, that this is the essential idea embodied in the organizations and institutions which that class creates: the working-class movement as a tendency, rather than all working-class people as individuals. (p.313)

Here, actual individuals are displaced: we have an 'essential idea' embodied (how?) in organizations and institutions created (how?) by a class, but floating free of the individuals who compose that class. This kind of abstraction – 'a massing and simplifying of actual individuals' – leads towards a socialist idealism which is either ineffective (unable to command the support of its supposed constituents) or repressive (knowing the 'essential idea' despite the vagaries of working-class individuals and groups). Williams partly acknowledges this when he says that the notion of 'the ladder' – of individual upward mobility – 'has produced a real conflict of values within the working class itself' (p.318). If actual working-class people adhere to, or are drawn to, the idea of individual upward mobility, by what right can we say that this is not a working-class idea (or, more precisely, an idea of some working-class people), even if we accept the debatable claim that its provenance is middle-class? This is not to say that the idea of individual upward mobility is now the dominant working-class idea, or that the collective idea is in fact a middle-class projection on to the working class as a whole. It is rather, as with the notion of 'masses', to suggest the need for a more complex account of individual and collective modes and motivations.

The Long Revolution (1961) develops some of the concerns of *Culture and Society* and broaches new ones. By the 'long revolution' Williams means a complex process of change that has transformed people's lives and continues to offer the possibility of greater freedom and participation. This process involves 'the struggle for democracy, the development of industry, the extension of communications, and...deep social and personal changes' (1965 edn, p.12). For Williams, the 'long revolution' is not inevitable, nor, necessarily, gradualist or conflict-free. It has been, and is, opposed and blocked in many ways, and there are disparities between rates and modes of change in different aspects of the process – its industrial and democratic aspects, for example. But he seeks to endorse this 'revolution' in almost Newmanic terms: 'In naming the great process of change the long revolution, I am trying to learn assent to it, an adequate assent of mind and spirit' (p.13).

Williams's explorations develop in a range of important though not always fully integrated ways. To challenge the distinction between 'art' and 'ordinary experience', he takes up a theory of perception based partly on contemporary work in biology: that our 'seeing' – our interpretation of sensory input according to a set of rules – is largely a learnt activity rather than a 'natural' one: 'reality *as we experience it* is...a human creation'. This creation has two main sources: 'the human brain as it has evolved, and the interpretations carried by our cultures' (p.34). Though the brain provides a common basis for our interpretative activity, our ways of seeing are not fixed and constant. Different cultures see the world in different ways, and ways of seeing within a specific culture change over time – or, more precisely, human beings change them, in response to the interactions between learnt, culturally inherited patterns and the contemporary environment. The artist also responds to these interactions and communicates his experience, and thus participates in the process of change. 'Art' and 'ordinary experience' are not separate: art is an aspect of the general process of human creativity and communication. Art, like culture, is ordinary.

This does not mean that art, or culture and society, are simple in actuality, or easy to analyse. *The Long Revolution* proposes a complex approach to social and cultural understanding. 'The truth about a society...is to be found in the actual relations, always exceptionally complicated, between the system of decision, the system of communication and learning, the system of maintenance and the system of generation and nurture' (p.136). Williams challenges the notion that any one sector alone – politics, economics, education, art, the family – can provide the key to comprehension and change. On one view, Williams's stress on complexity might seem to evade the problem of causation and to sanction a liberal complacency about the difficulty of explaining change and of contributing to it by such explanation. In another perspective, it can be linked with the Marxist idea of 'overdetermination', which Williams, in *Marxism and Literature* (1977), defines as 'determination by multiple factors' (p.83). As Williams points out in *Towards 2000* (1983), the problem might then be to establish a hierarchy of determinants (1985 edn, p.15).

The primary aim of *The Long Revolution* is to develop and apply concepts and approaches for the analysis of culture. The 'theory of culture' is defined as 'the study of relationships between elements in a whole way of life'; the analysis of culture is 'the attempt to discover the nature of the organization which is the complex of these relationships (p.63). Williams's totalizing approach – the attempt to see a whole structure and a whole process – is an important shift in cultural analysis away from a focus on isolated disciplines. *Culture and Society* delineated the development, in the late nineteenth century, of an approach that used the quality of art as the index of the quality of a civilization; the Leavisian ideology inherited this approach, though narrowing 'art' to a particular idea of 'literature'. The totalizing tendency of *The Long Revolution* is a definite break from that approach, if still a partial and understated one.

The concept of 'a whole way of life' raises problems, however. What constitutes the 'wholeness' of 'a whole way of life'? By what criteria are the boundaries of such 'wholes' drawn? In dealing with, say, a small, enclosed group – an isolated tribe, for example – the boundaries may seem relatively simple, though even then they may waver, and the investigator's own activity may change them. In a more complex, modern situation, it is much more difficult to draw boundaries. Are they to be temporal (a 'period', a decade), national, regional, linguistic, attitudinal, etc.? And are the singular case and holistic adjective adequate? Shouldn't we talk of 'ways of life' and keep 'whole' under erasure?

To provide a heuristic device for the investigation of organizations of life, Williams develops the concept of 'structure of feeling' which he had first introduced in a book written with Michael Orrom,

Preface to Film (1954, pp.21-2). Williams's definition of this concept in *The Long Revolution* is complicated, but we should attempt a summary, given its importance throughout his work. He says that a structure of feeling 'is as firm and definite as "structure" suggests, yet it operates in the most delicate and least tangible parts of our activity' (p.64). In one sense, the 'structure of feeling' is the culture of a period. It is not learned in any formal way, but each new generation creates it – using, in part, elements from the past – as it shapes its response to the unique world it inherits. A 'structure of feeling' corresponds, in some ways, to the dominant 'social character' – Erich Fromm's term, which Williams uses to denote 'a valued system of behaviour and attitudes' (p.63); but, more importantly, it expresses the interaction between the dominant 'social character', alternative 'social characters', and lived, experiential reality. In all actual communities, it is a very deep and wide possession, since communication depends on it: but it is not uniform throughout a society, and is primarily evident in the dominant productive group. At this level, however, it is different from any distinguishable 'social character' as it has to cope not only with the public ideas, but also with their lived omissions and consequences.

With the concept of 'structure of feeling', as with the 'wholeness' of 'a whole way of life', we may ask what constitutes it *as* a structure – why 'structure' rather than, say, a field of attitudes and affects? How far is 'structure' more than a metaphor for 'firmness' and 'interconnectedness' – the metaphor which the later twentieth century prefers to that of 'organic unity'? The temporal dimensions of the concept are also a problem. 'Structure of feeling' has synchronic implications, but Williams's stress, throughout his work, is diachronic, concerned with history, change. How do 'structures of feeling' change, and in what sense, when they change, do they remain 'structures'? *The Long Revolution* seems to suggest that they change with 'the new generation... feeling its whole life in certain ways differently, and shaping its creative response into a new structure of feeling' (p.65). But if a 'structure of feeling' changes with each new generation, there remain the difficulties of delimiting a 'generation' and of accounting for the possible persistence and co-existence of 'structures of feeling' across and within generations. In his later work, Williams sometimes tries to define the concept of 'structure of feeling' more closely, but it remains a shifting signifier.

Structuralism and poststructuralism have deployed the notion of 'structure' in a challenge to the idea of the free, autonomous individual; it is claimed that structures make men, not men structures.

In *The Long Revolution*, however, Williams stresses the role of human agency, indeed human creativity, in the shaping of 'structures of feeling'; and this creativity is not confined to the artist, who partakes, rather, of a general human process of creativity and communication. Up to a point, Williams also commends the existentialist stress on authenticity, much in vogue in the 1950s. But he seeks to situate and complicate the then-current notion of the lone 'outsider'; an especially interesting analysis redefines what might be seen as a range of social 'types' – subject, servant, member, rebel, exile, vagrant – as *modes of relationship* within a society. This redefinition contributes to a wider challenge to the abstract notion of the 'individual', particularly when that notion is counterposed with a no less abstract notion of 'society'. Williams does not dissolve the idea of the 'individual'; rather, he affirms: 'It is right to recognize that we became human individuals in terms of a social process, but still individuals are unique, through a particular heredity expressed in a particular history' (p.117). He counsels a balanced approach to the issue: 'the experience we now have to interpret includes both the gains of individualism and its limits' (p.113). The individual/society, or, in more recent parlance, subject/structure dichotomy is re-understood dialectically:

> To begin with, individuals have varying innate potentialities, and thus receive social influence in varying ways. Further, even if there is a common 'social character' or 'culture pattern', each individual's social history, his actual network of relationships, is in fact unique. These are the basic individualizing factors, but again, as the unique potentialities and the unique history interact, the very fact of the growth of self-consciousness produces a distinct organization, capable both of self-scrutiny and self-direction. This 'autonomous' self grows within a social process which radically influences it, but the degree of gained autonomy makes possible the observed next stage, in which the individual can help to change or modify the social process that has influenced and is influencing him. (pp.100-1)

To ground his political perspective, Williams also proposes a kind of ontology, based partly on biology and partly on sociology: 'If man is essentially a learning, creating and communicating being, the only social organization adequate to his nature is a participating democracy, in which all of us, as unique individuals, learn, communicate and control' – a 'common process' (p.118).

In *Culture and Society* and *The Long Revolution*, Williams had kept his distance from Marxism, working instead to develop a kind of socialist humanism. His later thinking about culture moved much closer to Marxism, though he retained a humanist emphasis. *Marxism and Literature* (1977) aims to promote a flexible and responsive Marxism which insists on 'the full social and historical material process' (p.206), dissolves static abstractions, and takes full account of specificity and variability. In some Marxist thought, especially as it bears on culture, Williams detects a 'basic error': the 'reduction of the social to fixed forms' and the 'taking [of] terms of analysis as terms of substance' (p.129). So he rejects the rigid schema of 'base' and 'superstructure'; he charges that the latter idea is not materialist enough, that it repeats an idealist dualism. The abstracted, dematerialized, frozen elements of the 'superstructure' must be returned to the whole social material process, grasped as actively *produced* in that process. This stress on process, on actively producing a culture, a society, a political order, informs his exploration of further concepts: the 'hegemonic'; selective traditions; formal institutions and cultural formations (that is, artistic and intellectual movements and tendencies such as the Godwin circle, the Pre-Raphaelites and the Bloomsbury Group); and the 'residual', 'dominant' and 'emergent' aspects of a cultural and social material process.

In *Marxism and Literature*, Williams once more deploys, and further defines, his concept of 'structure of feeling'. Indeed, he gives it a whole chapter. As if to answer our earlier question – what constitutes it *as* a structure? – he proposes that it is a structure in that it is 'a set, with specific internal relations, at once interlocking and in tension' (p.132). This develops the metaphor and adds a new one ('set'), but it still remains questionable how far the concept, though suggestive, is more than a rhetorical device which gives the semblance but not the substance of precision.

Williams stresses that 'structure', in the term 'structure of feeling', does not imply stasis: a 'structure of feeling' is a social experience 'in process', 'in solution', as distinct from other, 'precipitated' social semantic formations (another metaphor enters here). It is never a mere flux, however, but 'a structured formation... at the very edge of semantic availability' (p.134), with many characteristics of a 'pre-formation'. The concept is very relevant to art and literature as 'structures of feeling' can especially manifest themselves in these fields.

Williams strives to retain a sense of the specificity of the practices that have, in his view, been abstracted and isolated as 'art' and 'literature'. Indeed, 'structure of feeling' sometimes seems like an attempt to preserve such specificity in what is, in his terms, a politically and sociologically respectable way. But he cannot *replace* the concepts of art and literature: all he can do is to *displace* the experiences for which those concepts stand into a generalized socio-political awareness which especially manifests itself in particular artistic practices.

The central problem with *Marxism and Literature* is suggested by Williams's remark, in the Introduction, that his contact with international Marxist thought in the 1970s gave him 'the sense, for the first time in my life, of belonging to a sphere and dimension of *work* in which I could feel at home' (pp.4-5). This sense of being 'at home' in an enclosed world which takes itself for the whole world is a particularly telling synecdoche for the general ethos of *Marxism and Literature*. To stay within that ethos demands the *a priori* acceptance of the primacy of historical materialism. Williams's insistence throughout the book on 'the full social and historical material process', helpful as an emphasis, becomes all-enveloping; despite his reiterated stress on creativity, the 'full social process' is totalizing, transcendent. It will not leave us, but prevents us everywhere. It is not far from another name for God.

In 'Crisis in English Studies', a lecture delivered in 1981 in the wake of the Cambridge controversy over Colin MacCabe, Williams summarizes the 'controversial positions' in the debate, and concludes by defining the controversial position that he himself has now reached – the position that emerges from *Marxism and Literature*. This is 'cultural materialism...the analysis of all forms of signification, including quite centrally writing, within the actual means and conditions of their production' (*Writing in Society*, 1983, p.210). *Culture* (1981) develops that position. In this book, Williams wants not to abolish the category of literature or do away with discrimination among art-works, but to secure 'their serious recognition as social processes...of a highly significant and valuable kind' (p.126). He affirms that it is important not to set up a category of the aesthetic that is an abstraction, from the variety of specific historical uses of the term, 'to one exclusive set of practices or one exclusive intention or set of intentions'. This does not mean, however, 'that everything, including the most specifically artistic and most specifically aesthetic processes, has to be dissolved into some indiscriminate general social or cultural practice' (p.129).

Williams contends that attempts at a sociology of culture have been too ready to analyse a society and then simply apply this analysis to the cultural practices of that society, instead of recognizing those cultural practices as *part* of the 'general socio-cultural process' (p.143). For instance, 'to analyse the soliloquy in English

Renaissance drama is necessarily, first, a matter of formal analysis, but not as a way of denying or making irrelevant a social analysis; rather as a new and technically rigorous kind of social analysis of *this* social practice' (p.142). We may acknowledge the value of Williams's approach here but question the quasi-scientific ring of 'technically rigorous', and also suggest that 'formal analysis' is itself, within Williams's own perspective, a social practice, and therefore historically mutable: modes of analysis themselves, as well as their putative objects, need to be historicized, and cannot offer a 'pure', timeless technical rigour.

Culture also takes up the vexed questions of 'determinations' and 'relative autonomy'. Williams proposes 'the hypothesis of variable autonomy' – and, thus, variable 'cultural reproduction' – 'according to the degrees of distance between the conditions of a practice and otherwise organized social relations' (p.193). He points to the relative distance of newspaper and television production as compared with writing poems or making sculptures. We can query that spatial metaphor of 'distance', but the attempt to identify, in relation to specific practices, what 'variable autonomy' consists in, is valuable. Otherwise, such a notion may simply become a loose if suggestive way of saying that art, or any other social practice, has some degree of freedom, is not wholly determined by, or homologous with, the economy or any other single determinant. A more precise analysis must specify the kind and extent of such freedom in regard to particular practices.

In the light of Williams's earlier work, *Culture* is especially significant for its proposal that the concept of culture as 'a whole way of life' be replaced by 'the concept of culture as a *realized signifying system*' (p.207). Williams acknowledges the value of the concept of culture as 'a whole way of life' in stressing a general system and challenging separated analysis (for example, of 'the economy', 'politics', 'private life', 'leisure', etc.). But its weakness can be 'a crucial absence of significant relational terms beyond it' (p.210). This links with the problem we pointed out in our discussion of *Culture and Society*: how to establish the boundaries of 'a whole way of life'? With the new definition, 'the social organization of culture, as a realized signifying system, is embedded in a whole range of activities, relations and institutions, of which only some are manifestly "cultural". For modern societies, at least, this is a more effective theoretical usage than the sense of culture as a whole way of life' (p.209). In fact, the problem of boundaries remains in this new formulation. How do we determine the boundaries of 'a realized signifying system' and of that 'whole [note how the adjective creeps back in] range of activities' in which it is 'embedded'? And what precisely are we to understand by metaphors such as 'realized' and 'embedded'? In his work, Williams moves a long way towards a theory of culture; but, despite his progress, crucial concepts still remain unclarified.

Culture shows Williams at his most abstract and theoretical – though not, perhaps, quite theoretical enough. The book also offers a most interesting discussion of dramatic forms, which draws valuably on another major aspect of his work: his study of drama. It is to this that we will now turn.

Definitions of Drama

In 1945, when Williams returned from the war to his studies at Cambridge, he took Ibsen as his topic for the 15,000-word thesis which ex-servicemen could submit towards their degree. The plays of Ibsen spoke most closely to his own condition at that time – to his sense of a political and social *impasse*. He found 'exactly my sensation' in the motif, in *When We Dead Awaken* (1900), of coming 'to a tight place where you stick fast. There is no going forward or backward' (*Politics and Letters*, p.62). Williams developed an interpretation of Ibsen which was vital to his own project: it seemed to him that Ibsen's drama enacted the idea that everyone is defeated in his work, but that this defeat, though crucial, never invalidates the original project nor entails its renunciation.

His work on Ibsen fed into his first book, *Drama from Ibsen to Eliot* (1952). Here his declared aim is to apply 'practical criticism' to drama; he seeks to reaffirm what Yeats called 'the ancient sovereignty of words in drama'. The book mounts a sustained attack on dramatic naturalism, which is said to limit the dramatist and threaten the achievement of dramatic totality. Williams strongly stresses the need for the author, the dramatist, to be in control; he presses a distinction between 'drama' and 'theatre' and he is reluctant to allow any freedom to what he classifies as 'theatre' – for example, to the actors, the director, the stage designer; he cites, with implicit approval, Yeats's desire to rehearse the actors of his play in barrels to keep them under control. There is little sense of the drama as a collaborative effort between author, actors, director, stage designer and others; little sense of enjoyment in the theatre.

The concept of drama which Williams opposes to 'theatre' is itself a questionable one. For example, he says: 'The substance of a play –

the total organization of words, and those visual elements which the author prescribes – either conveys the experience he wishes to communicate, or it does not' (1964 edn, p.99). This dogmatic statement begs many questions. It assumes, for instance, that the 'substance' of a play can be clearly distinguished from any specific production, in an act of reading or by actors in performance – for if it could not be so distinguished, how could we judge whether or not the dramatic communication had been successful? If it can be so distinguished, however, isn't the play, in effect, redundant? The statement further assumes that there is a clear-cut binary opposition between effective and failed communication – but why might we not admit the possibility of different degrees of communicative success? This question is an aspect of a more general issue which Williams does not confront in this book: is a simple communication model adequate to account for successful or unsuccessful drama?

The most significant innovation of Williams's next book, *Drama in Performance* (1954) is its stress on 'structure of feeling'. This is combined with the simple communication model of *Drama from Ibsen to Eliot*. Thus *Drama in Performance* states that the purpose of a play should be 'the communication, through [story, characters] of the structure of feeling which the dramatist first imagines and creates' (p.116). As we suggested in our discussion of Williams's analysis of culture, the notion of 'structure of feeling' is a slippery and ambiguous one in his work; we should note here, however, that 'structure of feeling' is seen as a product of the dramatist rather than as a more general condition which the dramatist articulates.

Drama in Performance mounts an inquiry into 'the relation between a dramatic text and a dramatic performance' (p.10). Its case-studies are the performances, in the inferred conditions of their times, of five very different plays; they range from Greek tragedy, through English medieval drama and Shakespeare, to Chekhov. In this book, Williams advocates not the 'practical criticism' which he promoted in *Drama from Ibsen to Eliot* but 'dramatic criticism': a combination of 'literary' and 'theatrical' criticism which considers 'play and performance, literary text and theatrical representation' as a *unity* (p.12). Unity and integration are important criteria for Williams in this book, and he feels that the text of a play should achieve these prior to any performance.

Drama in Performance might be seen as, in part, a corrective to the emphasis on the text in *Drama from Ibsen to Eliot*. Indeed, Williams affirms: 'A normal interest in drama ought always to include an interest, and a delight, both in dramatic literature and in dramatic performance' (p.107). But it is doubtful how far Williams obeys his own normative injunction (you *ought* to enjoy it!). As in *Drama from Ibsen to Eliot*, his pedestrian approach rather treads down delight. Furthermore, his continued insistence on the primacy of the text constricts his sense of the pleasure and purpose of performance. Ideally, it seems, the text should wholly control the performance, and performance is in no way necessary to the text: prior to any performance, the text is already complete. In the earlier book, the communication model made the play, in a sense, redundant, since we already had access to the experience of which it was the dramatic realization. In this book, it is performance that is redundant, an agreeable but inessential supplement.

In 1966, Williams produced a remarkable book which aimed to broaden the discussion of tragedy beyond the confines of a literary genre. *Modern Tragedy* outlines the 'many roads' by which we come to tragedy – as 'an immediate experience, a body of literature, a conflict of theory, an academic problem' (p.13) – and challenges the distinction between academic and popular uses of the term:

> The events which are not seen as tragic are deep in the pattern of our own culture: war, famine, work, traffic, politics. To see no ethical content or human agency in such events, or to say that we cannot connect them with general meanings, and especially with permanent and universal meanings, is to admit a strange and particular bankruptcy, which no rhetoric of tragedy can finally hide. (p.49)

His challenge to the distinction between 'tragedy' in its popular sense(s) and 'permanent and universal meanings' is combined with an attack on the 'universalist character of most tragic theory' (p.46) and particularly on the assumption of a permanent, universal 'human nature'. To reject that assumption necessarily transforms the problem: 'Tragedy is then not a single and permanent kind of fact, but a series of experiences and conventions and institutions... the varieties of tragic experience are to be interpreted by reference to the changing conventions and institutions' (pp.45-6).

There is, however, a contradiction between Williams's attack on such assumptions and his implication that the experiences popularly called 'tragic' are indeed such. He seems to shift between a rejection of universalism and a desire to endow experiences excluded from some academic definitions of tragedy with 'universal', or at least general, significance. His definition of tragedy is very broad: 'all that is common, in the works we call tragedies, is the dramatization of a particular and grievous disorder and its resolution' (p.53). But this could surely also apply to many works usually called 'comedies' or 'romances'.

Williams also wants to wrest the idea of tragedy away from assumptions of the impossibility of change, the ineradicability of evil, the inevitability of suffering. He seeks to analyse 'the structure of tragedy in our own culture' (p.62) and to question 'the complacencies of our fashionable despair [and] the grossness of our defensive cynicism' (p.202). He challenges the apotheosis of death as an absolute in a world without God or immortality:

> The life-death contradiction is limited, in fact, to the kind of individual consciousness especially characteristic of bourgeois philosophy. 'I exist – I shall die' seems absolute, within this experience, but Camus sometimes recognized, at the limits of his strength, that 'we exist' is a permanent alternative proposition, and if this is so, then 'we exist – we shall not die' is in fact a resolution, and one which many men have in practice attained. (p.188)

But these propositions are not, as Williams implies, mutually exclusive. The dialectic of death is precisely the tension between 'I exist – I shall die' / 'we exist – we shall not die': precisely the contradiction between the fact that while this individual existence will be cancelled, other existences will, presumably, persist. Williams moves close to a form of bad faith here, to an attempt to assimilate the 'I' into the 'we', to forget death as a personal reality in an abstraction which in fact only gains its significance from the fact that death *is* a personal reality.

This relates to Williams's assimilation of revolution to tragedy in this book and to the uneasy aestheticization of revolution which such an assimilation produces: for the idea that 'we shall not die' may serve to diminish the significance of individual deaths in the revolutionary process. Williams does not formally endorse such diminishment:

> The tragic action, in its deepest sense, is not the confirmation of disorder, but its experience, its comprehension and its resolution. In our own time, this action is general, and its common name is revolution. We have to see the evil and the suffering, in the factual disorder that makes revolution necessary, and in the disordered struggle against the disorder. We have to recognize this suffering in a close and immediate experience, and not cover it with names. But we follow the whole action: not only the evil, but the men

> who have fought against evil; not only the crisis, but the energy released by it, the spirit learned in it. (p.83)

We must not cover suffering with names: Williams stitches suffering into a tragic pattern, which he then seeks to rehumanize, but in terms of a totalizing perspective which subsumes individuals and their sufferings. It may be, in fact, that the dialectic of tragedy, the constant difficulty of defining it, is active exactly in this tension between an aestheticization of suffering and an agonized apprehension of it, but Williams seems to seek, in his attitudes to tragedy and to revolution, to dissolve this tension into a perspective which will acknowledge but distance the suffering. This leads to confusion, evasion, and a loss of the dialectical tension which generates tragedy.

In 1967 Williams became Reader in Drama at Cambridge University, and in 1968 he issued substantially revised and expanded versions of *Drama from Ibsen to Eliot* and *Drama in Performance*. In the revised version of the former book, 'Eliot' had, significantly, been replaced by 'Brecht'. Williams said that he felt that these revised books formed a set with *Modern Tragedy*. In *Drama from Ibsen to Brecht*, the simple communication model of *Ibsen to Eliot* has largely disappeared. Instead, Williams employs the term 'structure of feeling' to indicate an 'essential relationship': 'the continuity of experience from a particular work, through its particular form, to its recognition as a general form, and then the relation of this general form to a period' (p.17). In this perspective, the 'structure of feeling' is both within a play, in that play's particular form, and also in a specific historical moment; it is neither wholly 'aesthetic' nor wholly 'historical'.

Williams's attack on naturalism in *Ibsen to Eliot* is amended in *Ibsen to Brecht* by means of a distinction between 'naturalism' and the 'naturalist habit'. In the great naturalist drama, there is a precise internal relationship between a particular 'structure of feeling' – the passion for a whole and wholly human kind of truth – and the effective conventions for articulating that structure in a specific dramatic action – the direct representation of human actuality. It is this relationship which characterizes 'naturalism'. When the naturalist conventions became established and lost precise relation to the 'structure of feeling' which they had been developed to express, they became self-sufficient dogmas and degenerated into the 'naturalist habit' which, for instance, crippled T.S. Eliot's later plays.

Williams identifies both a historical succession and, in authentic work, a continual co-existence, of naturalism, private and social expressionism, and the theatre of illusion and of the absurd. In this succession and co-existence, Brecht's work is seen as 'the most important and original in European drama since Ibsen and Strindberg' (p.277). It is work which both develops and criticizes a dramatic tradition and which offers a revolutionary and historical 'objective viewpoint' – a 'complex seeing' which both shows but then critically explains thwarting and destruction.

The revised version of *Drama in Performance* develops an important general argument which ultimately relates to film and television. Williams contends that 'the equation of drama with theatre . . . is now our most evident difficulty'. 'Theatre' here is being used in a rather different sense from the one that it had in *Drama from Ibsen to Eliot*; it means, not so much the actor, directors, etc., but the physical site of performance and the practices which sustain it as such. Drama in its early stages was 'a moving and open art' (1972 edn, p.183), but became static and framed as the walls of theatres were built and as broader changes in politics, society and 'structures of feeling' occurred. Dramatic writing and action were divided, and action was specialized to the sensational – crime, murder, fighting, spectacle. This specialization has continued, even with the development of film and television, which potentially have a greater flexibility and freedom. For Williams, a particularly significant corollary of this specialization is that 'any decisive action, in which men in general try to change their condition, is unconsciously ruled out'. Modern drama can grow by going 'where reality is being formed, at work, in the streets, in assemblies, and [by engaging] at those points with the human needs to which the actions relate' (p.184). At present, film and television are still largely locked in older modes, and in limiting economic and social structures. But they offer an unparalleled opportunity for a 'newly open and mobile experience', for an 'essential continuity of creation and production' (p.186), and for the control, by the dramatist, of his work, though possibly in co-operative effort. This last proviso marks a difference from the stress on the isolated dramatist in the earlier version of *Drama in Performance*.

In 1974 Williams became Professor of Drama at Cambridge. This was a new Chair, with no department attached, although as Williams pointed out in his inaugural lecture, drama was hardly a new concern for the University. This lecture, 'Drama in a dramatised society', focused on a new phenomenon:

> for the first time a majority of the population has regular and constant access to drama [and] drama, in quite new ways, is built

> into the rhythms of everyday life... This is part of what I mean by a dramatised society... What we now have is drama as habitual experience. (1975 edn, p.5; *Raymond Williams on Television*, 1989, p.4)

The medium which saturates everyday life with drama is television; and it is to Williams's concern with television that we shall now turn.

Raymond Williams on Television

Williams's study *Television: Technology and Cultural Form* (1974) does not merely retain its relevance today; it matters more than ever. In this study, Williams makes a crucial distinction between television as a technology and television as a 'cultural form'. His prime conceptual target is 'technological determinism' – the view that 'the steam engine, the automobile, television, the atomic bomb, have *made* modern man and the modern condition' (p.13). This is partly a covert polemic against Marshall McLuhan. Williams also challenges the inverse idea of 'determined technology' – the view that those who wanted a technology developed wholly control its uses and effects – and the notion of 'symptomatic technology', which sees 'particular technologies, or a complex of technologies, as *symptoms* of change of some other kind' (p.13).

For Williams, the crucial objection to all these ideas is that they each *isolate* technology – as cause, effect, or symptom. Instead what is required is a complex, dialectical understanding of the processes and practices in which, in specific social situations, technologies are deployed and developed. '[T]echnology... is at once an intention and an effect of a particular social order' (p.128). Williams sees the shape of broadcasting in modern society as a social product of a distinctive tendency which he terms 'mobile privatization': televsion serves a way of living that is 'at once mobile and home-centred' (p.26).

Williams also challenges the concept of 'programming', of thinking of television in terms of self-contained units or 'programmes'. Instead, he proposes that 'the central television experience [is] the fact of flow' (p.95), not only within but also between programmes. His analysis of a British news and news-magazine sequence suggests how 'a directed but apparently casual and miscellaneous flow operates, culturally, following a given structure of feeling' (p.111). The flow of a particular television service is 'the flow of meanings and values of a specific culture' (p.118). Williams generates here an important concept which enables a kind of analysis that does not only isolate and examine particular programme but also studies the flow (and thus the culture) in which they occur. The spread of video recorders in the home, which empower the viewer, to a limited extent, to intervene in, arrest and alter the 'flow' would complicate such analysis today.

Finally, Williams considers the technologies which were emergent in the 1970s and are now much more developed. These technologies include new types of receiver, such as large-screen; cable systems; visual information systems; satellite communications; video cassettes and cameras; reactive and interactive devices. They all pose questions of cultural form. They could enable 'inexpensive, locally based yet internationally extended television systems, making possible communication and information-sharing on a scale that not long ago would have seemed utopian', but they might also be

> the tools of... a short and successful counter-revolution, in which, under the cover of talk about choice and competition, a few paranational corporations, with their attendant states and agencies, could reach farther into our lives, at every level from news to psychodrama, until individual and collective response to many different kinds of experience and problem became almost limited to choice between their programmed possibilities (p.151).

It is, of course, the latter scenario which is being prepared at present.

Williams's concern with television grew partly out of his concern with the older and broader mode of drama. Another older mode with which he was even more actively engaged, not only as a critic and a theorist, but also as a practitioner, was the novel, and it is Williams the novelist we shall discuss next.

The Claims of Fiction

Raymond Williams's fiction seems to have been very important to him. Asked in an interview whether it was 'in a curious sense your novels, your fiction, that you care most deeply about and would like to be remembered by', Williams replied 'I think so'. Tony Pinkney, who quotes this exchange at the start of his study of Williams's novels (p.11), clearly feels that the novels have been overshadowed by Williams's cultural and political writing. The implication is that it is the weight of his achievements in these fields that has prevented due recognition of his stature as a novelist. There is another, harder way of seeing the matter: that, if it had not been for Williams's achievements as a cultural and political writer, his novels would have received even less attention than they have done: that they lack the power in themselves to command an appreciative readership. If it is the case, as Kevin Davey suggests, that '[t]hose who follow [Williams's] criticism or cultural theory turn only rarely' to his novels (*PN Review* 51, p.40), this may be because the novels are not all that good. Williams's intentions and ideas, as we infer them from his fiction, are certainly interesting; the question is whether his skills as a novelist are adequate to realize them.

Williams's first novel, *Border Country*, was published in 1960. The story starts as Matthew Price, a lecturer in London, arrives back in Glynmawr, his native village, to see his father, who has suffered a coronary. The novel shows Matthew's attempts to communicate with his father and with others who have stayed on in the village, and intercuts this with flashbacks of his own and his father's past. Matthew is brought to consider his own relationship with his father, the community, and the past, and to recognize his estrangement from them: 'I hardly know myself here': 'I feel so far outside' (pp.277, 279). He leaves the village, and his father starts to recover. But on his way back to London after a second visit, a sudden summons recalls him to Glynmawr. It is bad news; but as he travels to the village once more, he feels 'a deep flowing-back of energy...the recovery of a childhood which at the moment of recovery was a child's experience no more, but a living connexion between memory and substance' (p.317). He goes home from his father's funeral with 'the feeling of exile ending. For the distance is measured, and that is what matters. By measuring the distance we come home' (p.351).

The themes of *Border Country* are division, exile and loss of identity, and the partial recovery, in a necessary distance, of identity, connection and continuity – and not in a solely 'personal' integration. *Border Country* is, in a sense, an anti-escape novel: it challenges, even as it partly employs, the narrative of upward mobility in which the hero rejects and escapes from a constricting environment. In *Border Country*, the hero is, in a way, the father as well as the son, the man who stays as well as the man who goes – with the father's friend, Morgan Rosser, who experiences partial upward mobility, as the intermediate term. The novel seeks not to reject the village community but to acknowledge it, even in its distance from Matthew and in its recognized limitation. The story strongly evokes Matthew's personal crisis, but the focus is not on him alone. Williams seems to want to avoid what he calls, in *The Long Revolution*, the 'fiction of special pleading', in which the focus is on the consciousness of the protagonist, and other consciousnesses are diminished, seen only in the protagonist's terms (p.311).

Border Country is competently executed in a careful realist style. Williams writes convincing dialogue which eschews a stereotyped 'Welshness', although he is perhaps too anxious to exorcise the spectre of Dylan Thomas. Occasionally his style seems predictable, especially in his physical descriptions of people, but in its concern for detail, especially the detail of manual work, it can be quietly effective, and sometimes moves into a richer mode:

> One day as [Matthew] rode up the lane from school, he heard a strange high shouting, beyond the patch. He ran his bike along the hedge by the holly, and followed the shouting. Across the drying green, by the apple-trees, Harry and Jack Price were shouting and dancing, clapping their hands above their heads. Above them, twenty feet in the air and still rising, a swarm of bees moved in a gathering brown cloud. Will [Matthew] had seen many swarms, but the first thing he noticed, now, was the way his father and grandfather were dancing; the bees seemed only an excuse. And then Ellen arrived, carrying a zinc bath full of pans, and they all took the pans and began a furious drumming and clattering on them. The brown cloud rose steadily higher, above the apple trees. Still the tanging continued, and the excited shouting. (p.193)

Here, work and leisure, nature and culture, male and female, parents and children, come together, in a controlled, purposive exuberance.

Second Generation (1964) takes two interlinked families of Welsh origin – the husbands are brothers – who now live next door to each other in a town which is the site both of a car factory, where the husbands work, and of an ancient university. The strongest aspect of the novel is the portrayal of Peter Owen, the son of one of the families. Peter is torn between two worlds, and trying to find a way of connecting them – one of Williams's most characteristic themes. He still lives at home, and he is engaged to the girl next door, his uncle's stepdaughter; but he is a research student at the ancient university. As he tells his academic supervisor, Robert Lane – who is himself of humble stock, but now assimilated: 'I'm asking for the connection, between work and living'... 'The connections are deeper than we ever suspected: between work and living, between families, between cities. You surrendered by breaking the connections, or by letting them atrophy. We shall try not to do that, in this generation. We shall hold to the connections and ride our history' (pp.252, 253).

The account of Peter's inner and outer conflicts perceptively anticipates the conflicts of some of the young student rebels of the later 1960s. While by no means wholly endorsing Peter's behaviour, the novel suggests that his rebellion cannot simply be dismissed as 'immature', as what Robert Lane defensively calls 'adolescent ranting' (p.254). In the interviews with Williams collected in *Politics and Letters* (1979), Williams compared his own state as a student in the early 1940s with that of some student militants in the 1960s (p.52). *Second Generation* does not focus only on Peter: to do so could bring it close to 'the fiction of special pleading'. It also tries, for example, to explore the situation of Kate, Peter's mother, as she too goes through a crisis of relationship, connection and direction. And, on a more obviously 'political' plane, it gives an account of an unsuccessful strike at the car factory.

The imaginative and technical resources of *Second Generation* are inadequate, however, to its ambitious range and its repertoire of potentially rich themes. Its narrative prose and dialogue are undistinguished. Williams lacks a sufficiently subtle and powerful language for the evocation and exploration of emotion. His attempt to register the consciousness of his women characters is slack, trivializing. Such as they are, the sexual scenes are embarrassingly bad. Indeed, *Second Generation* shows a certain prim, Old-Left aversion to sexual 'immorality', personified in the dubious figure of Arthur Dean, the supposedly radical don who is, for a time, Kate's lover, and whose new book proclaims: 'All the great radicals have been sexual radicals' (p.35). Kate repudiates their affair to him as 'the old bourgeois fantasy' of 'the personal break-out, through sex' (p.272). But the old bourgeois fantasy of family life is accepted uncritically in the novel.

The Fight for Manod (1979) brings together Matthew Price, of *Border Country*, and Peter Owen, of *Second Generation*. Peter's former tutor, Robert Lane, who now works for the government, takes them both on as consultants to look into a plan to build a new city in Wales which will be structured on modern communications technology. Matthew is older now, ill and tired; he seems trapped in a 'structure of feeling' – and a social structure – like that epitomized, for Williams, by the motif in Ibsen's *When We Dead Awaken*, of coming 'to a tight place where you stick fast. There is no going forward or backward'. An exchange with a friend sums up his condition:

'...I want the pattern to break, to some new possibility.'

> 'But that's what's wearing you out. You can't push a whole system.'
>
> 'Neither push it nor settle inside it'. (p.187)

The friend tells him: 'you are not history. You're one man working against the grain. All you can do you've done'. But Matthew will not accept this 'kindly sentence' (p.188).

Peter's Owen's itinerary since *Second Generation* has been varied. He has fulfilled the intention announced at the end of that novel, and worked in the same car factory as his father; he has spent six months in prison for assaulting a policeman during an anti-Vietnam march; and he has written a successful book, *Industrial Estate*. But he remains restless, unsettled.

The Fight for Manod contrasts, but does not choose between, two kinds of radicalism: Matthew's belief in 'working where I can... working *for*, always. And...working against only when I finally have to'; and Peter's more actively oppositional stance, summed up in his reply: 'You have to now' (p.186). Peter is younger, more urgent, more militant, more confused, more selfish, and, in some ways, more effective. As they explore the Manod scheme in their respective ways – Matthew staying close to the locality, Peter following a devious trail to London and then to Europe – they, and we, start to get a sense of the complexities and pressures of the situation, of the links between local and national needs and desires, and paranational capitalism and corruption. *The Fight for Manod* conveys the difficulty of penetrating and connecting complex and mystified social and political processes, and links this with the needs and desires of human beings.

In contrast to *Second Generation, The Fight for Manod* cuts down on description and relies a lot on dialogue. As with the earlier novel, there are weaknesses which, interestingly, very much resemble those weaknesses in drama which Williams attributed to the 'naturalist habit': a loss of rhythm within scenes and perhaps over the whole book, and much realistic 'business' – the characters spend a lot of words drinking, eating, driving, and opening and closing doors. Such banal details seem to be used to prop up and pad out the novel. An example: 'Susan came in and said that she had made lunch: nothing much, just soup, bread and cheese' (p.137). This also exemplifies the central function of women in Williams's novels: some feeble pro-feminist concessions cannot stop the constant slide towards a cosy acceptance of women in a wife-mother-cook-waitress role.

In the year before *The Fight for Manod* was published, a novel by

Williams of a different sort came out. *The Volunteers* (1978) partakes of the form and idiom of both the thriller and the 'future fiction'. It is set in an imagined late 1980s Britain which has a National Government and where no general socialist opposition is in evidence; the narrator, Lewis Redfern, at one point recalls the 1970s and 'a Labour government (that name takes you back)' (p.67). Redfern, once a man of left-wing convictions, can still summon socialist perspectives on occasion, but now for the most part sports a dismissive, or defensive, semi-comic cynicism – 'get anyone on to the end of social democracy and it's a fact that they'll never get up in the morning' (p.78). His discourse is a mixture of clipped, hardboiled slang – 'I played it straight down the line' (p.31) – and a more complex mode suggestive of his uncertainties and of his repressed intelligence and conscience.

Redfern's pursuit of the truth about an incident in Wales in which a government minister was shot and wounded leads him into a labyrinth in which he comes to suspect the existence of the 'Volunteers'. This seems to be an association of people vowed to infiltrate the institutions and power structures of contemporary society with the ultimate aim of effecting radical change. Redfern finds himself drawn, or pushed, towards this association, and his own uneasy detachment is called into question: 'I wanted the cement that keeps so many lives together: the experience of belonging to something, of confirming an identity in the identification with others' (pp.165-6).

In Williams's fiction, and perhaps in his work in general, *The Volunteers* marks a significant development, both in its partial break from realism, and in its increasing sense of obscurity and ambiguity. It dramatizes the difficulty of penetrating and connecting the processes of a complex, opaque, divided, mystified society; it also dramatizes the problems of commitment – of if, how, where, and to what to commit oneself (even while recognizing that one is in a sense committed anyway, simply by living in a particular society). With this novel we are in a world where simplicities, in so far as they ever seemed to exist, have vanished.

Loyalties (1985) returns to realism to some extent; but, like *The Volunteers*, it has a 'thriller' element. It tends towards the hermeneutic complexity of a Le Carré novel, though in a more moralized and politicized way – an interesting development, given that Williams denounced such fiction in *Towards 2000* (pp.141-2). Like *The Volunteers*, it conveys an increasing sense of the difficulty of commitment, of loyalty, and of penetrating the processes and grasping the connections of a complex society, not only at a given moment but also over stretches of time. The novel's historical reach is long: it covers most of Williams's lifespan. As Mike Westlake pointed out in his review of the novel, 'all the best material is there' – Spain, the Second World War, 1945, Hungary, Suez, '68, the 1984-5 miners' strike (*PN Review* 51, p.64).

This material is under-used, however. For example, the account of a Normandy tank battle in the novel is less vivid and harrowing than Williams's 'war memoir' in the *Politics and Letters* interviews (pp.55-9). The celebrated anti-Vietnam demonstration in Grosvenor Square is weakly evoked. The tensions *within* the mining communities during the 1984-5 strike are evaded, unexplored – the pit in Danycapel is 'unpicketed because of the local solidarity' (p.334). We might defend this as a deliberate 'alienation effect' to draw attention to the difference between lived history and its representations, or to the failure of potentially liberating movements. But neither the novel itself, nor Williams's declared aesthetics of fiction, offer any warrant for this.

There are other problems. More than any of Williams's previous novels, *Loyalties* props up dialogue with banal 'business': 'Norman sipped his wine'; 'he finished his coffee'; 'Norman lit a cigarette'; 'Norman stubbed out his cigarette' (pp.188, 202, 260, 263). The novel seems psychoanalytically naïve in regard to the 'family romance' element on which it turns – Gwyn is the product of a brief union between the upper-class Communist, Norman, and the working-class Welsh girl, Nesta. To see this apparent naïvety as a trap for psychoanalytic gullibility would be to attribute to the novel a degree of sophistication (perhaps that dreaded, decadent 'postmodernist' sophistication which *Towards 2000* deplores) which it does not seem to possess.

The characterization in *Loyalties* is poor – though 'Monkey', Monk Pitter, has his moments, indeed is evoked with an exuberance that Williams normally lacks or represses. As usual, the women come off worst. Gwyn's Jill is a pale stereotype of a supportive wife. Emma, the committed communist, unshaken by Hungary or Czechoslovakia, seems potentially interesting, but the picture is undeveloped. To compare *Loyalties* with Doris Lessing's *The Golden Notebook* (1962) and *The Four-Gated City* (1969) is to bring out the lack of tension and insight in Williams's portrayal of the communist left, and more generally of women, especially radical women.

Loyalties does not hierarchize its characters or achieve closure as clearly as Mike Westlake suggests in his review. Norman, for instance, remains an effectively ambiguous figure, and the novel ends with the words 'open questions'. We might see this, of course, as itself a form of closure, one suspiciously congenial to the modern reader; though we should recall Williams's remark that 'open questions' are always 'specific historical questions' (*Marxism and Literature*, p.197). But the novel's 'open questions' lack power, pressure.

Williams then turned to concentrate on 'a historical novel of a different kind'. *People of the Black Mountains* was intended to take Williams's native Black Mountain area as 'it is inhabited in different periods...by different kinds of people, manifesting different social relations, and exercising different ways of using the land' (*Politics and Letters*, pp.301, 302). The novel was to stretch from neolithic times to the twentieth century and perhaps slightly into the future. Williams's aim was to show 'history' in an active sense, as human shaping, and to bring out the continuities and connections over time between the people of the place, even when those connections had apparently been broken.

The first volume of the novel was published posthumously, in 1989. Its timespan runs from around 23,000 BC to around AD 51, from the Ice Age to the Roman occupation of Britain, with some interpolations from the late twentieth century. It challenges the narrow 'bourgeois' conception of the novel by its collective concern; a concern for 'people' as well as for the doings of discrete individuals and for a common rather than largely self-centred memory: 'The mountains were too open, too emphatic, to be reduced to personal recollection: the madeleine, the shout in the street. What moved, if at all, in the moonlit expanse was a common memory, over a common forgetting' (p.11). *People of the Black Mountains I* also challenges three attitudes to history. One is the attitude which confines history largely to written traces, thus writing off 'ten thousand generations of conscious life and memory'. Another is the identification of history with the narratives of dominant groups – 'what becomes history is a selection by the winners' (p.325). A third, at the other extreme from the 'bourgeois' isolation of individuals, sees history *only* in terms of large collective movements over time: 'In one kind of history the generations are seen as epochs: single herds which move through the country, acknowledged as innumerable but seen as common. Little else can be felt as the generations appear to rush past. Yet the true pace, always, was local and day by day' (pp.82-3). Williams does not deny the importance of history; but he wants to open a more complex seeing, to suggest that there are other stories.

It is stories that this novel mainly offers, close-up accounts which are focused through a few figures. These accounts are often of typical and/or crucial moments: birth, marriage, death; hunting, herding, sharing, building, feasting, singing, fighting; the meeting of hunters and shepherds, the development of the power of measurement, the division between mental and manual labour, the growth of private property, the advent of armies. The problem is how to link these moments together over such a long timespan, to suggest their epochal and/or crucial quality, and to give a sense also of epochal movements.

Williams's approach to this problem employs three techniques. One is the recurrence of names, sometimes with slight variations, in generations widely separated in time: the effect is of a distant, not quite congruent echo. The second is the return, in the form of old tales and legends, of what was first represented in an immediate way: we see how the passage of time transforms the up-to-the-minute into myth. The third and most important technique is the use of the frame tale of Glyn, a man of our time, of the late twentieth century, searching the Black Mountains, on a moonlit night, for his grandfather, Elis, who has failed to return from a long walk. As Glyn anxiously scours the landscape, calling 'Taid! Taid!' – the old Welsh name for 'grandfather' (p.9) – voices seem to sound and we move back into the past (but a past that was present for those who lived it); we return to our present and to Glyn from time to time. Glyn is thus, nominally, the 'totalizing consciousness' who brings out the continuities and connections over time.

Such success as the novel achieves is patchy. Some of the accounts of past moments are vivid and forceful. There is, for example, the rape of Seril by her stepfather, her flight and marriage into another tribe, the murder of her husband by her stepfather, her own suicide, and the implied reconciliation, after the stepfather has confessed to the murder, of the tribes: a birth of tragedy here, perhaps. And to some extent these accounts do build into a broader chronicle that stays in the mind. But there is little in them that a good 'popular' writer could not do as well, perhaps better. The style can be sharp – 'the long dazzle of the lake', for instance (p.49), and over longer stretches, it can attain a restrained lyricism. Some of the novel, especially in its early sections, seems a version of pastoral, though not sequestered from threat, or serving to mask inequality: it is a pastoral of plenty and sharing. 'Families and children, grass and flocks, trees and beasts for the hunt, abounded in these good mountains and valleys, under the kind skies' (p.215). But the style can also be awkward, clotted with clumsy material detail. Admittedly the sense, particularly earlier in the novel, of living on the edge of survival, opens a new perspective on the 'business' of preparing and consuming food and drink in Williams's earlier novels: such activities are, after all, the essential activities of living, without which no physical life, let alone intellectual and emotional life, could take place, a fact the 'bourgeois' novel of personal relationships may forget. Who wants for food in Henry James? But it is open to question whether the 'people' Williams wants to portray themselves saw these activities in the banal way in which he often describes them.

The technique of Glyn as the 'totalizing consciousness' of the novel quickly breaks down, within most of the sections that start with him, into what is, in effect, an 'impersonal narrator' who summarizes change over long timespans and draws out some of the general implications of the stories we have been told. This narrator also takes over sometimes in the sections that deal more directly with the past – 'The Lords of Banavint', for example. This impersonal narration can be interesting, when we hear Williams's characteristic tones and nuances, but at times it comes across as partly undigested, and fairly low-level, 'research'. The very last part of the novel, about half a page long, tries to bring the novel back to Glyn, and to its beginning: 'His search for Elis on the high moors was part of a quest for himself, for a history and a landscape that had shaped his being' (p.358). To some extent, this seems like an attempt to draw the work back into the bottle of the self-corked 'bourgeois' novel from which Williams has been working to free it. It might be seen as an attempt to 'balance' the individual and the collective, to see the 'person' as produced out of, and still depending on, 'people', but it has a rather hasty, inadequate quality.

Above all, *People of the Black Mountains I*, despite its anti-imperialist aims, practices what the postmodernist Jean-François Lyotard calls a 'soft imperialism'. Its style, moving between the lyrical and the pedestrian, remains largely uniform, and works to efface difference, to draw its diverse stories into a totalizing, homogeneous narrative of people who are, *mutatis mutandi*, not unlike Williams himself. Williams does not try to write different sections in markedly different styles, for example, and though linguistic difference is referred to, it is barely exemplified in the prose. The 'imperialist' impression is reinforced by the sense that 'knowledge' lies in the totalizing consciousness of the 'impersonal narrator'. Epistemological issues about the difficulty of knowing the past are raised in the sections nominally concerned with Glyn – there are references to 'the strong yet uncertain evidence of those distant times' and to the tale of

Menvandir and the Company of Measurers as 'a possible construction, from the many traces' (pp.236, 237). But these uncertainties do not inform the structure or style of the whole text.

The siting of knowledge in the narrator is an aspect of what might be called the 'educational model' of human development which tends to homogenize the stories. Williams shows human beings developing rationally, facing and trying to deal with dangers and problems, sometimes making mistakes and falling back into error and superstition, but continuing that long revolution towards an educated and participatory democracy. Human history is a large adult education class. We can see the value of this, in contrast to accounts of early people which, at one extreme, stress their ignorance and brutality and use it as a model for an essential 'human nature' (William Golding), or, at the other extreme, propose that modern man is no wiser or better off, and indeed may be less so, than his 'primitive forebears' (Lévi-Strauss). But we may also feel that the orders of life, the orders of consciousness and practice, that Williams seeks to render were stranger, more intense, more complex, more valid in their own right, than he allows. In this respect, it is notable that his treatment of the *mentalités* of early peoples, especially when they fall outside a conventionally rational framework (in the area of myth and religion in particular) tend to be simplistic and at times slightly patronizing. The homogenizing movement of this novel can be seen as part of a general tendency in Williams's whole *oeuvre* – though to say this is also to homogenize! That tendency exposes Williams to the critique of socialism and Marxism which comes, not only from traditional conservatism, but also, today, from post-modernism: that those *grand récits*, the gross and incestuous children of the Enlightenment, utilitarianism, and Hegel, work, even against themselves, to deny difference, to enforce a homogeneous model of rational collective man.

The Country and the City

The sense of complexity which Williams aims for but does not achieve in his fiction is especially evident in what may be his richest book: *The Country and the City* (1973). This combines most of his concerns: his preoccupation with the divisions and movements between town and country, and mental and manual labour; his desire to demystify and historicize abstract essentialist notions; his awareness of the processes, as well as the products, of human labour;

his feeling for the natural world; his engagement with literature; his contained utopianism; his political commitment. His desire to historicize does not simply dissolve the apparent endurance or recurrence of ideas across historical moments: 'We have to be able to explain, in related terms, both the persistence and the historicity of concepts' (1975 edn, p.348). But while he fully acknowledges the positive realities of rural living, he works to repudiate the idea of a lost pastoral paradise, a Golden Age, an 'organic community'; or more precisely, to relocate that idea in a dimension which is mythical, and often mystifying, rather than historical in any direct sense. In scotching the myth of the organic community, Williams settles a particularly irksome account with Leavis.

In *The Country and the City*, Williams seeks to convert a contemplation, a visual consumption, of the countryside and the country house into a comprehension of the practices which produced and sustain it: 'Think it through as labour...' (p.132). He dismantles the stereotype of an immemorial rural order destroyed by urbanization and industrialization: the rural order was not static but, like the city, penetrated and changed by the capitalist mode of production. Capitalism is firmly denounced as the chief culprit, although Williams deprecates Marx and Engels's reference, in the *Communist Manifesto* (1848), to 'the idiocy of rural life', and he acknowledges, if too briefly, the brutality of Stalin's treatment of the Russian peasants (pp.363-4). But the experience of formerly and actually existing socialism makes it painfully clear that the absence of a capitalist mode of production within a country does not preclude, and may promote, the depredation of rural life.

To demystify the myth of the country is not, for Williams, to deny that myth all substance, to dismiss it as ideological illusion. Instead, he advocates a different relationship with the 'country', and thus with the 'city', in which socialism and ecology could unite (pp.359-63). His remarkable conclusion argues that the country/city split now exists less as an internal feature of the 'advanced' countries than as the division between the 'developed' and the 'undeveloped' world. He relates this to the even wider problem of the division of labour, and he stresses the need to tackle this through rigorous analysis, proposal and practice in new forms of co-operative effort. Admittedly this is a rather vague rhetorical exhortation to a task which, as Williams defines it, somewhat contradictorily seems to require the partial pre-existence of its purported objective: the division of labour must already have been overcome to some extent to make possible the new forms of co-operative effort which aim to overcome the division of labour. Williams's long exploration of the country/city split develops, as the book ends, into a perspective which is both utopian and, he believes, urgently necessary.

Towards 2000

The break-up of an old order and a radically unknown future face us as we move towards the second millennium. This is even more evident in the 1990s than it was when Williams's *Towards 2000* first appeared in 1983. *Towards 2000* aimed to give a comprehensive assessment and analysis of contemporary conditions and prospects, and thus help to generate the will, vision and sense of direction necessary to meet the future and to work for change. Williams poses a choice between two prospects. There could be an increasingly authoritarian capitalist order in which élites accept perpetual danger and crisis, and constantly calculate for temporary advantage with no concern for communal well-being: this is what Williams calls, without wanting to imply a conspiracy theory, 'Plan X' – the X indicating that its objective is 'A willed and deliberate unknown' (1983 edn, p.244). The alternative possibility would be a new kind of co-operative, communal, democratic, and ecologically aware socialism.

Williams criticizes the ideas of a 'post-industrial' or de-industrialized' society, pointing out that even manufacturing decline will not do away with the structures and processes of industrial capitalism. He challenges what he sees as the idealization of 'parliamentary democracy' and proposes a more direct, participatory kind of democracy. The unholy alliance 'of technological determinism with cultural pessimism' is attacked and some positive prospects for technologies and cultural forms are outlined.

Compared with *The Long Revolution* and with much of Williams's previous work, the later part of *Towards 2000* makes a crucial break by extending the analysis to a global scale. Williams seeks to dismantle the still-dominant idea of 'the nation', but also recognizes its force and rejects a facile internationalism. Instead, he recommends a 'cultural struggle for actual social identities' combined with 'the political definition of effective self-governing societies' (p.193). He also tries to unpick the notions of 'East-West' and 'North-South' as inadequate ways in which to conceptualize the world, and argues carefully for a redefined concept of 'multilateral disarmament'.

Much of this analysis is impressive, within the perspectives and values that it assumes. The criticisms of parliamentary democracy strike home. There are feasible and inspiriting proposals for deploying new technology in democratic decision-making, in cultural production, in information systems, in voluntary associations, in co-operation and consultation in work, and in education. The analysis of the image and realities of 'development' is complex and telling. The difficulties of 'unilateralism' receive sensitive and intelligent clarification. But it is the assumed perspectives and values which are the problem, which need to be argued for.

In regard to this assumption of common ground, the provenance of the early drafts of some of the material is significant: *New Left Review, New Socialist, Socialist Register, Marxism Today, The Forward March of Labour Halted?* (1981). Terry Eagleton has remarked that Williams had 'a socialist commitment so deep and unyielding that you sometimes felt he literally could not imagine how anyone could believe otherwise' (*Raymond Williams: Critical Perspectives*, p.7). To some extent, Williams could imagine this; for example, there is his observation on how a realization of 'the human weight of revolutionary change' could cause people to shift to the right (*Politics and Letters*, p.383), or his article 'Hesitations before Socialism' (*Resources of Hope*, pp.288-94). But his reach into non-socialist perspectives and sympathies was limited.

In particular, Williams seems to think 'capitalism' is the source of all our discontents. In this respect, he sometimes moves close to what he calls, apropos of Orwell, 'generalized swearing' (*Orwell*, p.87). It is as if, in certain company, he has to affirm his Marxist credentials. He goes so far as to claim, for example: 'it is, in the modern epoch, capitalism which has disrupted and overridden natural communities, and imposed artificial orders' (p.184). Only capitalism? This is a careless, and callous, statement from the man who, in *The Country and the City*, said that Stalin's drive against rural communities was conducted 'on a scale and with a brutality which made that "victory" over the peasants one of the most terrible phases in the whole history of rural society' (pp.363-4). For much of *Towards 2000*, Williams plays down and partly exculpates the cruelties of 'actually existing socialism'. Yet that socialism has also perpetrated, sometimes more extensively, all the oppressions with which Williams charges capitalism – though to say this is not, of course, to justify capitalism. Indeed, the very phrase 'actually existing socialism', which Williams takes from Rudolf Bahro (see *Problems in Materialism and Culture*, pp.252-73), and which implies that another kind of socialism is possible, itself functions, in Williams's apologetics, partly as a rhetorical exculpation that Williams would hardly permit to a liberal or conservative who spoke, with a similar implication, of 'actually existing capitalism'.

Williams's global analysis in *Towards 2000* is inadequate because it does not incorporate the complex realities of those societies which called and call themselves socialist or Marxist. One of his epigraphs is from Thomas Hardy's 'In Tenebris' (1895): 'Who holds that if the way to the Better there be, it exacts a full look at the Worst'. But Williams does not look at the 'worst' of 'actually [or formerly] existing socialism'. Only his conclusion starts to offer some criticisms. He speaks, for instance, of 'the continuing appropriation and exploitation of the world as raw material in the "communist" or "actually existing socialist" economies' (p.261), and when he acknowledges that the concept of 'mode of production' is useful but criticizes it as 'at some important points a prisoner of the social orders which it is offering to analyse' (p.263), he implies that some of the difficulty may lie, not simply in the deformation, but in the primary discourse of Marxism.

This failure adequately to attack and analyse actual and former socialist societies relates to a fundamental weakness in *Towards 2000*. Despite his careful clarifications of problems, his specific proposals (in regard to technology, for instance), his suggestive intimations, and his frequent exhortations to detailed enquiry and discussion, Williams remains vague about the kind of socialism he wants and how to achieve it. The adjective 'new' is much used: 'new kinds of communal, co-operative and collective institutions'; 'a new kind of socialist movement'; 'a new definition of the general interest'; 'new political forms'; 'new and radically alternative kinds of relationship'; 'new kinds of monetary institutions'; 'new kinds of auditing of resources'; a 'new orientation of livelihood' (pp.123, 174, 199, 217, 256, 258, 266). The lack of detail is vitiating. It leaves Williams open to the charge which R.W. Johnson lays against *Resources of Hope*: 'Williams never actually spells out what socialism is for him. It seems, in the great tradition of British wooziness, to be all about values and community and wholeness; in a word, Christian socialism and brown bread' (p.138).

Of course, *Towards 2000* is partly a call to common enquiry, to collaborative effort, to participation in defining the 'new forms'. The very principles of Williams's project means that it cannot be a one-man job. But, as with his exhortation to co-operative effort at the end of *The Country and the City*, there is an aporia: the kind of collective activity needed to define the 'new forms' could only occur in the kinds of conditions which would prevail if the new forms were already in existence. Impasse: you come to a tight place where you stick fast: there is no going forward or back. But Williams taught us to see that an aporia is not an absolute.

10 Zapping the Foundations: Stanley Fish

'This man is a Jewish swindler, he wants to use me from behind and shit on my head'. According to his own later report, this was what the Wolf-Man thought of Freud, shortly after first meeting him. Stanley Fish thinks that the Wolf-Man got it right. In the essay which concludes *Doing What Comes Naturally* (1989), Fish analyses how Freud, in that celebrated case-study, structures his release of information – in particular as to the manner in which the Wolf-Man, as an infant, supposedly interrupted his parents' lovemaking – in order to engage and disarm the reader. But the point of this *exposé* is not to prove that Freud distorted the 'truth'. For Fish, there is no 'truth' outside rhetoric – which is not to say that there is no truth. His difference with Freud is that, while psychoanalysis holds 'that one cannot get to the side of the unconscious', Fish holds 'that one cannot get to the side of rhetoric' (p.553). His primal scene is 'the scene of persuasion' (p.547). His attack on Freud is, in fact, energized by his admiration, perhaps his envy, for that professor's persuasive abilities. Indeed, we may – and the essay's position at the end of *Doing What Comes Naturally* strengthens the impression – see more than a little resemblance between Fish and Freud. For Fish too is a formidable rhetorician, if in a different, distinctly American, mode: hard-hitting, provocative, engaging. Even the sternest poststructuralist, ready to repress reference the moment it starts to poke through the skeins of signification, must have wondered, in a moment of backsliding, whether Fish is the model for Morris Zapp in David Lodge's novels.

Fish is an anti-foundationalist. He holds not that there are no foundations but that, in any given situation, what count as foundations are historically and culturally specific. Whatever we identify as a foundation or a constraint will never simply be *there*, though it will certainly feel that way, but will be a product of interpretation, and subject to change. Fish is now a Professor of both English and Law at Duke University – a rich university which, as David Lodge points out in *After Bakhtin* (1990, p. 182), like an unsuccessful baseball or football team, has dramatically increased its prestige and performance by hiring stars, such as Fish and Fredric Jameson, at high salaries – and he cross-examines, with the forensic force of a Perry Mason, a wide range of witnesses from the literary and legal world who attempt to distinguish literal from metaphorical meaning, or to posit enduring constraints on interpretation that emanate from a text or from a body of previous juridical or scholarly decisions. In his dealings with jurisprudence, Fish's literary training – he is a Renaissance specialist and a Miltonist – is particularly useful in enabling him to seize on naïve literary examples used by writers on law such as Ronald Dworkin and Richard Posner. His three assaults on Dworkin suggest that he must, in the 1960s, have been a fan of *Rowan and Martin's Laugh-In*, since their tone is very much one of 'Look, dumb-dumb…'.

A central claim Fish makes – it is both radical and recuperative – is that an awareness of the relativity of foundations has no consequences. So he takes issue, on the one hand, with those cultural conservatives, and Marxists, who fear that anti-foundationalism will mean chaos come again or capitalism rampant, and, on the other hand, with those, for example in radical critical theory and the Critical Legal Studies movement, who see it as potentially liberating – as long, of course, as it stops short of their own values. To be aware that we are constrained, Fish argues, does not mean that we will, or can, cease to be so. Chaos will not come because constraints, of one kind or another, will always be in place; liberation will not occur because one 'escapes' from one set of constraints only into another set, and any feeling of liberation is an illusion; one is no less constrained, and one loses as much as one gains. Neither the fears nor the hopes raised by 'theory' can ever be realized: partial lucidity changes nothing; total lucidity is a chimera. We can never make all our constraints explicit. There will always be unspoken assumptions – Fish calls on Polanyi's concept of 'tacit knowledge' – and any situation, because it is mutable and temporal, will always stay ahead of any attempt wholly to articulate it. From some perspectives, this may seem enervating, but Fish's message is – we can paraphrase it in a song refrain, since he seems to be fond of those – don't let it bring you down. Constraints are not merely repressive; they are, in fact, necessary and enabling. Without constraints, one could not choose or act at all, since any choice or act must take place within a framework of constraints to give it meaning. Anti-foundationalism does not entail apathy; indeed, it claims total apathy is impossible, since that would mean complete escape from constraints. Whether we are anti-foundationalists, humanists, Christians, Marxists, or whatever, we will still choose, act, fight for what we believe in, go on making foundational assertions: there's no stopping us. We're just doing what comes naturally.

Is Fish right? After the 554 pages of bruising if blood-quickening conflict in *Doing What Comes Naturally*, it would be nice to able to declare roundly, in one of his own favourite locutions: The answer is no. But it is not so simple. Fish is often right on local matters – for example, on anti-professionalism among teachers of literature. He contends that a literature teacher's denial that s/he is a professional – whether it takes the traditional form of seeing the role as a vocation, or the modern one of seeing it as that of cultural revolutionary – is, in fact, a form of professional behaviour. In a sense, by Fish's own arguments, it is only on local matters that he *could* be right: but his position does of course entail general claims.

The first and now familiar (though not thereby invalid) objection to the anti-foundationalist case is that it is self-contradictory: it asserts the kind of transhistorical truth – that all foundations are culturally and historically specific – whose very possibility it denies. Fish is 'naturally' – that is, as a result of the constraints that make him an academic intellectual – aware of this objection, and he tries, briefly, to pre-empt it in his Introduction; otherwise it is passed over in this long book. His pre-emptive strike claims that those who make the self-contradiction charge mistakenly believe that anti-foundationalists hold that there are no foundations: Fish can then easily incinerate this straw man by making the point that the anti-foundationalist case does not deny that there are foundations, but rather holds that 'foundations are local and temporal phenomena, and are always vulnerable to challenge from other localities and other times' (p.30). But the case as Fish states it here still affirms what it denies: a transhistorical, transcultural truth. To know that all foundations are always local and temporal is to be able to transcend one's particular local and temporal moment to comprehend that which is the case in all local and temporal moments. But if one can do that – and Fish *implicitly* claims that he can as he *explicitly* claims that no one can – then one has demonstrated that there is a truth that is not local or temporal: namely, that all foundations are local and temporal. And this truth serves as a foundation which is necessary to the anti-foundationalist case but also disproves it. The paradox is intriguing, however Fish does not pursue it – it would result in a very different kind of book. Anti-foundationalism is a powerful springboard, but it depends on the forces of gravity.

A further problem, which Fish does address, is that of change. In a traditional model, change in a system of thought – or, in Fish's terms, an 'interpretive community' – comes about when it is unable to incorporate some aspect of an 'external' reality that is, at least partly, independent of it. Fish's model of change is that the perception of the aspect of reality that provokes change is already inherent in the system of thought, or 'interpretive community', which changes

> when a community is provoked to change by something outside it, that something will already have been inside, in the sense that the angle of its notice – the angle from which it is related to the community's project even before it is seen – will determine its shape, not *after* it has been perceived, but *as* it is perceived. (p.147)

But how could this effect *foundational* change? If the community is already implicitly prepared for, and determines in perceiving it, the shape of whatever changes it, it need never change its fundamental interpretative processes, its basic structure of constraints, since it will only ever receive what that structure can cope with.

It is not only difficult for Fish to explain *how* foundational change occurs: it is also difficult for him to explain how we *know* that it occurs. If, as he claims, we can never make explicit all the constraints that are operative in any given situation, then how do we know that the same 'tacit' constraints may not be operative in apparently very different situations? Given that Fish posits the existence of 'tacit' constraints, how does he know that they all change? Indeed, he himself affirms that they do *not* change in one respect, when he argues that the feeling of liberation one may experience in moving from one set of beliefs to another is an illusion – that the degree of constraint is always the same. This implies that there is an underlying 'deep structure' of constraint whose pressure is always equivalent in any historical or cultural situation, however it may change in other ways. We slide, once more, into a transhistorical claim.

Change might also be explained as due to a conflict, not between an 'interpretive community' and 'external' reality, but between different 'interpretive communities'. Fish acknowledges that 'each of us is a member of not one but innumerable interpretive communities in relation to which different kinds of belief are operating with different weight and force', and he offers a cheerful self-portrait:

> I am, among other things, white, male, a teacher, a literary critic, a student of interpretation, a member of a law faculty, a father, a son, an uncle, a husband (twice), a citizen, a (passionate) consumer, a member of the middle class, a Jew, the oldest of four children, a cousin, a brother, a brother-in-law, a son-in-law, a Democrat, short, balding, fifty, an easterner who has been a westerner and is now a southerner, a voter, a neighbor, an optimist, a department chairman. (pp.30-1)

It is, of course, questionable whether each of these does constitute a distinct interpretive community; it might be better to speak, in some instances, of 'roles', as indeed Fish quickly starts to do, when he acknowledges 'the possibility of *conflict* between the various roles I am called on to play' and argues that one 'is often "conflictually" constrained, that is, held in place by a sense of a situation as requiring negotiation between conflicting demands that seem equally legitimate' (p.31). But Fish's claim that any interpretive community already contains the 'angle of notice' which will determine the shape of what changes it presumably also applies to what conflicts with it: any interpretive community will only conflict with any aspect of any other interpretive community that it can already recognize as conflictual, and it will determine the shape of that aspect as it perceives it. So, as with change, there can be no conflict that assaults fundamental interpretive processes: each interpretive community is already, in those processes, compatible with any aspect of any other interpretive community with which it might conflict. It is hardly surprising that, after this brief concession to the possibility of inter-community conflict, Fish speaks for much of the book as if the 'interpretive community' were a single, isolated, ongoing entity. For in Fish's model, all interpretive communities are fundamentally the same: each changes and engages in conflict only on its own terms: each has an equivalent pressure of constraint. Behind Fish's cheery pragmatism we see that older kind of American literary criticism which stressed enduring patterns and archetypes. *Plus ça change.*

11 Pragmatic Protocols: Robert Scholes

Robert Scholes is an heir to John Dewey in his concern for education and democracy, but he has also been strongly influenced by hermeneutic modes of European provenance, especially structuralism. As a critic and teacher, he wants to avoid both the anarchy of interpretative freeplay and the authoritarianism of what he calls, in *Protocols of Reading* (1989) 'textual fundamentalism' (p.52) – the appeal to the 'one right meaning' which is, for those with eyes to see, manifestly *there* in the text. He seeks to promote a pragmatic ethos which permits a range of critical approaches while eschewing an easy eclecticism.

Protocols of Reading draws a distinction between 'centripetal' and 'centrifugal' approaches to reading (p.8). The former approach assumes, and seeks, a 'centring' of the text on a specific and essential meaning, while the latter pursues the endless dissemination of meanings for which the text is only a 'pre-text'. Scholes suggests that the 'centrifugal' approach has, of late, been unduly privileged, due to the dissemination of deconstruction. Moreover, he argues that the American assimilation of deconstruction – most notably by J. Hillis Miller – isolates reading from extra-literary ethical and political concerns, in a deconstructive re-run of the New Criticism.

Scholes is neither overwhelmed nor outraged by Derrida, and has some amusing remarks on 'Limited Inc a b c...', Derrida's famous response to the attack upon him by the philosopher John Searle:

> We might expect [Derrida] to be, as we say, philosophical about it and accept misreading along with *différance* (and original sin, which it closely resembles) as the fate of readers and writers doomed to iterability in this world – but no, iterability yields all too readily to irritability, and Derrida calls in what he refers

> to when others invoke it as the 'language-police', just as any property owner calls the cops when a burglar arrives...All of Derrida's jokes about copyright and property in 'Limited Inc a b c...' are an index of his own investment in the takeover of the Communications Corp. (or core or corps or corpus or corpse) by Writing Unlimited, J. Derrida, Prop. (pp.61, 65)

Protocols of Reading is a gracious, witty, intelligent essay, copious in examples drawn from a broad cultural range; Scholes takes in, for instance, Ruskin, Proust, D.H. Lawrence and Mann writing (on) Venice; the lives, as textually reconstituted, of three figures born in the 1880s whose lives and cultural situations had certain significant similarities but who defined themselves very differently in relation to modernism in art and to political commitment – Joyce, Mussolini and Lukács; a magazine advertisement for Guess Jeans and a television advertisement for Budweiser beer which shows a black baseball umpire making a close call under pressure and finally being acknowledged, by the white manager who originally protested, as having done the right thing; Judy Garland's carefully calculated tear-jerking performances; and George Eliot's *Middlemarch*.

All these texts, Scholes suggests, can be read – indeed, for adequate understanding, *have* to be read – within larger cultural texts. In the case of the Budweiser advertisement, the larger cultural text is that of twentieth-century America, with its myths of the racial melting-pot, upward mobility, and strict and fearless judgement. In the case of *Middlemarch*, it is nineteenth-century England, with its uneasy amalgam of Protestantism and capitalism. As well as being read within larger cultural texts, specific texts also have to be read within the 'text', the weave, of one's individual life – at both the beginning and the end of the book, Scholes cites Barthes's axiom that reading is 'rewriting the text of the work within the text of our lives' (pp.1, 10, 155). He recalls his own experience, on first reading *Middlemarch* forty years ago, of 'the ethical shock of finding myself far too closely mirrored in the character of Fred Vincy...one of those "young gentlemen whose consciousness is chiefly made up of their own wishes"'. Scholes also reports a friend's response to this recollection: that 'was before you grew up and turned into Casaubon' (p.139).

In some respects, the synthesis Scholes suggests is congenial. It combines the ethical approach in which reading literature contributes to a process of moral self-shaping with an awareness of the politics of reading and interpretation and of what Scholes called 'textual power' in an earlier book of that title: the sense of literary and other texts as rhetorical acts that, to a greater or lesser extent, have effects in the world. His synthesis moves between attention to 'literary' texts in the traditional sense and the texts of 'popular culture', as in advertising and video. It is, in fact, a synthesis which enables the critic to move into the field of 'cultural studies' while not abandoning literature.

One problem arises, however, in relation to Scholes' educational concerns. In this book, as in *Textual Power*, Scholes seems far closer to the realities of teaching than some theorists. *Protocols of Reading* is fertile in examples that could be employed in, and adapted and extended for, the classroom and seminar: but questions of priorities are evaded. The case for teaching the broad 'cultural text' – across the media of print, film, television, video, etc. – and for doing so with the intention of understanding rather than simply deploring the practices of 'popular culture' is now irresistible within any project of humane education. It is within this broad cultural text that we all live, and any effective resistance to, and rectification of, its objectionable aspects must start from an attempt to comprehend the whole field. It is also true, as Scholes argues, that the 'texts' of 'popular culture' may engage complex modes of understanding. The Budweiser advertisement, for example, presents what George Steiner has called, in respect of poetry, 'modal difficulties' (*On Difficulty*, 1978. 1980 edn, pp.27-33) to those who lack comprehension of the protocols and practices of American baseball, of the uncertain role of blacks in American sport and society, of the myth of equality of opportunity and so on; and Scholes cites a German visitor who, shown the video of Judy Garland's performance, read her tears as a sign of respiratory distress. Furthermore, it can hardly be denied that 'popular culture' and literature are not, in some absolute and rigid sense, distinct. Scholes enjoys himself for several perceptive and entertaining pages when he seeks to demonstrate 'that poetry, advertising, and propaganda are not different in kind or in method but are always intermingled, drawing their strength from this very mixture more often than not' (p.110). The question then arises: in teaching, in reading, how much time should be allocated, respectively, to, say, poetry and 'popular culture'? It is possible that the study of poetry, and other forms of literature, will be swamped by the study of popular culture.

Whatever sophistication cultural theory achieves, the study of *Dallas* is still likely to be easier than the study of Dryden (or, for that matter, of Derrida). It may be, as T.S. Eliot suggested, it is a part of education to learn to interest ourselves in matters for which we have no aptitude; and while T.S. Eliot's notions may fit ill with Scholes' democratic principles, the spread of cultural studies may in one way threaten those principles. Like many older advocates of such studies, Scholes, thanks to a fusion of native nous and traditional training, can move with facility from George Eliot to Judy Garland, Valéry to the video text. But will this facility be preserved, except by a tiny élite, in the cultural studies programmes which will increasingly assimilate literary studies in the future?

In more general terms, Scholes's pragmatism may seem a little too easy, especially to those shaped by Anglo-Saxon secularized Protestantism (George Eliot's formative matrix) or by a European philosophical and literary tradition darkly shadowed by tragedy and barbarism (Paul de Man is now the haplessly exemplary figure here). In *Protocols of Reading*, Scholes hints at his own complex formation – Northern and Southern European, English and Italian, Protestant and Catholic – but with the implication that he has escaped from intense and specific cultural identifications and can mediate between them. Like the ump in the Budweiser ad, he himself embodies the American myth of the melting pot and upward mobility (he is now Professor of English and Comparative Literature at Brown University). But it can be suggested that his approach might have difficulty in coping with the fierce investments people may make in their beliefs – investments which may be deplored (especially when the beliefs appear to be unsympathetic) but which need to be understood if they are to be mitigated.

Moreover, in the field of textual interpretation, fierce investment in particular beliefs may not be wholly deleterious. As Paul B. Armstrong points out in his *Conflicting Readings* (1990), 'the most powerful approaches to interpretation often owe their depth of insight to the radical one-sidedness of their beliefs' (p.9). Indeed, Scholes' notion of textual economy, of an organized system involving exchanges of power and pleasure between text and reader, helps to suggest why this should be so: if texts have power and give power, then a powerfully one-sided interpretation, a 'strong misreading' in Harold Bloom's terms, may be in some senses the most effective means of tapping into the sources of that power. And it is difficult to countervail this without sliding into a pragmatism which itself becomes fundamentalist, paradoxically, by proscribing radically one-sided readings. The dilemma is that interpretative fundamentalism, whether of a Leavisian, Marxist, psychoanalytic, deconstructive or any other kind, has been, and sometimes still is, powerfully motivating and enabling; but it is also the case that it cannot provide what Scholes calls 'a framework within which to negotiate our differences' (p.51). It may be that we shall have to live on the horns of this dilemma, to develop the difficult, democratic, dialectical skill of combining intense commitment with a tensed openness to alternative approaches and to the possibility of error. In this, we will need pragmatic protocols.

12 Deconstructive Débâcle J. Hillis Miller

The career of J. Hillis Miller has taken him to the centres of American academic prestige and power: a chair at Yale from 1972 to 1986 and the Presidency of the MLA in that year. From Yale, he moved to the well-cushioned Chair which he now holds at the University of California at Irvine. Miller was born in 1928 and had a traditional kind of higher education at Oberlin College in Ohio where, as he recalls in *Theory Now and Then*, he read Homer, Chaucer, Shakespeare, Milton, Pope, Wordsworth, Tennyson, Arnold, Newman, Mill, Huxley, T.S. Eliot; 'not a woman among them' (p.389). Miller remembers the time, in the mid-1940s, when the New Criticism was indeed new and mounting its challenge, but in *Tropes, Parables, Performatives* he attributes his own close-reading commitment not to the New Criticism but to 'an initial and persistent fascination with local strangenesses in literary language' (p. vii). He showed an early interest in post-war Continental developments in literary and critical practice, especially in the 'criticism of consciousness' of Georges Poulet (then in fact Miller's colleague in the United States). Miller was thus well-placed to understand and assimilate the extraordinary explosions of structuralism, poststructuralism and deconstruction that have transformed literary studies in the past two decades. He is a very good technical critic, who combines structural comprehension with precise textual focus, but he has not sought to create a general theory of his own. He has, however, become identified with two theories – Poulet's phenomenology, then Derrida's deconstruction – and he does sometimes give the impression that he would defend Derrida, and de Man, against all comers. But his primary interest is in reading and interpretation rather than in pure theory. As his preface to *Theory Now and Then* puts it: 'We need theory now and then, to help us get on with the serious business of reading' (p.vii).

In *Theory Now and Then*, Miller is, as a rule, consistently serious, weightily expansive; he sometimes comes close to the pomposity of the podium. For the most part, he gives the impression that he has comprehensively exhausted the topics he takes up (despite his formal acknowledgement that, deconstructively speaking, such closure is never possible). This makes his attacks on, for example, the metaphysical assumptions and inattentiveness to language of M.H. Abrams's *Natural Supernaturalism* for the conflation of Heidegger, Derrida and William Carlos Williams in Joseph Riddel's *The Inverted Bell*, devastating. Though Miller prefers to define rhetoric, *à la* deconstruction, as the study of the figurative work of language that undermines the grammatical and logical structure of any text, he is in fact a master of rhetoric as the art of persuasion, and his rhetorical techniques in this sense should be watched with care.

Miller's focus throughout his work has been on the canon of nineteenth and earlier twentieth century literature. *Tropes, Parables, Performatives* discusses, among others, Hardy, Lawrence, Woolf, Conrad, Stevens and Williams, and a third recent volume, *Victorian Subjects*, includes essays on Dickens, George Eliot, Trollope and Carlyle. In a question-and-answer session reprinted in *Theory Now and Then*, he states that 'there's too much attention paid to modern literature', instancing Virginia Woolf as a modern writer 'whom you can spend too much time studying' (despite his own work on her). Miller welcomes feminism to the field of literary and cultural studies, but it does not seem to have penetrated his critical practice: his focus, as on his Oberlin course, is overwhelmingly on male authors (including, at a stretch, George Eliot). He recalls that the American curriculum of his student days 'was oriented primarily toward preparing white Anglo-Saxon middle-class males for professions... [and] white Anglo-Saxon middle-class women to be better wives, mothers, hostesses, and community servants' (p.389). He affirms that 'deconstruction is conservative as far as the canon goes' (p.194), though he acknowledges that there has now been 'an irrevocable breakdown of the canon' (p.391). Miller has not given extended attention to recent literary production – to the American postmodernist fiction of Barth and Pynchon, for example; he exemplifies the point made by the novelist and critic Christine Brooke-Rose, in *Stories, theories and things*, that 'the Deconstructionist School in America paid little attention to the deconstructing "postmodern" literature all around them' (p.264). One would like to know more about Miller's views of such fiction, for instance in the light of his interesting remarks on 'character' in the traditional realistic novel in *Theory Now and Then*. In contrast to Robert Scholes, Miller has also paid little attention to popular culture. He has only recently and, one feels, reluctantly, affirmed the need for 'training in reading all the signs', including 'movies, television, the newspaper' (*Theory Now and Then*, p.392).

If one wanted, in a rough kind of way, to construct a history of recent American criticism from *Theory Now and Then*, it would something like this: New Criticism gave way to deconstruction, but deconstruction, in Miller's version was, in a sense, a continuation of New Criticism by better means, a necessary development of that close focus on the words on the page that the New Criticism had made central to critical activity. Deconstruction began its triumphal march through the interpretations and institutions. That march was not unimpeded; but the opposition from conservative New Critics, ill-informed and inexperienced in this kind of controversy, was quickly seen off. Miller recalls Paul de Man as saying – this is Miller's own paraphrase – that '*the* task of criticism in the coming years would be a kind of imperialistic appropriation of all of literature by the method of rhetorical reading often called "deconstruction"' (p.385). The imperialists then met resistance, not from the old guard, but from younger, radical critics, often skilled in deconstructive techniques but keen to adapt them to activist causes. This was a much stronger threat. Deconstruction went on the defensive, both stressing the importance of rigorous deconstructive reading while claiming that this was, none the less, of the highest political importance in that it provided a crucial means by which to critique and contest ideological mystifications. This defensiveness is exemplified in 'The Ethics of Reading', a well-known essay first published in 1987 and now reprinted in *Theory Now and Then*. Here Miller acknowledges that 'the relations of literature to ethics, to history, and to society' have become important again (p.334), but he affirms that 'the primary ethical obligation of the teacher of literature is to the work of literature', and – echoing his Oberlin course – that '[t]he rare ability to see the object, in this case a poem, a novel, a play, or a work of philosophy, as in itself it really is, to borrow Arnold's phrasing... is the one thing necessary in the good teacher of literature' (pp.338, 339). Miller reconciled Arnold with Derrida by arguing that the Derridean method was essential to achieve the Arnoldian objective, although that would never be achieved but always deferred, displaced. This attempt to square the circle, to stop deconstruction devouring its own, was doomed. Like Lear divesting himself of authority yet seeking to 'retain / The name and all th'addition to a king', Miller soon found himself with only a handful of knights facing Regan's implacable question: What need one?

Miller's fall was spurred by the bastard: Paul de Man. It has to be said that Miller's responses in *Theory Now and Then* to the de Man revelations are a moral and intellectual disgrace. In 'a matter of this gravity', as Miller himself calls it (p.373), why does he offer only two brief and bad-tempered articles on the matter? A substantial and scrupulous essay was surely in order. But he tells us in his preface and in a later footnote that, in these two pieces, he has had his 'say' (pp.x, 357 n.7) – and that 'say' displays an intolerance of alternative interpretations of de Man that becomes almost apoplectic: Miller here is deconstruction's Dr Johnson, who seems to want to 'say' '*there's* an end on't'. But there will never be an end of it.

Miller presents one of the now-standard defence stories: that de Man's later deconstructiveness was a reversal, a putting into question, of the mystifying organicism, the literary, racial and political nationalism that had once made him less than hostile to the Nazis. This may or may not be true – the evidence remains insufficient, and there will always be, as any good deconstructionist should recognize, differences of interpretation. But what is notable is the narrative structure of that story: it tells the tale of a man who does wrong, sees the error of his ways and, more or less consciously, spends the rest of his life trying obliquely to atone and to prevent others repeating his mistake. It is, in fact, a story as old as those Christian narratives of sin and redemption which Miller rebukes M.H. Abrams for applying to the Romantics. But why not deconstruct that narrative? Why this violent, hierarchical opposition between 'early' and 'late' de Man? Why privilege the writer of 'The Resistance to Theory' over the non-resistant who wrote, for example, an article called 'Les Juifs dans la littérature actuelle' in a special anti-Semitic section of the then collaborationist Belgian newspaper *Le Soir* on 4 March 1941 in which he said (it is one of the few sentences Miller quotes, although he omits, without marks of ellipsis, the 'donc' that follows 'on voit' in the original): 'En plus, on voit donc qu'une solution du problème juif qui viserait à la création d'une colonie juive isolée de l'Europe, n'entraînerait pas, pour la vie littéraire de l'Occident, de conséquences déplorables'. In the translation Miller gives: 'In addition, one sees that a solution to the Jewish problem that would aim at creation of a Jewish colony isolated from Europe would not result, for the literary life of the West, in deplorable consequences' (p.371). By what absolute right does Miller relegate this de Man to the margins, to a superseded stage? Why does he not, in the first movement of the deconstructive operation, reverse the hierarchy, and privilege early de Man, and then hold the two de Mans in a mobile suspension, refusing conclusively to privilege one over the other?

Instead Miller, with much self-righteous bluster, falls back on an élitist disdain for journalism, dark hints about defamation, a violent mobilization of the truth / falsehood hierarchy, and a positivist appeal to 'the facts' and 'the documents'. Now it is true, as Miller protests, that deconstruction, in its more qualified and careful versions, does not dispense with protocols of validity and verification; but it is also the case, which Miller elides, that deconstruction encourages the idea that there are no facts, only interpretations, that any reading is, necessarily, a misreading and can never be 'adequate', that the 'documents' can never finally be demarcated, decoded, or prioritized, and that language always escapes the control of those who think they use it and is disseminated and grafted into new contexts in which it acquires different meanings. Miller is at his most abject when he attempts to police the conduct of the debate by invoking 'what de Man actually said' (p.360), thus falling, with no apology and no acknowledgement of the aporia, into the once mocked rhetorical procedure of those who attempted to refute deconstructive readings by appealing to – for example – 'what Hardy actually said'.

Miller is right to reject crude couplings of deconstruction and fascism and to argue that the anti-Semitic and fascist associations of a writer do not, in themselves, cancel out his work or ideas – if they did, the twentieth century literary and philosophical canon would have to empty rapidly. But the de Man case has done mortal damage to deconstruction, not because it has shown deconstruction to be in some sense inherently oppressive, but because it has demonstrated that deconstruction can supply no intellectual or moral resources with which to cope with such a fundamental crisis. Deconstruction provides Miller with no distinctive forms of comprehension and consolation with which to apprehend and ameliorate his distress.

Miller also fails to grasp that when he affirms de Man's 'learning, rigor, and original insight into major works' (p.374), he exacerbates the enormity of de Man's dereliction. If de Man were a mediocre hack, it would be another matter. George Steiner's *Language and Silence*, published in 1967 long before de Man was even heard of, offers, in its sustained and searching encounter with the dark aporia of culture and barbarism, an apprehension of what is at stake in these matters that puts Miller's sophistries to shame.

We have entered a post-deconstructionist phase: what of the

future? In *Stories, theories and things*, Christine Brooke-Rose proposes the important concept of 'palimpsest history' to indicate a kind of fiction (more commonly falling under the rubric of 'magic realism') 'that has lately burst on the literary scene and thoroughly renewed the dying art of the novel' (p.182). She instances Carlos Fuentes' *Terra Nostra* (1976), Milorad Pavíc's *Dictionary of the Khazars* (1983), and Salman Rushdie's *The Satanic Verses* (1988). These novels, in their distinctive ways, create alternative histories that, to follow up the palimpsest metaphor, are written over an effaced 'actual' history whose traces none the less sometimes show through, or are inscribed on the reverse of the monumental brasses on which 'official' history is engraved. *The Satanic Verses*, for example, offers an 'unauthorised version' of the history of 'two palimpsest countries, India and England', and of the scripture of 'one palimpsest religion, Islam' (p.182). 'Palimpsest history', palimpsest fiction, is, we might argue, one means of orientation, of contributing to that 'global cognitive mapping' in the postmodern world for which Fredric Jameson calls. (Jameson wants that mapping to be Marxist – but what about a 'palimpsest history' of Marxism in theory and practice, a satanic version of that sacred scripture?) Palimpsest history may help us to cope with that crisis which Brooke-Rose identifies in a key passage:

> We have been going through a more and more generalized crisis of representation at all levels: not only have our political systems, both totalitarian and democratic, become incapable of efficient political representation, but societies and their complexities are no longer imaged for us except through the distortions of media conventions. Perhaps it always was so, but less visibly and less fast, and today the 'representation crisis' even seems institutionalized for the profit of the culture-and-information purveyors who live on it... our old beliefs in the 'truth' of people and events as represented has long collapsed, and we seem to live in a simulation-cabin that gives us detailed illusions of movement and control, all the while keeping us immobile and observed. (p.172)

J. Hillis Miller's forgivable error was to suppose that deconstruction was a way to deal with that crisis – but, as its difficulties in 'representing' the de Man case demonstrate, it was more of a symptom than a salve. The insights of deconstruction should not and will not be dismissed, but should become, to adapt a Derridean image, part of the old cloth in which the break – past the postmodern? – will be inscribed. Miller is right enough when he says in his Preface – written early in 1990 – that 'we are on the threshold of an enormous transformation both in cultural practices and in their understanding through theory and reading', and that 'rapid technological changes are moving us all out of the Gutenberg era into an era of multimedia, hypertext or hypermedia, a mixing of alphabetic, iconic, and auditory signs' (p.x) – though one might want to question his McLuhanesque technological determinism and political complacency. Christine Brooke-Rose's sense of crisis is vital here. In the 1990s, there is a need for new cultural, social and political forms to cope with the representation crisis. Our success or failure in creating these forms will, as in the 1890s, help to determine whether the next century is closer to nightmare or nirvana.

13 Goodbye to Dada: Fredric Jameson

Tzara was the Dada of them all – all the cultural, or rather anti-cultural manifestations which were starting to be called postmodernist: that was the kind of argument you heard in the 1960s. Postmodernism, in other words, was little more than an enervated and entropic repetition of the wilder and less weighty impulses of a modernism whose classic achievements were those defaced but still noble monuments such as *Ulysses* and *The Waste Land*. This argument was, in effect, an assurance that the academy need not bother too much with postmodernism, which was merely the smaller and less vital variety of the modernist beast it had, at last, painfully tamed.

Such an argument has become much more difficult to sustain in the last decade, not only because of the burgeoning bibliography on the topic, but also because of the changes in the world we inhabit – in architecture, in communications technology, in modes of personal and collective consumption – which mean that even 'traditional' cultural positions function in a different force-field and are thereby changed. The criticisms of postmodernism made from such positions – that it is, for example, frivolous, superficial, complicit, commercialized, ephemeral, ahistorical, indifferent (in both modern senses) – can all be, in a way, pre-empted by postmodernism itself, which subverts or simply ignores the hierarchies which privilege, for instance, 'depth' over 'surface' and which may indeed proudly accept such charges as signs of merit, as well as pointing to the ways in which those who make them partake of and profit from the cultural moment they denounced; jeremiads against cultural decline can top best-seller lists.

To talk of 'postmodernism' is to imply that it is a unitary, clearly defined concept or entity. This in itself, in postmodernist terms, a paradox, since postmodernism denies notions of unity and fixed definition; such notions are also suspect to an older empiricism wary of 'labels'. But concepts that indicate cultural styles and periods are never fixed in precise and universally shared definitions; they are better understood as roughing out areas of debate about the identity and relationship of a range of phenomena which are partly, but not wholly, constituted by that very debate. Since postmodernism is, however, a concept intended to indicate a condition we are currently living, the debate presses more immediately than it might with such concepts as 'baroque' and 'medieval', and is complicated by the problem – well-recognized, though not necessarily as a problem, by postmodernism itself – that definitions of the present may influence that present: they may become self-fulfilling prophecies. Such pressures and problems are less reasons to eschew such debate than promptings to pursue it further.

Postmodernism, with its destruction of organic and originary metaphors, would reject the notion of the 'seminal text', but the term still seems appropriate to Fredric Jameson's essay, 'Postmodernism, or, The Cultural Logic of Late Capitalism', which first appeared in *New Left Review* in 1984 and which now provides the opening chapter and title of this remarkable book. Jameson's work, in that and further essays also gathered here, such as 'Reading without interpretation: postmodernism and the video-text' have stimulated widespread discussion. But Jameson is not a fully paid-up postmodernist in the same way as, say, the ex-Communist Jean-François Lyotard, or Jean Baudrillard. He remains, in many ways, an old-fashioned Marxist, with an unashamedly neo-Hegelian totalizing aspiration, whose *The Political Unconscious* (1981) affirmed a vision of human history as 'a single great collective... struggle to wrest a realm of Freedom from a realm of Necessity' (1983 edn, p.19). There is no reason to suppose that Jameson has departed from this vision, and this book on postmodernism, like his earlier book on structuralism, *The Prison House of Language* (1972), is an attempt to wrest Marxism from the maw of its most powerful and popular competitors and to show that it can comprehend, ingest and transcend these. Today, structuralism has long since been seen off, but more by poststructuralism – which is, for Jameson, a subsidiary form of postmodernism – than by Marxism: the mirage of a structuralist Marxism having finally been buried with Althusser. And postmodernism remains a potent force, now slugging it out with Marxism on what *The Political Unconscious* called the 'Homeric battlefield' of interpretation (p.13) – with the balance of youth and numbers currently favouring the postmodernist side. Jameson's great strength, however, is that he does not merely engage in denunciations of postmodernism – as both traditional Marxists and humanists have sometimes tended to do – but seeks to understand it and to perceive what he calls its dialectical character, that is, the tension within it of progressive and regressive forces. And his openness to the present is informed by his grasp both of the often sombre *Kulturkritik* of Western Marxism – his other recent book, *Late Marxism* (1990), is a relatively austere study of Adorno – and of the wide range of past European literature discussed in *The Political Unconscious*.

Jameson proposes that postmodernism is the 'cultural dominant' of the present, the 'cultural logic', the necessary cultural consequence, of the most recent changes in the capitalist system. Obviously not all current cultural production is postmodernist, but postmodernism is the 'force field' in which it emerges (p.6). Postmodernism, however, is different from previous cultural dominants in that, today, the traditional boundaries of culture have dissolved, so that culture, along with capital, permeates every aspect of life; nature, still a residual presence in modernism – in, say, Eliot, Lawrence, Heidegger – has disappeared: we cannot speak of it without scare quotes. And the expansion of culture has also collapsed the distinction, stressed in the last-ditch defence operations of modernism, between 'high' and 'low' culture. The materials of popular culture are no longer 'quoted' in order to place, deprecate or transform them – as in Eliot or Joyce – but are simply part of the text. The mimicry of a 'popular' or indeed 'high' style in order to satirize it and imply a proper norm is replaced by a widespread neutral practice of pastiche, of what Jameson calls 'blank parody, a statue with blind eyeballs' (p.17).

Perhaps the most prominent feature of postmodernism for Jameson is 'a new depthlessness' (p.6); a rejection of the distinction between a 'deep' reality and a misleading or mendacious surface, whether this takes the form of a distinction between 'inside' and 'outside', essence and appearance, imaginary and real relations to the conditions of production (as in Marxism), manifest and latent content (as in psychoanalysis), authenticity and inauthenticity (as in existentialism), signifier and signified (as in what must now be called old-style semiotics) and structure and event (as in classical structuralism). It can be seen that this makes a clean sweep of the major modern Western cultural movements! Instead, postmodernism argues, we live in a culture of the image or simulacrum – Plato's term for a copy of which there is no original: a culture of surfaces, practices, discourses, games. But this, for postmodernism, was always the 'reality' of culture anyway, and is not to be deplored; it may, in some postmodernist writing, be celebrated; but in any case, it simply *is* – though without any weight of Heideggerean *Sein*. It is an attitude epitomized in Andy Warhol's remark that 'if you want to know about Andy Warhol just look at the surface of my paintings and films and me and there I am. There's nothing behind it' (quoted in Simon Wilson, *Pop*, 1974, p.18). And it is Andy Warhol's 'Diamond Dust Shoes', contrasted with the Van Gogh painting of a pair of peasant shoes that is central to Heidegger's *The Origin of the Work of Art* (1935), which provides Jameson, in a virtuoso comparison, with his paradigm of the difference between high modernism and postmodernism.

This new depthlessness weakens the sense of history, in both public and private terms. We lose a sense of collective identity as constituted by a public past with which we have continuities and differences, and we also lose a sense of our individual identity as formed by a personal past that feeds into our present. In a way, we may seem – more so in Britain than in America, as Robert Hewison's *The Heritage Industry* (1987) suggests – to live in a nostalgia-ridden culture which, to a greater extent than ever before, can produce image after image of the past; but this nostalgia is not the anguished Romantic-modernist yearning for a lost childhood, or for a vanished aristocratic and/or peasant community. It is depthless and painless, a consumption of images of 'the past' which, by their very sophistication, are in a sense images of the *present* – of a capacity to achieve a simulacrum of a past that never existed in that glittering, hi-tech form. Postmodernism is a shift from a temporal to a spatial emphasis. Especially in its architectural manifestations, postmodernism involves 'mutations in the lived experience of built space itself' (p.6); for example, the combination of delight and disorientation evoked in Jameson's account of the Westin Bonaventure Hotel in Los Angeles designed by John Portman. It is this experience of what Jameson calls 'postmodern hyperspace' (p.44) that exemplifies 'a whole new type of emotional ground tone' (p.6) – a kind of 'postmodernist "sublime"' (p.49) in which euphoria and disequilibrium are interfused – and also serves as a possibility of 'cognitive mapping' (p.54), of finding individual and collective location and direction, in 'the bewildering new world space of late or multinational capital' (p.6).

The addiction which may seriously damage your cultural health has progressed from the novel, in the early nineteenth century, to film in the twentieth century, then television, and now video. It is video which Jameson sees as the privileged mode of postmodernism, the form most fitted to and exemplary of it. In video – whether of a commercial or 'art'/'experimental' kind – the flow of images, their rapid succession, juxtaposition, repetition, and variation, disrupt more traditional interpretative operations – extracting themes, collecting images, finding hidden meanings. The machinery of video 'uniquely dominates and depersonalizes subject and object alike, transforming the former into a quasi-material registering apparatus for the machine time of the latter and of the video image or "total flow"' (p.76). But Jameson's purpose is not merely to deplore this, but to understand it, and, moreover, to suggest its positive aspect. For this disruption of traditional hermeneutic modes is also a kind of liberation, and the materiality of video foregrounds the materiality of all culture, freeing it from spiritual reductionism. In an important passage in his Conclusion, Jameson speaks of 'the *relief* of the postmodern generally, a thunderous unblocking of logjams and a release of new productivity that was somehow tensed up and frozen, locked like cramped muscles, at the latter end of the modern period' (p.313). Postmodernism, in this respect, was a revolt against, and release from, a modernism that had become institutionalized and inert.

To suggest the positive aspects of postmodernism is not, however, wholly to applaud it, and Jameson offers an interesting perspective on contemporary literary and cultural theory, seen as an aspect of postmodernism. Such theory has often been perceived and presented as a challenge to a dominant conventional wisdom enshrining obsolete metaphysical notions like the substantial unity of the self. While not denying the interest and value of such theory, Jameson suggests that

> the critique of the metaphysical shadows and traces that persist within modernity paradoxically turns around into a replication of that very postmodern triumph over the metaphysical remnants of the modern, where to call for the shedding of any illusions about psychic identity or the centred subject, for the ethical ideal of good molecular "schizophrenic" living, and for the ruthless abandonment of the mirage of presence may turn out to be a description of the way we live now, rather than its rebuke or subversion. (p.339)

This, of course, leads to a crucial question: how can a valid cultural criticism emerge that is not the product and prisoner of what it purports to criticize?

By means of Marxism, perhaps, which links cultural criticism to an anti-capitalist political perspective? In this case, *Postmodernism, or, The Cultural Logic of Late Capitalism* would stand as an example of such criticism. But Jameson's book holds out a temptation implied in its very title: to take the cultural analysis without the political critique. In Jameson's perspective, the joke of the title might be that it models the operations of late capitalism by puporting to offer consumer choice where really there is none: we cannot, in his view, truly choose between postmodernism and late capitalism; it is a package deal, with no options. In practical analysis, one suspects, the political baggage may be jettisoned. If, in one sense, this might seem to reinforce Jameson's analysis of late capitalism – in which Marxism becomes merely another cultural commodity, mainly consumed by intellectuals – it also points to the more serious question of the status of Marxism. For the commodification of Marxism may be related, not only to the absorptive power of late capitalism, but also to deficiencies in Marxism's explanatory and energizing power – deficiencies evident in some equivocations in Jameson's book.

Jameson is a fine writer. His sentences are both relaxed and periodic, so that the reader is reassured and elevated, smoothly raised, as in the see-through lifts of Portmans's Hyatt Regencies which, as Jameson puts it, rise 'like great Japanese lanterns or gondolas' (p.42) into a position in which global cognitive mapping, a totalizing grasp, seems at least possible. Coming down to earth (a possibility, of course, which postmodernism excludes), we may find the cartography rather more complex. Jameson remarked in *Marxism and Form* (1971) that 'any concrete description of a literary or philosophical phenomenon – if it is to be really complete – has an ultimate obligation to come to terms with the shape of the individual sentences themselves, to give an account of their origin and formation' (p.xii). Relating this specifically to Marxism, and extending it across a whole range of cultural forms, we may say that any adequate Marxist cultural theory should be able to give an account of the origin and formation of the smallest elements of the cultural phenomena it considers. By this criterion, we may find Jameson's assertion that postmodernism is the 'cultural logic' of 'late capitalism' wanting. For what, precisely, are the relations between 'late capitalism' and the specific and general features of postmodernism? In this area, Jameson is loosely suggestive in such a way as to lay himself open to the postmodernist charge that Marxism is merely one interpretative option among others. He seeks to establish its priority less by trying to demonstrate that it provides the most complete and compelling explanation of the relationship between a certain mode of economic and of cultural production than by a rhetorical movement between the invocation of late capitalism and specific cultural analyses which do not seem to depend, for their effectiveness, on his general Marxist premiss. The effect is at moments like that process of 'channel switching' which Jameson takes from the media theorists (p.373) as a useful model for the postmodern perceptual operation in which incompatible discourses and modes are perceived in juxtaposition without any attempt to unify them, though they may 'infect' each other (as in video). We move, in this book, between a Marxist rhetoric that sometimes has an old-fashioned 'feel' – as in the 1930s-style reference to 'the Russian comrades' (p.274) or the very 1960s gesture of calling Castro 'Fidel' (p.354) – and up-to-the-minute cultural analysis, without a worked-out synthesis of the two.

This incompatibility is compounded by a confusion as to whether cultural or economic determinants are primary; at times Jameson seems to suggest, for instance, that both the dominance of Thatcherism and the decline of socialism were due as much to cultural as to economic factors (e.g., pp.207-8, 263-4). This confusion could be seen to confirm his analysis of 'late capitalism' as characterized by a hitherto unprecedented interfection of culture and commerce; but it clearly poses a problem for any project of cognitive mapping, let alone of radical social and political change. If one cannot grasp the causes and relations of things, how can one hope either to interpret the world or to change it?

There can be no doubt, however, about the power and insight of Jameson's specific cultural analyses. This book demonstrates definitively that we have moved into a new phase, that modernism is no longer the cultural dominant. Postmodernism may not have come of age, but it has said goodbye to Dada.

14 Politic Evasions: Terry Eagleton

Terry Eagleton's *Literary Theory* (1983) signals the failure of the radical project crystallized, for British intellectuals, by Perry Anderson's 1968 essay 'Components of the National Culture': the quest for a totalizing theory which would comprehensively explain the whole range of political, social and cultural phenomena in such a way as to promote revolutionary change. Eagleton had tried to produce such a theory in *Criticism and Ideology* (1976); *Literary Theory* implicitly jettisons that attempt and presents this abandonment, in a skilful sleight of hand, as up-to-date and liberating. And maybe, in a sense, it is; but it is much closer than Eagleton might like to believe to the postmodernist, anti-totalizing approach of, say, Jean-François Lyotard. It may be objected that it is only the possibility of a totalizing *literary* theory that Eagleton's book rejects; but the book fails to offer not only a totalizing literary theory but a totalizing social and political perspective within which literary theory can be understood. In so far as a totalizing perspective is implied, it is a political one; but it is not an articulated, comprehensive and coherent theory. Furthermore, Eagleton's political thought is exiguous. It may seem strange to say this of such a high-profile left-wing critic: but Eagleton is no political thinker.

In *Literary Theory*, Eagleton distinguishes between 'different forms of politics – between those who subscribe to the doctrine that history, society and human reality as a whole are fragmentary, arbitrary and directionless, and those who have other interests which imply alternative views about the way the world is'. It is questionable, in fact, whether this distinction can be sustained – an important aspect of Eagleton's argument in the book depends on the view that the doctrine of fragmentariness, arbitrariness and directionlessness comprises a definite, and thus, in a sense, non-fragmentary ideology.

Moreover, Eagleton's coyness about 'alternative views' – an almost Leavisian refusal of definition – is telling: in *Literary Theory*, it is his own world-view which seems 'fragmentary'. Having drawn his dubious distinction, he goes on: 'There is no way of settling the question of which politics is preferable in literary critical terms. You simply have to argue about politics' (p.209). This is precisely what Eagleton does not do in the book. Instead of argument, there is emotive rhetoric and evasive sloganizing. One of the most useful functions of the final chapter, comically entitled 'Political Criticism', would be as a source of examples for a manual on how to avoid political thought.

Consider this, for instance, from near the start of that chapter:

> As I write, it is estimated that the world contains over 60,000 nuclear warheads, many with a capacity a thousand times greater than the bomb which destroyed Hiroshima. The possibility that these weapons will be used in our lifetime is steadily growing. The approximate cost of these weapons is 500 billion dollars a year, or 1.3 billion dollars a day. Five per cent of this sum – 25 billion dollars – could drastically, fundamentally alleviate the problems of the poverty-stricken Third World. (p.194)

The use of the first person singular and the present tense gives a sense of immediacy, indeed of that 'presence' of which deconstruction teaches a reader to be sceptical. This form of authorial authority is both subverted and reinforced by the intertextual allusion to the opening words of Orwell's 'The Lion and the Unicorn' (1941; *Collected Essays*, p.74). The apocalyptic note, the warning of Armageddon, is given a 'factual' grounding by the deployment of unsubstantiated statistics. To examine Eagleton's rhetorical techniques in this way might be interpreted as a defensive displacement, a distortion of priorities, an evasion of the urgent realities which Eagleton invokes; but Eagleton himself, having invoked them, hardly tries to face up to them. His implicit political perspective is inadequate to the challenges and complexities they represent. For example, it is implied that a simple transfer of funds could automatically help a 'Third World' which is both personified, and patronizingly turned into an object of charity rather than seen as a site of agents in their own right; Eagleton's discourse here is a mixture of that of a Victorian philanthropist and a twentieth-century, paternalistic social-worker. The dangers of nuclear war, the sufferings of the poor, are briefly invoked, then dissolved as immensely difficult actualities to leave a residue as emotional tokens in Eagleton's rhetorical strategy.

This combined invocation-and-evasion of politics is evident throughout *Literary Theory*. For example, he contrasts what he regards as the liberal humanist view of democracy, 'the abstract one of the ballot box', with 'a specific, living and practical democracy which might also somehow concern the operations of the Foreign Office and Standard Oil' (p.207). The adjectival insistence on specificity, aliveness and practicality is unsubstantiated by any proposals for 'full, concrete, practical applications' (p.208) and collapses into the vagueness of 'might also somehow concern'. Somehow, but how? One can imagine how Eagleton would castigate such an evasion in a 'liberal humanist' text. Eagleton calls liberal humanism 'the impotent conscience of bourgeois society' (p.199). Today that role is surely reserved for socialism.

Eagleton is no more able than the liberal humanism he assaults to articulate the connections between his politico-moral stance and political actuality. When he turns, all too briefly, to 'actually existing socialism' he does no better. Invoking what he calls 'the tyrannies in Eastern Europe', he claims that 'what would be necessary to bring down such tyrannies would not be just more free speech, but a workers' revolution against the state' (p.208). This is indeed a glib slogan-remedy, in a century in which the concept of 'a workers' revolution' has come into question time and again, in theory and practice. (And from the hindsight of the 1990s, we know that, when the tyrannies did collapse in Eastern Europe, it didn't happen quite like that.) Eagleton's remark might be permissible as simply a momentary blow-off: it is hardly appropriate in a chapter that asserts the need for explicit attention to and argument about politics. The only time in *Literary Theory* that Eagleton comes near to practicalities is when he affirms that 'the democratic control of these ideological apparatuses [television and the popular press], along with popular alternatives to them, must be high on the agenda of any future socialist programme' (p.216). He goes no further in being 'specific' about what forms 'democratic control' or 'popular alternatives' might take, or how the enabling conditions for them might be created: instead, a note refers us to Raymond Williams's *Communications* (1962) for 'some interesting practical proposals' (p.222, n.3). It is hardly surprising that *Literary Theory* ends not with an agenda but an allegory.

This paucity of political thought is evident elsewhere in Eagleton's writing. Consider this analysis of the 1984-5 British miners' strike, which occurs in the course of an attack, in an essay, upon an abstracted 'liberal humanism':

> Very recently, in Britain, we have been witness to a form of creativity rich in concrete experience, subtly discriminating, sensitively alert to nuance and particularity. I am referring of course to the attempt by the National Union of Mineworkers to bring down the Thatcher government. In many ways this attempt is absolutely exemplary of everything the liberal humanists speak of. For where, after all, could you find a more creative and authentic mode of experience, more spontaneous rightness of response (as Leavis himself might have said), a more richly lived sense of value and meaning, than that manifested in the pitched battles between strikers and police at the pit heads, or in the work of the women's support groups. ('The Subject of Literature', p.102)

Eagleton wants to suggest, provocatively, that the strike could be seen to exemplify liberal humanist values, even though liberal humanists themselves might not care to recognize such values in that context. But from a liberal humanist perspective it would be possible to reply that it was precisely the lack of subtle discrimination in certain key respects, of sensitive alertness among the strike's leaders and supporters to nuance and particularity, which contributed significantly to the strike's failure. In particular, there was a failure subtly to discriminate among and to be alert sensitively to the different feelings, needs, aspirations, interests, beliefs, experiences, of miners and miners' wives and children, within the same geographical areas, or in different geographical areas. One major cause of the strike's failure, it might be argued, was its failure to respect individuality and difference, its reliance on a fantasized, abstract, monolithic 'unity' which never materialized. It is notable that in this passage Eagleton avoids the use of the term 'miners' and refers instead, first to one of the mining unions – the NUM – and then to 'strikers' and women's support groups. To use the term 'miners' would be inaccurate and inconvenient, and might foreground the scandalous, unnerving truth that not all miners, or miners' wives, supported the strike, and that some of them played a part in bringing about its collapse. Subtle discrimination and sensitive alertness to nuance and particularity would have to confront these painful facts. Eagleton perhaps prefers what he commends, later in the essay, as a 'proper insensitivity' (p.103): we might see this as exemplified by those who supported the NUM strike from a safe distance (contributing, of course, to the strikers' Christmas Appeal – see *The Miner*, 11 December 1984, p.5) and who now employ it as an image in their rhetoric: not for them the bitterness of lost jobs, broken communities and families, debt, prison. They have enjoyed the thrill of vicarious participation in pit-head battles and the sentimental drama of defeat; these voyeurs can move on to the next abortive revolution.

In view of this evasion of political thought, it is hardly surprising that, in a later essay, Eagleton remarks:

> In the end, critics divide not in terms of theories, methods or 'approaches', but in terms of whether they do or do not instantly understand and appreciate Walter Benjamin's comment that "there is no cultural document which is not at the same time a record of barbarism". A critical practice founded upon this centrally important insight is quite irreconcilable with one which ignores it. ('Literature and History', p.25).

The wheel has come full circle. We return here to something very like the 'intuitionism', the appeal to those who 'know already', the rejection of rational argument in favour of instant insight, which the quest for theory, of both a literary and socio-political kind, set out to combat.

If Eagleton is no political thinker, he remains a lucid commentator on cultural topics, and *The Ideology of the Aesthetic* (1990) is his most substantial book so far. In Eagleton's Marxist perspective, the aesthetic as a theoretical category emerges in the early capitalist era as economic and cultural production start to break out of the traditional confines of church, court and state, and 'individual' and 'society', the sensuous body and abstract reason, 'fact' and 'value', begin dangerously to diverge. A major problem of the society of that era is that the ideology of the free, autonomous individual which its economy requires is, potentially, in conflict with the social cohesion that it also needs. Thus the function of the aesthetic in such a context is to reconcile, on the imaginary plane, individualism with social harmony. It seeks to work through the body. Alexander Baumgarten, the German philosopher who first defined the notion of 'aesthetics' in his book *Aesthetica* (1750-8), saw the aesthetic as concerned, not first of all with art, but with the whole of lived sensory experience. The body is the site on which sensuous and spiritual, abstract and particular, the law and the sentiments, fact and value, meet, where you can feel your civic duty as immediately as the odour of a rose. But this makes the aesthetic a dangerous, unstable, double-edged category: for the body which bourgeois hegemony needs to flesh out its ideology can rebel, dropping out of the nets of reason to leave them void, or rising up to tear them asunder.

Eagleton tracks this instability with energy and relish. He strives to maintain a dialectical comprehension: that is, he does not simply dismiss the category of the aesthetic – or imbricated categories such as the liberal humanist subject or bourgeois society – but tries to grasp them as simultaneously dynamic and destructive, life-denying and liberating; to take Marx's point that history progresses by its bad side. He is attentive to the intricacies of specific theories, and can empathize not only with the thinkers one might expect – Walter Benjamin, for example – but also with less likely figures such as that intransigent Protestant individualist and political reactionary, Søren Kierkegaard. Furthermore, he can make sharp criticisms both of 'bourgeois' philosophers and of Marxist ones, including Adorno and Marx himself.

The trouble with the aesthetic, it seems, is that, hired by the bourgeoisie as a benign schoolmaster, it becomes a naughty child, a cynical jester, a holy fool, a raving lout, a double agent, a committed militant. It subverts what it should support, figures the contradictions it is meant to conceal. Thus, for instance, Hume and Kant find, in their respective ways, that the aesthetic tends to infiltrate and undermine the cognitive. Schiller's aesthetic sphere, the hinge of the sensuous and the rational, which suspends all determinations and discloses boundless possibilities, is both a critique of a fragmented society, and an image of that society's dream of untrammelled freedom. Fichte's absolute ego becomes the aesthetic womb of the whole world, an immaculate conceiver which invents but threatens to ingest the objects it needs for its own activity. Schelling's 'aesthetic intuition' of an 'absolute identity' that transcends subject and object in an 'indifference' to both is famously dismissed by Hegel as the night in which all cows are black. Hegel himself seeks to resolve Kant's subject/object dichotomy by turning Kant's aesthetic fiction – the unity of subject and object in the act of judgement – into an ontological myth in which the subject's free activity conveniently uncovers the rational totality of the world. But as totality can only ultimately be grasped by the theorizing mind reading Hegel, it cannot be felt through the body, in practical activity, and its ideological function is thus impaired. As Kierkegaard protested, Hegel's system cannot be *lived*.

Schopenhauer sees human beings as driven blindly on by desire, by the voracious will of which reason and subjectivity are illusory products. The only escape from appetency is into an aesthetic attitude to reality in which desire drops away and the world emerges as it really is – but this entails the virtual disappearance of the ego, which is bad news for the bourgeoisie. Kierkegaard opposes an intransigent, anguished religious commitment to an ethical sphere of empty, abstracted idealism and an aesthetic sphere of degraded desire, and thus provides a proleptic critique of the bourgeois society that is only just starting to emerge from the near-medieval absolute monarchy of his time.

Marx, Nietzche and Freud all, in their distinctive ways, seize upon the body, the potentially subversive element of the aesthetic, and try to build their thought up from it: 'Marx with the labouring body, Nietzche with the body as power, Freud with the body of desire' (p.197). Marx accepts the goals of the aesthetic – the fusion of feeling and reason, fact and value, the sensuous and the 'spiritual', the idea that society (and material production) should be, like the work of art, ends in themselves – but sees these as awaiting achievement through a practical and theoretical struggle that would transform the material conditions of human existence. Nietzche demystifies aesthetic disinterestedness and throws one traditional aim of the aesthetic, social harmony, to the wolves of the other, individual self-actualization. But it's a family argument. 'If the furious dynamism of the *Übermensch* terrifies the stout metaphysical citizen, he may also figure as his fantastic *alter ego*, in the sphere of production' (p.259). Freud follows up Nietzche's assault on disinterestedness by scandalously (a favourite Eagleton term) bringing the libidinal and aggressive drives into the utilitarian and cultural spheres, while his concept of desire as lack undermines the phallic fullness of Nietzche's 'self-actualization'. But Freud himself was still phallocentric, and he didn't have much time for socialism.

Heidegger, darkly implicated in a fascism that aestheticized politics, dismisses the aesthetic only because he universalizes it: the aesthetic is a way of relating to a Being that eludes the concept, though art can disclose its very movement. But the Marxist aesthetics of Lukács 'are a left mirror-image of the dominant model of bourgeois aesthetics' (p.325) that Eagleton's study has analysed – though Eagleton does not deny the value of Lukács's theory of realism. Walter Benjamin's revolutionary politics are in all kinds of ways aesthetic, but only because he has subverted most traditional aesthetic notions – beauty, harmony, totality, appearance – and found faint Messianic flickers in 'what Brecht called the "bad new things" ...the structure of the commodity, the death of storytelling, the vacancy of historical time and the technology of capitalism itself' (p.338). Adorno seeks to hold on to the traditional aesthetic project, but with an anguished awareness, after Auschwitz, of the body of suffering rather than of pleasure, and in a tense dialectic of fragmentation and totality, of art as fetishized commodity and utopian *ahnung*. In his last chapter Eagleton charges that postmodernism has lost this dialectic.

The crucial problem that arises from the book is the cognitive status of its metanarrative. Eagleton sees the aesthetic as an 'incipient materialism', and stresses its importance in Marx's own thought and in subsequent Western Marxism. This prompts the subversive question: what if Marxism itself were one more example of 'the ideology of the aesthetic', rather than, as Eagleton assumes, the master code which can not only decipher the aesthetic but also enable its material realization? What if the function of Marxism were to maintain bourgeois hegemony by offering an imaginary resolution of real contradictions that was the more enchanting because it claimed that such a resolution could be achieved through political action?

The obvious objection to seeing Marxism as aesthetic in this sense is that it has apparently motivated many to action, and has legitimated a number of violent revolutions and repressive regimes. This could strengthen the point: the failure of Marxism in practice might be seen as a very likely result of an attempt to realize the aesthetic in non-aesthetic actuality: 'actually existing Marxism' might be seen as an excess, not of reason as is often claimed, but of imagination, wrongly applied. And what greater gift has there been to bourgeois hegemony than the Marxist regimes of the twentieth century?

The last chapter of *The Ideology of the Aesthetic* and many of its earlier asides show that Eagleton is now threatened by a cultural revolution which he helped to foment. For Marxism is open to all the charges which, in *Literary Theory*, Eagleton made against the category of literature: it is a recent historical invention, it has no fixed essence or boundary, and it promotes bourgeois hegemony, though it may also offer a marginal site of resistance. Epistemological scepticism is a powerful weapon, but it can blow up in your face. The flabby liberal humanist can take a breather for a moment, leaner and fitter for his hot encounters: it's open season on Marxism now, as postmodernists and postmarxists take to the field.

Eagleton counter-attacks on three fronts. First, he tries to reclaim for Marxism a humanist, even Christian vocabulary. Tabooed terms, shorn of scare quotes, gush from his pen: 'fundamental human values'; 'loving kindness' (p.354); 'human nature' (p.409); 'love' (p.413) – though he stresses that these need to be realized at the level of the whole society. Secondly, he affirms the need for a normative discourse:

> The universal...is not some realm of abstract duty set sternly against the particular; it is just every individual's equal right to have his or her difference respected, and to participate in the common process whereby that can be achieved. Identity is to this extent in the service of non-identity; but without such identity, no real non-identity can be attained. (pp.414-5)

Thirdly, while acknowledging the partial validity of attacks on the oppressiveness of totality and metanarrative, he points out that you need totality to fight totality, and that postmodernists, and Stanley Fish-style pragmatists, themselves promote the totalizing metanarrative of the end of totalizing metanarratives. Much of this is welcome but it fails to address a key question: why should we accept Marxism as our totalizing metanarrative?

In *The Signficance of Theory* (1990), Eagleton remarks: 'The only good reason for being a socialist, in my opinion, is that one cannot quite overcome one's amazement that the fate of the vast majority of men and women who have ever lived and died has been, and still is today, one of fruitless, unremitting labour' (p.33). But this is a very poor reason for being a socialist – certainly of a Marxist kind – unless one believes that socialism will change this condition in the future. Eagleton does of course believe this, but many others, no less appalled than he at human misery, will have grave doubts, given that in the twentieth century Marxism in practice has meant, not the body, but bodies.

15 Modern Tragedy: Perry Anderson

In 1917, or even in 1970, a different scenario for the end of the century might have seemed credible: one in which some beneficient form of socialism swept over the world, a decayed and discredited capitalism collapsing before it. Even in the 1980s, the advent of Gorbachev produced hopes that the Soviet Union might change in such a way as to realize some of the hopes originally invested in it. It was not to be. Now socialism can look rather as Christianity looked to Thomas Hardy in the post-Victorian twilight; at best, the object of a vague, sentimental, aspiration: 'Hoping it might be so'.

It is in this conjuncture that Perry Anderson's *English Questions* and *A Zone of Engagement* (both 1992) appear. The essays of which these volumes are comprised cover a span of nearly thirty years, the earliest dated 1964, the latest ones 1992. Anderson has been a significant figure on the British intellectual Left. His position in regard to English society has been that of an inside outsider: educated at Eton, he is of what he himself, in the Foreword to *English Questions*, calls 'residual Anglo-Irish' origins (p.7), and it is perhaps relevant to observe that in 'The Figures of Descent' in that book, he points out that 'the neediest and least reputable branch of the [gentry] class, its Anglo-Irish extension...provided most of Britain's leading commanders down even to a century later, in a line stretching from Wellington to Roberts, Kitchener to Alanbrooke, Montgomery to Templer' (pp.135-6). Anderson's own command skills were applied not to the battlefield but to another site of struggle, to the running of *New Left Review*, which he took over from Stuart Hall and E.P. Thompson, and to the establishment of New Left Books, later to become Verso. His efforts and those of his associates were important in importing and disseminating a wide range of ideas, particularly those of Western Marxism from Lukács to Althusser.

The creation of a successful magazine and publishing house was hardly Anderson's overriding aim; rather the hope was that the intellectual production he promoted would link at some point with actual political struggles that would transform society. In the late 1960s and early 1970s, those struggles looked as though they might materialize. Anderson's *In the Tracks of Historical Materialism* (1983) acknowledged the spread of intellectual and political reaction and the retreat of Latin Marxism, but continued to affirm his commitment to Marxism as the most comprehensive theory of historical development available. In 1986, however, the first volume of Michael Mann's *A Theory of Social Power* appeared; while critical of it in important respects, Anderson none the less saw this, as he acknowledges in the Foreword to *A Zone of Engagement*, as 'a developed analytic theory of the pattern of human development, exceeding in explanatory ambition and empirical detail any Marxist account' (p.xii). It is not, in fact, altogether clear from these books whether Anderson still defines himself as a Marxist; but he is strongly aware of the challenges, beyond those of the more obvious conservative or liberal kinds, which have come to Marxism from both recent history and theory.

The very appearance of two volumes of essays – with the inevitable diversity that essays written at different times and at different occasions will have – is significant in this respect, marking a retreat, or at least a vacation, from the desire to develop a 'totalizing' account of human history which was evident in two earlier books, *Passages from Antiquity to Feudalism* and *Lineages of the Absolutist State* (both 1974). The Foreword to the latter book promised two sequels which would deal, respectively, with the chain of great bourgeois revolutions and with the structure of the capitalist states that emerged from them. These have not so far appeared. The division, with some overlaps, between these two latest volumes relates to Anderson's ongoing attempt to comprehend both the national and the global context of historical, political and cultural development. He has been an acute analyst both of the structural development of British society over the centuries and of mid and late twentieth-century British intellectual culture. These analyses comprise the bulk of *English Questions*. He has also been concerned with international political, social and cultural developments, particularly in Europe but also in Russia and America, and with placing British developments in that broader context. His range is polyglot – French, German, Italian, Russian – and polymath, covering sociology, historical, political theory and cultural analysis. Thus *A Zone of Engagement* considers the theories of historical development of Michael Mann and W.G. Runciman, two English thinkers covered in a more compressed way in *English Questions*; the links and differences between Max Weber and Ernest Gellner, the latter also discussed more briefly in *English Questions*; the materialist reinterpetation of the ancient world by the historian and classicist Geoffrey de Ste. Croix; the book *Two Kinds of Ruin* (1986) by the German historian Andreas Hillgruber and the controversy over historical representations of the Final Solution which it fuelled; the work of the Marxist historian and biographer of Stalin and Trotsky, Isaac Deutscher; the pursuit across a vast historical and geographical canvas of the motifs of nocturnal flying and animal metamorphoses in the work of Carlo Ginzburg; the exploration of French national identity in Fernand Braudel's last book; the attempt to combine liberalism and socialism in the political thinking of Norberto Bobbio; the theories of empowerment of the Brazilian-American writer Roberto Unger; the liberalism of Isaiah Berlin; the account of the relations between modernity and revolution in Marshall Berman's *All That is Solid Melts into Air* (1982). *A Zone of Engagement* concludes with a discussion of Francis Fukuyama's end-of-history thesis and a survey of the prospects for socialism.

Anderson's intellectual approach is of a rather traditional kind in today's context. His discussions of ideas, as he himself acknowledges in the Foreword to *A Zone of Engagement*, 'are centred on individual authors – not concepts, discourses or texts – whose work they aim to reconstruct, so far as possible, as an intentional unity, situated within the intellectual and political currents of their time'. He engages in careful explication of these authors – that very word itself is provocative today – and tries 'to locate specific contradictions of argument where these occur, generally treating them...as symptomatic points of tension, either within the body of thought itself, or with the evidence beyond it' (p.x). The reference to 'evidence' is also characteristic; *In the Tracks* affirmed that 'the *distinction* between the true and the false is the ineliminable premise of any rational knowledge. Its central site is evidence' (p.48). These latest volumes maintain that stance, against those approaches which would tend to see 'evidence' as merely the construction of specific discourses, with no purchase outside those discourses. For example, Anderson's discussion of Hillgruber is also, in part, an argument against Hayden White and more generally against those philosophies of historiography which assert the superiority of narrative emplotment over evidence. Narrative strategies in historical writing always operate within exterior limits set by the evidence – for instance, no historical representation of Nazism or the Final Solution could deny the existence of either the regime or its crimes – and also operates within a double interior limit; some kinds of evidence preclude some kinds of emplotment – 'the Final Solution cannot *historically* be written as romance, or comedy' (p.180) – and any generic emplotment can only weakly determine the selection of evidence. Narratives 'are never plenipotentiaries of the past' and history cannot be reduced to rhetoric. This is part of a broader campaign against what he called in *In the Tracks of Historical Materialism*, with particular reference to structuralism and poststructuralism, the '*exorbitation of language*' (p.40) – the attribution to language of some primary determinative power exceeding that of any other potential determinant. Anderson is arguably too neglectful of the role of rhetoric in historical writing and in intellectual work more generally; indeed his own work – for example, the historical narrative of 'The Figures of Descent' in *English Questions*, sweeping through centuries of British history from the Civil War to the Thatcher era – is doubtless responsible to the evidence but gains some of its persuasive force from its skilful rhetorical presentation. He is a master of the concise, assured summary and dissection; image and epigram pepper his pages; he enjoys alliteration; he is fond of the recondite word, and, his public school education perhaps showing, of the occasional Latin tag. His comparative lack of attention to rhetoric – not least, in any self-reflexive way to his own – is a lacuna in his armoury of analytic skills.

If he was too dismissive, in *In the Tracks*, of poststructuralism, he is rather too dismissive, in these volumes, of postmodernism. It is witty to say that '"*Le capital fait jouir*" – Lyotard's lesson – is the slogan of Dionysus in Disneyland' (*Zone*, p.48-9), but that dismissal, with its neat alliterative fusion, itself smacks of sloganizing (and is surely itself, in its fusion of élite and popular cultural reference, exemplary of postmodernism). The force of postmodernism, beyond its fatuities, is not registered – Anderson pays no attention, for example, to the ways in which its emphases on discontinuity and the difficulties of representation have entered into the work of postcolonial critics such as Homi Bhabha (indeed, this whole area of work is notably absent from Anderson's survey of British intellectual culture in *English Questions*). Anderson is still deeply drawn to 'totalizing' approaches, and this is all well and good; but any such approaches could only benefit from confronting the serious questions posed by postmodernism.

What overall themes emerge from these volumes, besides the many illuminating local discussions they contain? In *English Questions*, two themes stand out: the contraction of British power and the expansion of English culture. 'Origins of the Present Crisis', first published in 1964, and 'The Figures of Descent', first published in 1987, both offer a historical aetiology of British decline. The first essay saw that decline as due to the subordination of the industrial bourgeoisie to the landowning gentry, a subordination which had meant that the bourgeoisie had failed to make the structural changes which would have been necessary for Britain to continue to compete successfully once it had lost the easy advantage that its headstart in the Industrial Revolution had given it. That argument had been based, however, on the view that Britain was exceptional in that its dominance by a land-owning class had begun in the 'bourgeois revolution' of the Civil War and continued into the twentieth century. 'The Figures of Descent' acknowledges, however, that Britain was not exceptional in either of these respects. 'The Figures of Descent' therefore attempts to explain the British crisis of the mid-twentieth century, not merely as a result of continued land-owner dominance, which turns out to have been a much more general phenomenon, but by a more specific analysis of the particular patterns this took in the context of, for example, the growth of Britain's maritime Empire, the priority Britain enjoyed in the Industrial Revolution, and the freedom of Britain in the twentieth century from invasion or occupation. The general conclusion is that the structural changes in British government, economy and society that would have been necessary to revive Britain's flagging economic fortunes have not been made, and that, in view of 'the radical internationalization of the forces of production [and] circulation' (p.192), a purely 'national' solution may no longer be possible.

Anderson's general account is, by and large, convincing. His verdict on the Thatcher regime, acknowledging but not applauding its innovations in privatization, while pointing to the continued failure to achieve real structural change or truly to revive Britain's economy, seems even more valid than it might have done on the first publication of the essay, when Thatcher's reign still had three years to run. For all Anderson's awareness of the failures and depredations of capitalism, however, there are moments when one might be reading a rather more right-wing kind of diagnosis of British inefficiency and amateurism; it is significant that he applauds Martin Wiener's *English Culture and the Decline of the Industrial Spirit* in which the anti-industrial ideology of British intellectuals is 'incomparably depicted' (p.147), or, in a footnote, praises Correlli Barnett's *The Audit of War* as 'the most detailed and devastating panorama of the misery of British industry yet to have appeared, and the most radically wounding to national illusions' (p.155 n.63). Both of these studies are indeed very good in some respects, but in both there is an underlying assumption that a wholehearted commitment to industrial capitalism is desirable and that those who do not subscribe to it are misguided, ignorant or lazy; Barnett courteously calls British workers 'coolies' (p.187). In a way that seems to support Leavis's charge, cited by Anderson in *English Questions*, that Marxism merely reproduces the economic emphasis of capitalism (pp.100-2), Anderson sometimes appears to take the view that economic performance is the priority and proving-ground of a nation. Marx and Margaret Thatcher here join hands. But, as Sissy Jupe knew, there are other measures than that of National Prosperity. National Prosperity seemed, of course, rather less vulnerable in 1854 than in 1987, but the continuing British resistance to those frequent exhortations to become more like Japan or Germany is not neccesarily merely the product of structural inertia; it may also be, in part, a tacit trade-off of a certain degree of prosperity for other less calculable priorities.

Anderson's assumption of the priority of economic indicators is related to another assumption: that the norm for a nation is that it should not be in a state of 'crisis' and that to be in such a state is to be in a deviant condition. Obviously, one might distinguish different uses of the term 'crisis': it is clear that, whatever apocalyptic scenarios may have been sketched from the 1960s onwards, Britain has not been and is not in a state of 'crisis' in the sense of tottering on the brink of dissolution; Anderson himself remarks that 'the UK state has long been uniquely formidable as a constitutional structure for securing the active consent of the population to the political order; it is now equipped with the most experienced and professional apparatus for the exercise of coercion in any domestic emergency as well' (p.189). Of course apparently stable states can dissolve very quickly; Anderson, in his discussion of Britain, does not use 'crisis' to denote this kind of extremity, but to indicate a longer-term process of difficulty, anxiety and uncertainty. It is arguable, however, that this kind of 'crisis' is an inevitable feature of any government – that economic, social and political conditions may vary, but any government will have to cope with both long-term structural problems and unforeseen and more immediate contingencies. The norm of a nation free of 'crisis' in Anderson's sense of the term may be valuable as an ideal and as a standard, but it is difficult to actualize – indeed, impossible to do so under capitalism as Anderson, and Marx before him, conceived it.

A more general question that arises from Anderson's analysis of the British 'crisis' is that of the relationship between structure and agency. Or, to put it bluntly: could things have been any different? Anderson's delineation of the structural constraints upon change sometimes tends to suggest that the answer is no; on the other hand, he is often judgemental in a way that implies that it would have been possible to act otherwise. For example, his judgement on the Labour government that came to power in 1945 is, in his own terms, harsh: 'The whole effort of Labour's rule was not to transform the historic structures of Britain's economy, much less state, but to restore them' (p.164). But much of his previous argument suggests that it would have been very difficult for Labour to act otherwise. Earlier, he speaks of the improvement in Labour's position that came about during the Second World War 'not as the fruit of conscious purpose or collective struggle, but as a historical windfall' (p.163). There, the productive role of 'conscious purpose or collective struggle' is allowed, in an abstract way, but Anderson has already shown why 'conscious purpose or collective struggle' of a kind that might have enabled Labour to be a truly transformative party would have been most unlikely to have penetrated it or to have arisen within it, given its formation and structures. (The metaphor of the 'historical windfall' is also a curious one, implying as it partly does a role for chance that is not elsewhere made explicit or theorized in Anderson's argument.) The problem of structure and agency, of determination and possibility, is not confined to Anderson's diagnosis of the British malaise but is a general one for any political or historical analysis that is related to the prospects of political change.

Each of these essays on the British crisis comes in tandem with an essay on British intellectual culture. The first essay, 'Components of the National Culture', appeared in the *annus mirabilis* (or otherwise) of 1968. It begins with a reference to student revolt, but aims to open 'another front... against the reactionary culture inculcated in universities and colleges, which it is one of the functions of British higher education to instil in students' (p.48). This was to be a very influential essay, not least in literary studies. Anderson argued that British culture was organized about an absent centre – that it lacked a 'totalizing' overall account of itself that could have been produced either by a classical sociology or a national Marxism. This was because the structural features of British society analysed in 'Origins of the Present Crisis' precluded the emergence of the revolutionary challenge from below that would have made a 'totalizing' account seem necessary. Instead, British intellectual life had been dominated by 'White' emigrés in flight from political unrest in their native lands, who often identified themselves with Britain as a country of stability and order. The disciplines had been parcelled out among these emigrés; Wittgenstein in philosophy, Malinowski in anthropology, Namier in history, Popper in social theory, Berlin in political theory, Gombrich in aesthetics, and (to move, for Anderson, to a very low intellectual level) Eysenck in psychology. Despite the impressive intellectual contributions of some of these figures – Namier and Gombrich, for instance – their overall effect had been to encourage a way of thinking that was piecemeal, rejecting the category of the totality. Psychoanalysis had developed impressively in England, not least through the contributions of another emigré, Melanie Klein, but it had remained a separate enclave, largely cut off from the wider culture. Isaac Deutscher, an able Marxist scholar working in Britain, had enjoyed no formal recognition. Only in two areas had the category of the totality reappeared; in anthropology, where the imperatives of imperial administration had provoked a need for a totalizing vision of native societies – but here, of course, the totality had been, like the wayward younger son, packed off to the colonies; and, surprisingly, in the literary criticism of F.R. Leavis, with his claim that English was 'the chief of the humanities' (p.96). But there were major contradictions in Leavis's position: he affirmed that ostensive demonstration – pointing to certain texts – should be enough to carry a general argument, any explication of which he famously refused, yet such ostensive demonstration could only work in a situation where there was a shared, stable system of values which, by Leavis's own account, was disappearing. This diagnosis is strengthened by Leavis's subsequent attempt both to maintain the ostensive approach – pointing to Lawrence in *Thought, Words and Creativity* (1976), for example – and, in *The Living Principle* (1975), to support his case with philosophical authority, such as that of Polanyi – a tacit admission that ostensive demonstration was, in itself, inadequate to sustain his case.

The effect of 'Components of the National Culture' is summed up by the critic Bernard Sharratt: 'In the wake of Anderson's argument, and his editorial policy at *New Left Review*, therefore, a whole generation of British socialist intellectuals spent nearly a decade trying to arrive at (or simply import from Continent thinkers)... totalizing concepts and theories' (*The Robert Tressell Lectures*, 1988, ed. David Alfred, p.97). Given the role that Anderson had granted literary criticism as the 'displaced home of the totality', it was not surprising that his ideas appealed, on their first appearance, to young, leftish literary critics like Sharratt and Eagleton. But the elevation of literary criticism was coupled with a demotion of one form of literature: the contemporary novel. It is interesting to see that a long footnote in the version of 'Components of the National Culture' which appeared in the volume *Student Power* (1969) has shrunk to a sentence in the version in *English Questions*. In that footnote, Anderson claimed that the 'novel has declined as a coherent genre' because 'it has disappeared into the abyss between everyday language and the technical discourses inaugurated by Marx and Freud'. He adds: 'The gap will only be closed by the reintegration of revolutionary ideas into unreflective linguistic practice, which would make possible a coherent novel once again. Such a change, of course, presupposes a changed society' (p.283). The suppression of most of this footnote is understandable, but taken with the rest of the essay it was influential, as Sharratt's account, which paraphrases the argument of the footnote and indeed makes it appear central in Anderson's essay, testifies. Not least, of course, it contributed to a demotion not only of modern fiction – in this Anderson was after all, though in a different vocabulary, only following Leavis – but also of the novel in general. Indeed, Sharratt's account of the effect of the Anderson essay is in part an attempt to explain why he 'was put off for a very long time from reading *The Ragged Trousered Philanthropists* not just because of its title but simply because it was a novel' (p.93). Leavis had suggested that certain kinds of novels were, as it were, modes of knowledge: the effect of the quest for totalizing theory in literary criticism was to make novels seem imperfect and inadvertent modes of knowledge which needed to be supplemented and completed by theory (this was very much the approach promoted by Althusser and evident in Eagleton's *Criticism and Ideology*). Footnote number 72 of the earlier version of Anderson's essay has its place in the elevation of theory above literary text.

The quest for the totalizing theory was not, of course, to be successful. None the less it contributed to what Anderson himself calls 'a large change' (p.194) and which he explores in the essay 'A Culture in Contraflow', first published in 1990. While the political unrest of the 1960s was suppressed, 'it altered the intellectual climate of the country durably. For the first time there emerged in Britain a stratum of radicalized graduates of a certain numerical mass – one which... was reinforced under the impact of the industrial battles of the early seventies' (pp.194-5). The old conformity and insularity has now gone, and a range of powerful work has emerged; for example, the distinctive historical sociologies of Anthony Giddens, Michael Mann, W.G. Runciman, Ernest Gellner, and Jack Goody (breaking down the barriers between anthropology and sociology); the art history of T.J. Clark, Michael Baxandall and Norman Bryson; the analysis of aesthetic ideology of Terry Eagleton; the philosophical work of Dummett, Parfitt, and Honderich; the ethical inquries of Alasdair MacIntyre, Charles Taylor and James Griffin; the economics of James Meade and Amartya Sen; the work of Quentin Skinner and James Pocock in the history of ideas; and feminism, which Anderson inserts rather awkwardly at the end of his survey of other intellectual fields which, as he partly recognizes, it cuts across and extends beyond; he seems to find difficulty in knowing which way to have it. Much of this intellectual work is contrary to prevailing political currents, even though it has not necessarily taken a socialist or Marxist direction. Indeed, one of the ironies of the assimilation of Marxist ideas into English culture which *New Left Review* and New Left Books promoted so actively and so successfully is that it has not led to the dominance of Marxist or even radical socialist ideas either politically or intellectually. Marxist and, to use the old term, marxizing ideas are certainly widely available; but the price of their dissemination seems to have been a diminution in their potency. A question Anderson does not wholly address is why such ideas should have ceased to arouse the resistance that they once did; one reason may be that they no longer carry the radical charge that they once did, that they have themselves become commodified as pleasurable objects of consumption, offering an imaginary compensation for the supposed lacunae of an omnipresent capitalism.

The final essay in *English Questions* surveys the condition of Britain in relation to Europe and the problems of socialism and social democracy in the European arena. Written in 1992, before the outcome of the British General Election was known, it cautiously adumbrates the possibility that Major might follow the fate of Home, but it is under no illusions about the subaltern status or internal structural inequities of the Labour Party. The union block vote is memorably denounced as 'the working-class version of the rotten borough – Old Sarum inverted [which] over time...raised up a Leviathan of dead souls' (p.349). Not for the first time, Anderson's rhetoric here would not be out of place in the columns of the *Spectator*. The possible ways of breaking 'the present logjam of the Left in advanced capitalism' with which the esssay concludes, modest though they may seem by comparison with the revolutionary proposals of the

1960s, would be less welcome to *Spectator* readers: targeting company law to make top management more accountable, highlighting the dangers and costs of a permanently unemployed underclass, guaranteeing a basic income to all as a social dividend, committing far greater resources to the school system, assaulting gender inequality by establishing maternity entitlements at the same level as wages. In so far as these could be articulated into a combined programme, they would constitute a formidable challenge; how or by whom they might be combined remains an unanswered question.

An unanswered question – 'Socialism?' – also dominates the closing section of *A Zone of Engagement* and might be seen as the underlying theme of the whole book. Its wide and illuminating discussions of a range of thinkers and ideas concludes, as mentioned above, with an exploration of the 'end of history' thesis of Fukuyama, which sets it in the context of the earlier concepts of the end of history of Hegel, Cournot and Kojève. Fukuyama's thesis, which has become widely disseminated, is that, in the formulation from 'The End of History' (1989) quoted by Anderson, 'the unabashed victory of economic and political liberalism' means 'not just the end of the Cold War, or the passing of a particular period of history, but the end of history as such: that is, the end-point of mankind's ideological evolution and the universalization of Western liberal democracy as the final form of human government' (p.333). Empirical events will continue and conflict and suffering will persist, but they will do so within the parameters set by liberal capitalist democracy. Anderson points out a range of objections to this notion – most notably, perhaps, that the economic and ecological resources of the earth preclude the global universalization of the levels of consumption of advanced liberal capitalist societies. He does not see these as comprising a conclusive refutation, however: 'for Fukuyama's case to fail, it is not enough to show that it understates or overlooks the defects in the world order dominated by liberal capitalism. It must be possible to indicate a credible alternative to it' (pp.357-8). That alternative might once have been socialism, and 'the test for the validity of socialism as an alternative to capitalism lies in whether it retains a potential for solutions to the problems confronting the latter in its hour of historical triumph' (p.360). Does it still do so?

Anderson does not quite answer that question, but he does draw from history 'a range of ideal-typical outcomes' which suggest four possible futures for socialism (p.367). The attempts to build socialism in the twentieth century might, like the Jesuit experiment in forming Guaraní tribes into egalitarian communities in Paraguay between the 1610s and the 1760s, come to be regarded 'as a set of exotic aberrations in backward lands, fated to vanish after briefly disturbing the main course of history' (p.368). Socialism might reappear in a transvalued form, as the ideas of Leveller democracy re-emerged in the different idiom of the French Revolution. A third possibility is that, as the Jacobinism born in the bourgeois-democratic matrix of the French Revolution overlapped with and changed into modern socialism, so socialism might undergo a decisive mutation into a new kind of movement for the radical transformation of society – perhaps at the hands of feminism. Lastly the fate of liberalism – once seemingly doomed but now, as Fukuyama's thesis stresses, strongly re-emergent – may prefigure the fate of socialism which though now apparently doomed would re-emerge in redeemed form as a programme for a better world as the capitalist order buckles under growing strains. 'Oblivion, transvaluation, mutation, redemption: each, according to their intuition, will make their own guess as to which is more probable. Jesuit, Leveller, Jacobin, Liberal – these are the figures in the mirror' (p.375). Anderson does not say what his guess is; perhaps because it is not intellectually possible to do so – the invocation of intuition and guesswork is significant here. One can infer where his sympathies lie, however, and given those sympathies, and the remarkable industry and intelligence that he has brought to the Marxist cause, his sober and balanced conclusion must be commended. Evidence constrains emplotment: and it is hard now to see how the history of socialism could be written as anything but tragedy.

16 Woman's Wager: Jacqueline Rose

The repressed returns. In the 1930s, Q.D. Leavis conducted a campaign against a certain kind of feminism which – like *Scrutiny*'s related campaigns against socialism and Marxism – was, in conjunction with other political, social and cultural forces, successful for a time (see 'I'm Not Complaining' above). But the Women's Movement(s) which began towards the end of the 1960s, reviving in some of its aspects older, buried feminisms, and in other respects developing new themes and approaches, soon began to have an impact on literary studies. There were several reasons for this. Unlike, for example, nineteenth-century women painters, women writers already had an established place in the traditional literary canon: George Eliot was part of Leavis's Great Tradition, and Jane Austen was, so to speak, its offstage precursor. Even if the elevation of these ladies was in proportion to their escape from the denigrated signs of femininity – even if, to extend what may be Q.D. rather than F.R. Leavis's remark on George Eliot, their minds were in no way disabled by being women's – they were, unignorably, *there* – and, therefore, ripe for re-reading. Moreover, in both male and female canonical literary texts, women were amply represented, even if those representations were informed by sexist perspectives: women were major, sometimes central protagonists – Isabel Archer, Emma Bovary, Anna Karenina, Dorothea Brooke, Sue Bridehead – and they often seemed to produce what Roland Barthes, in *S/Z*, called '[un] trouble même de la représentation' (p.222), a partial destabilizing, a putting into question, of the regulating forms and ideologies of the novel. In the area of literary pedagogy, it was the case that most students were women, most teachers men – a distribution that was hardly commensurate with the distribution of formally or informally recognized ability – but at the same time there were distinguished women scholars such as Q.D. Leavis herself, M.C. Bradbrook and Helen Gardner who, while not necessarily feminists, could none the less serve to some extent as role models, especially once women began to articulate the inequities to which the academy subjected them. Literary studies was thus, in some sense, the soft underbelly of a male-dominated academic establishment – the metaphor is itself, of course, a *macho* one, originally used in relation to the perceived threat of communism in the 1950s America in which Sylvia Plath grew up.

In the 1970s and 1980s a wide range of feminist approaches to literary studies developed. These included the re-reading of canonical works in such a way as to draw out and analyse the kind of troubling of representation of which Barthes had spoken; the re-publication of, and renewed critical attention to, a range of lesser-known women writers, from Aphra Behn to Ruth Adam – the author whose novel *I'm Not Complaining* Q.D. Leavis so admired; the encouraging of women both to write about their own experiences, not least those which had been denigrated as 'feminine'; the attempt, often rather fraught, to develop more collective ways of working in magazine editing, book publishing, academic research and teaching; and the re-examination of both male and female critics to reveal their misogyny, their conscious and/or inadvertent sexism. Given the wider social and political concerns which were inherent and often explicit in feminist approaches, and the way in which they often went to the root of the matter, probing with fine instruments or tearing with rough justice at the splints and plaster which had held the old regime erect, they could hardly fail, particularly in combination with other interrogations of the founding concepts of literary studies, to burst the boundaries of those studies, to relate the analysis of literary texts to other kinds of visual and verbal discourses – religious, medical, legal, commercial, cinematic, televisual – and to social and political issues. In this respect, feminism both promoted and formed part of the expansion of literary into cultural studies: an ambiguous position, of course, since it could be seen to become, like Marxism, another element of the adjustments in the academy propelled by Thatcherism – itself a profoundly troubling phenomena for feminism – and a profitable branch of the culture industry. But, in contrast to Marxism, especially after the collapse of communism in Eastern Europe and the USSR, feminism has retained a radical political edge and efficacy which resists total absorption into an academic or cultural commodity. And it has clearly made a profound difference to what and how we (women, men) read.

One measure of that difference is the re-readings of texts by and the production of texts about a figure who has become a crucial stake in modern feminism, and indeed more generally in modern culture: Sylvia Plath. Like the stake driven through Daddy's heart in Plath's famous, notorious poem – which is, as Jacqueline Rose points out in *The Haunting of Sylvia Plath*, an ambiguous act, suggesting both an attempt at final exorcism and a continued investment (1992 edn, p.233) – the stake in Plath partakes both of aggression and desire, an urge to lay her ghost in both senses of the verb. In Rose's words, 'Sylvia Plath haunts our culture' (p.1) – that is, late twentieth century European (especially English) and (white) North American culture – and Rose's book is an exploration of some possible reasons for that haunting. Plath of course died before the modern feminist movement began, and one of the many unresolvable questions left by her early death is how she would have reacted to it. There is a sense, of course, in which she – the texts which survive her – have been made to react to it, read as admonitory or approving anticipations of feminism. Seized on initially by male critics as exemplary of a needed or nihilistic extremism – A. Alvarez and David Holbrook respectively – she has since been taken up by female and often feminist biographers and critics and deployed as a weapon against patriarchy, sometimes as incarnated in the figure of Ted Hughes, sometimes conceived of as a broader ideology of which Hughes is an example and an effect. Interpretation of Plath's life and work has at times taken on a peculiar bitterness because of the deep subjective investments which that life and work seem to produce, investments which are emotional, idological and, not least, financial (posthumous Plath is a money-spinner). Rose observes that 'the pull of the Plath story is that it calls up a language of victimization and blame with such force' (p.6). Given this, it is perhaps inevitable that such language spills over on to some of those who write about Plath, so it is not difficult, reading the introduction in which Rose gives her version of the disputes with Ted and Olwyn Hughes over her book – or the subsequent correspondence of Rose and Ted Hughes in the *Times Literary Supplement* (see Bibliography) – to feel oneself drawn into the judgement seat, casting each participant in the debate into the role of either victim or aggressor. In Jean Genet's play *The Balcony* (1956), the brothel client who takes the role of the Judge says, in an image which might have come from a Plath poem: 'The world is an apple. I cut it in two: the good, the bad' (1965 edn, p.17). It is that form of binary division – good/bad, aggressor/victim, inner/outer, high/low culture, poetry/prose, political/personal – which, in Rose's view, Plath's texts both solicit and challenge: Plath works on the boundaries, most fundamentally on the boundaries where language and identity begin.

Given the significance of Plath in feminist debates, Rose's book is – necessarily, but also explicitly – an intervention in such debates. One of the crucial current issues in these debates – as in other areas of cultural and literary criticism today – is that of how individual identity is to be understood. There is a range of possible positions. These include the liberal humanist idea of a reasonably coherent and integrated, largely conscious self; the Jungian (and Ted Hughesean) idea of an authentic, integrated self produced by the satisfactory fusion of archetypal components; and the Sartrean existential idea of a self as becoming rather than being, always free to choose but always liable to lapse into bad faith, that form of self-deception in which one denies one's freedom (a distinctly *passé* notion now, but an important one for the pioneering feminism of Simone de Beauvoir). There is also the idea of the self as determined to a greater or lesser extent by historical, social and political forces, and the related but distinct idea of the self as a changeable construction produced by a combination of social, political and psychical determinants. Each of these ideas – and variations and more or less uneasy combinations of them – has its feminist adherents. Provisionally mobilizing a binary opposition, they might be broadly subsumed under two rubrics: essentialist (the idea that there is a female essence which all women share) and constructionist (the idea that the female self is, as it were, a temporary habitation, a product of a kind of socio-psychical *bricolage*).

Undoubtedly in academic feminism (if less so in extra-academic, popular feminism, in so far as this binary division is permissible), it is the constructionist view that is now dominant, and this mainly takes the form of the idea of the self as a changeable construction produced by a combination of social, political and psychical determinants. For example, in her influential *Sexual/Textual Politics* (1985) – a must for most student reading-lists – Toril Moi slaps some essentializing sisters sharply on the wrists:

> What feminists such as [Elaine] Showalter and [Marcia] Holly fail to grasp is that the traditional humanism they represent is in effect part of patriarchal ideology. At its centre is the seamlessly unified self – either individual or collective – which is commonly called 'Man'. As Luce Irigaray or Hélène Cixous would argue, this integrated self is in fact a phallic self, constructed on the model

> of the self-contained, powerful phallus. Gloriously autonomous, it banishes from itself all conflict, contradiction and ambiguity. In this humanist ideology the self is the *sole author* of history and of the literary text: the humanist creator is potent, phallic and male – God in relation to his world, the author in relation to his text. (p.8)

There is a certain contradiction in this passage in that it is itself offering to the reader a position of power, the position of the possessor of insight who sees through to what is 'in fact' the case: in certain feminist perspectives, such a rhetorical strategy might itself be seen to partake of patriarchal ideology. The passage makes the assumption that some concepts can be identified unequivocally with patriarchal ideology and cannot be appropriated for feminist purposes: the feminists who think they are using them are in fact being used by them; like the pacifists whom Orwell called objectively pro-fascist, such feminists are, in Moi's perspective, objectively pro-patriarchal. It is perhaps not improper nor irredeemably macho to remark that the model of the 'self-contained, powerful phallus', 'gloriously autonomous' which Moi conjures up with uncertain irony might not seem wholly unattractive, that it might be an object of desire, not least to women who have been deprived of any sense of themselves as autonomous and integrated. To shut the idea of the integrated self behind a door marked 'Men Only' is, arguably, to repeat a form of patriarchal exclusion. The English feminist Alison Light, writing about a novel which can indeed be seen to celebrate the hard-won achievement of a sense of individual and collective unity – Alice Walker's *The Color Purple* (1983) – suggests that the idea of the unified self may still have an enabling value, as long as it does not become a means of finally fixing identity and wiping out difference: 'It is this sense of "self", a coherent and powerful identity, which we must recognise both as an effect of language and as the fiction which keeps us sane and active' (*Literature Teaching Politics* 6, p.131). In *Essentially Speaking*, the American feminist Diana Fuss asks whether 'essentialism' has 'received a bad rap' and points out that '[f]ew other words in the vocabulary of contemporary critical theory are so persistently maligned, so little interrogated, and so predictably summoned as a term of infallible critique (p.xi). Fuss aims to break or weaken 'the hold which the essentialist/constructionist binarism has on feminist theory' (p.1) and argues that 'essentialism underwrites theories of constructionism and that constructionism operates as a more sophisticated form of essentialism' (p.119). Each position, she suggests, has 'internal contradictions' and variable political possibilities.

The essentialist/constructionist division, as it exists both within and beyond feminism, has been exemplified in the debates over Sylvia Plath, in regard to her life and her work. Biographical and critical interpretations have sometimes sought to recover an essential Plath, but the Plaths produced have, of course, varied widely. Jacqueline Rose, who takes up a constructionist position strongly informed by psychoanalysis, contends that there is no way of recovering an essential Plath, of producing a unity from the multiplicity of her writings. The relationship of Rose's book to Plath's life may be summed up by the recent experience of a bookshop customer who asked for a copy of the book and was directed to the biography section, only to find that the book was not there. Rose states clearly that her book is not a biography, but she finds herself drawn into considerations of the writing of Plath biographies, and she has an extended – and deeply critical – discussion of the biography of Plath by Anne Stevenson, *Bitter Fame* (1989): Rose calls this 'something of a *cause célèbre* in the genre of abusive biography [which] shows the coercive nature of biography as a form of writing, the fantasy of omnipotence which supports it' (p.93). She also takes issue with Ted Hughes's distinction between 'the fantasia about Sylvia Plath' and 'the facts' (pp.11, 239 n.1).

There is, of course, a difficulty in Rose's position: for if 'the facts' cannot be established, by what means can Stevenson's biography, or any other, be contested? Only by contesting the general claim to truth which biography makes; a challenge which itself presents a metatruth, a fact about facts, and which is in effect a kind of general warrant indicting any biography or history, and many other kinds of non-fiction writing. The difficulty is that unless the writing of biography or history is to cease altogether – and the intense investments made in the idea of the definitive biography or history make such surcease most unlikely – the need to try to determine facts, to distinguish them from fantasies or falsehoods, will remain even when the necessary provisionality or impossibility of doing so has been acknowledged.

The problem is compounded because a significant strategy in Rose's interpretation of Plath is a comparison between Plath's published and unpublished texts and an analysis of the cuts made by her literary executors. That comparison frequently, perhaps inevitably, takes on the form of a scene of revelation. Rose is aware of this herself; as she observes in her comparison of the edited and unedited versions from Plath's journals of her first meeting with Ted Hughes, ' "so that's what really happened" – one can't help but react on reading what was taken out' (p.122) – although the reaction is perhaps more (the nuance is significant) 'so that's what Plath really said!' In Freud's analysis of 'Dora', there is a moment in Dora's second dream when she goes calmly to her room and begins reading a big book that lies on her writing-table. It is a moment which Freud's interpretation enables us to see as an oneiric fulfilment of her wish to find out 'the facts of life'. (*Case Histories I*, pp.140-6). In *The Haunting of Sylvia Plath*, we find ourselves, as it were, vicariously following Jacqueline Rose into the Sylvia Plath Collections at the Smith College Library and the Lilly Library at Indiana University and finding out, if not the facts of Plath's life, at least some facts about what she wrote. In this respect Rose, while rejecting the possibility of finally establishing the 'facts' about Sylvia Plath, inevitably offers some 'facts', even if these facts themselves require interpretations. Her book is not biography, but it slides into issues about biography. In this respect as in others, it exemplifies those difficulties of drawing clear boundaries which, in Rose's view, Plath's writing enacts.

Rose's interpretation of Plath's writing – and of her haunting, the way she troubles and enchants us – relates to a general model of the construction of subjectivity and of linguistic capacity. It is a model which draws on Julia Kristeva, and more distantly on Lacan and Melanie Klein. The model – as is often the way of these things, it is also a kind of narrative – looks something like this. The infant comes to recognize and identify itself as a body by a process of introjection and projection, that is, by drawing in and expelling fragments of the surrounding world. This process can be seen as the origin of thinking, but because it is experienced by the child as murderous, it is also the origin of guilt. And of fear. It is the realm of what Kristeva in *Powers of Horror* (1982) calls abjection; as Rose defines it, 'a primordial fear situated at the point where the subject first splits from the body of the mother, finding at once in that body and in the terrifying gap that opens up between them the only space for the constitution of its own identity, the only distance which will allow it to become a user of words' (p.33). The phobic object – a feared object which fills an even more frightening void – inserts itself into this gap. In Kristeva's words, as cited by Rose: 'Learning to speak is like trying to make one's own an oral "object" [ab-ject] which slips away, and whose necessarily deformed hallucination threatens us from the outside'. In this perspective, writing – in Derrida's extended sense, in which writing includes speech – is bound up with the fear which is at its origin. Kristeva defines the writer as 'a phobic who succeeds at metaphorisation so that, instead of dying of fear, she or he is resuscitated through signs'. Applying this model, Rose suggests that Plath seems 'to be laying out something which could be called a psychic economy of writing – that is, the unconscious and normally covered-over conditions or substrata of speech' (p.34).

Looked at like this, the fear and violence of Plath's writing are not to be understood primarily in thematic terms, although they are certainly evident as themes; nor are they to be interpreted simply as symptoms of her individual pathology or as intelligible responses to external male oppression – which is not, for Rose, to deny the reality of male oppression. Rather, they return us to the fear of the moment of separation from the mother and the violence of introjection and projection which lie at the origins of speech and of individual identity.

This perspective can be used to account plausibly both for certain formal features of Plath's poetry (the syntactic ambiguities as to the subject of a line or sentence, for example) and for the range and intensity of the responses her texts have aroused. It is characteristic of psychoanalytic scenarios in its melodramatic appeal and it possesses what Wittgenstein called the charm of Freudian ideas (see 'Euphoria, Ltd' above, p.48): such melodrama and charm might also be seen to characterize Plath's poetry. But Rose's model also displays the characteristic weakness of psychoanalytic theory. First, given that such theory is an attempt to understand very early pre- or sub-verbal processes, it is necessarily deeply speculative: the proliferation of psychoanalytic theories suggests the difficulty of controlling them by evidence. Secondly, such theory depends on a causal and/or structural homology or analogy between infant processes and later phenomena – those processes are seen as the cause or prototype of the later phenomena; it depends, that is, on assumptions about causality and/or homology or analogy that are themselves questionable. Thirdly, and related to the second objection, it moves away from specific phenomena to their presumed causes or prototypes and assumes that a knowledge of those presumed causes or prototypes deepens our understanding of the phenomena themselves – whereas, in fact, such knowledge, even if its status were much less problematic than it is in psychoanalysis, could be seen as, in part, a distraction from the phenomena, a loss of understanding.

This third objection is an important aspect of Wittgenstein's case against Freud (see Frank Cioffi, 'Wittgenstein's Freud', 1969). Consider what happens when a disaster such as a train or plane smash occurs. The response constructed by the media and the authorities is, in effect: Let's set up an inquiry to find out why this happened. A very proper and necessary response, too, producing a crucial kind of understanding; but one which also involves a movement of attention away from the horror of the disaster itself and thus, arguably in that respect a loss of another kind of understanding. An analogy might be drawn with certain approaches to Plath's writing; in so far as it can be viewed as a writing of disaster (this is not, of course, all that it is), it is often seen to demand, so to speak, an enquiry into the reasons for that disaster – whether those reasons are seen in terms of individual biography, of personal pathology, of patriarchal oppression, or, as in Rose's account, of a general model of the early formation of the speaking subject. In all these cases, understanding is conceived of as a matter of moving away from the phenomena themselves to their origins. It is that movement which Rose shares with the biographical or pathological explanations that she rejects and with the explanation in terms of patriarchal oppression which she accepts only in a qualified way. We have learnt, of course, in literary criticism as elsewhere, to suspect the idea of 'the phenomena themselves' – of 'the poem itself', for instance – and to ask questions about the contexts in which phenomena are produced and received as such; none the less, one can also still ask whether the foregrounding of context may not sometimes limit understanding of phenomena – or, more concretely, whether attention to the presumed origins or conditions of production of, say, a poem, however those origins or conditions of production may be conceived, might not in some respects restrict our apprehension of the poem. One could add that it might restrict our apprehension not only of the disaster Plath writes but also of the other effects which her poems can produce – effects (to be sure, with their ambiguities, their shadowings) of joy, of calm, of celebration – as, for example, in an aubade not discussed by Rose, 'Morning Song'.

A further aspect of Rose's model of the origins of subjectivity and language is, as she herself points out, that it is not gendered. Rose observes that for some time, feminist criticism 'has seemed to be divided between a reading of women writers which bemoans the lack of – or attempts to retrieve for them – a consistent and artriculate "I"' – for example, Sandra Gilbert and Susan Gubar's *The Madwoman in the Attic* (1979) – 'and one which celebrates linguistic fragmentation, the disintegration of body and sexual identity, in the name of a form of writing which has come to be known as *écriture féminine*' (p.26) – Rose instances Hélène Cixous's famous essay

'The Laugh of the Medusa' (1972). Neither of these approaches is, in Rose's view, appropriate to Plath; rather, Rose suggests, we need 'in relation to Plath (although not only in relation to her)...a conception of writing as neither marshalled nor fragmented, neither surplus order nor a hysterical body pouring out of itself' (p.25).

Clearly a more general approach to the interpretation of women's (and men's) writing is implied here. We might see, in the very manner of Rose's formulation, an updated version of what Barthes once called 'Neither-Nor' criticism (*Mythologies*, pp.81-3). What significantly differentiates Rose's approach from the liberal humanism with which it seems partly homologous is presumably that her 'neither-nor' seeks to offer not so much a comfortable transcendence – in which, to take up Barthes's image, one holds the scales in which each potentially exclusive component is balanced – as the awkward, intricate, sometimes painful tension suggested in the following proposition, which also employs the 'neither-nor' structure:

> Plath is neither one identity, nor multiple identities simply dispersing themselves. She writes at the point of tension – pleasure/danger, your fault/my fault, high/low culture – without resolution or dissipation of what produces the clash between the two. (p.10)

If Plath's writing works at the point of tension where language, identity and division are constantly being generated and constantly under threat, one crucial aspect of that work is the mobilization of fantasy, the production and occupation of, and the provisional but intense subjective investment in, a range of often contradictory positions: male/female, victim/aggressor, Nazi/Jew. It is this movement between subjective positions and fantasy identifications – a movement produced, in her poetry, by its syntactic shifts and ambiguities – which both invites the operations of binary division and judgement and also makes them impossible without reductiveness. For example, in the poem 'The Rabbit-Catcher' – a notorious crux for both literary and biographical interpretation of Plath – the simile 'a mind like a ring/Sliding shut on some quick thing' could allude to male and/or female violence – the violence of the male logos and/or of the female body, as Rose puts it, 'contracting (giving birth), shutting (pleasuring but also retaliating, in the very act of sexual consummation, against the man)' (p.141). Rose points out that 'his mind' was changed to 'a mind' in the first draft, a significant alteration in the way that it produces ambiguity and forestalls any easy allocation of blame. 'The Rabbit-Catcher' offers both an analysis of patriarchal power and of women's participation in, as well as subjection to that power – an uncomfortable analysis for any feminist approach which reads Plath solely in terms of external male oppression. As Rose says of the poem:

> Point of view of the woman (of women), we might say – on condition that we open up that concept to both its conscious and unconscious implications. He did it. I did it. Neither or both. Thus Plath sits on the edge of two contrary analyses of women's relationship to patriarchal power. (p.141)

If Plath, in her poetry, transgresses binary divisions and troublingly occupies different subject-positions, she also, in the whole *corpus* of her writing, moves across and challenges the high/low culture distinction which has been so important in later nineteenth century and early and mid-twentieth century literary and cultural criticism. Some of the cuts in her *corpus* appear as attempts to excise this engagement with popular culture, and they are compounded by presentations of her work which downgrade her more commercial writing, for instance some of her magazine fiction. Rose points to the link feminists have drawn between the denigration of popular culture and the denigration of women – for instance, women being seen as the passive consumers of romantic fiction – but suggests that Plath's own challenge to this doubled denigration has been largely overlooked, despite the feminist attention to Plath. Indeed, we might say that some of that attention has been concerned to increase Plath's status in the domain of high art.

Yet while aspiring to and, in the end, unequivocally achieving a place within high art, Plath also aspired to, and partly achieved, a place within mass culture. Rose quotes a number of passages from her journals which show how much she, in her own words, wanted 'to break into the women's slicks' (p.170). Plath published in a remarkable range of journals which ran the gamut from teenage popular to high-prestige literary; they included *Seventeen*, the *Christian Science Monitor*, the *New Yorker*, the *Ladies Home Journal*, the *London Magazine* and the *Sewanee Review*. In 1959, the year often seen as crucial for her poetry, she invented, in her journals the *persona* of Sadie Peregrine, who shares her initials, whose name alludes to the peregrine falcon and to sadism, and who is a producer of fiction: a persona who might be seen to connote some elements of Plath's complex relation to popular culture.

Plath's engagement with that culture, as a practitioner of some of its forms, did not mean uncritical acceptance of its ideologies – of the ideology of familial domesticity in the *Ladies Home Journal*, for example; but then popular culture can be seen to call into question its own ostensible ideologies, to some degree – as Rose observes, the *Ladies Home Journal* gives a 'sense of ideological ambiguity...its famous and unquestionable promotion of domesticity appears as constantly in danger *from itself*' (p.175). Plath's writing not only moves across high and popular culture but also inhabits contradictory positions within popular culture itself. Her pseudonymous novel *The Bell Jar* (1962) is indeed a literary novel but one which, Rose suggests, charts 'the coming-into-being of a writer across the fragments of...a multiplicity of cultural forms' (p.186), including the unnamed magazine where the protagonist, Esther, is a guest editor, *Ladies Day, The New Yorker*, the *Christian Science Monitor*, the scandal sheets and the cinema – technicolor football romances, *Gone with the Wind*, the Bette Davis movie made out of the book by Esther's benefactress. Although poetry is Esther's long-term desire, it is only one of these cultural forms, and her story is told as a novel, not a poem. A similar negotiation of cultural forms can be traced across Plath's writing. If she partly accepts the criticism of mass cultural conformity, and relates it to her political concerns, she also seeks to participate in, and contribute to, mass culture.

Plath's political concern is in fact powerfully articulated in the first sentence of *The Bell Jar*, with its reference to the execution of the Rosenbergs, an execution which becomes, within the novel, a kind of national electrotherapy; like the popular culture into which it is wired, it aims to annul the anxieties that it has helped to excite. But if Plath's concern with popular culture has been downplayed in the editing of her work, so has her concern with politics, and this latter process has helped to make the appearance of the Holocaust in her later poetry appear more gratuitous than it might otherwise have seemed. Rose seeks both to restore Plath's political profile and, in an extended discussion, to defend her treatment of the Holocaust – especially in 'Daddy' – from the charge that by linking the Holocaust with her own experience she trivializes the Holocaust and/or aggrandizes herself.

In this discussion, Rose suggests that it is metaphor which is in question: not only whether it is proper or possible for Plath to employ the Holocaust as metaphor, but whether the Holocaust itself can be represented figuratively – or indeed, whether it can be represented at all: 'the Holocaust is the historical event which puts under greatest pressure – or is most readily available to put under such pressure – the concept of linguistic figuration' (p.207). Rose seeks to ask what the Holocaust might tell us about the relationship between metaphor, fantasy and identification – an issue, as she points out, which is highly relevant to an understanding of Nazism itself – and to consider whether the discomfort produced by 'Daddy' is due to what it unleashes about that relationship. First, Rose focuses on the case-histories presented at the 1985 Hamburg Conference of the International Association of Psychoanalysis which focused on patients who were the children of concentration camp survivors or the children of Nazis. It emerged from those case-histories that

> the question of historical participation in no sense exhausted that of identification and of fantasy – it did not settle the question of from where, and in what form, memory takes place. For being a victim does not stop you from identifying with the aggressor; being an aggressor does not stop you from identifying with the victim. To which we can add a formula only deceptively tautological – that being a victim (or aggressor) does not stop you from identifying with the victim (or aggressor). Identification is something that always has to be constructed. Wherever it is that subjects find themselves historically, this will not produce any one, unequivocal, identification as its logical effect. (p.210)

It is this construction of identification which 'Daddy' can be seen to dramatize. The poem does not offer a simple fusion of the 'I' of the poem and the Holocaust victims; as Rose points out, simile and metonymy, which open a distance between the two terms, are more prominent than metaphor when the speaker of the poem begins to allude to herself as, possibly, a Jew ('like a Jew', 'I think I may well be a Jew', 'I may be a bit of a Jew'). The poem presents us with 'precisely the problem of trying to claim a relationship to an event in which – the poem makes it quite clear – the speaker did not participate' (p.228).

This intricate discussion is conducted by Rose with the intelligence, courage and tact which she shows throughout the book; none the less, it could provoke outrage if it were read – in an interpretation which would be both inaccurate and intelligible – as in some sense diminishing the reality of the Holocaust. As Rose knows, the charge that the psychoanalytic concern with fantasy leads to, indeed constitutes, a repression of reality, has in recent years been brought against the founding act of the concept of fantasy itself – Freud's abandonment of the seduction theory, which Jeffery Masson's *Freud: The Assault on Truth* presents as an evasion of the actuality of the child abuse, and particularly of the abuse of female children (for Rose's comments on this, see *Haunting of Sylvia Plath*, pp.13, 239 n.6, and her *Sexuality in the Field of Vision*, pp.12-14). From certain feminist positions, a prime objection to the focus on fantasy – in general terms as regards women, and specifically in relation to Plath – could be that it tends to diminish the reality of male oppression. And that could be the flipside of the kind of objection which Ted Hughes himself made to Rose's interpretation of 'The Rabbit Catcher' – that rather than fantasy diminishing reality, fantasy might be taken for reality. Rose's insistence that throughout the book she is talking about fantasy, not reality, founders both on her own recognition of the strength of fantasy, and on her own acknowledgement of the difficulty of establishing what reality is. *The Haunting of Sylvia Plath* maintains the importance of distinguishing reality from fantasy – and if we think of their confusion in Nazism, we can see how high the stakes are in this – but Rose does not really offer concepts or criteria which might enable such a distinction.

The charge that a concern with fantasy might result in a diminishing of reality relates to another charge – that a concern with fantasy might result in a diminishing of responsibility. If we consider Rose's formulation in the passage quoted above – 'being a victim does not stop you from identifying with the aggressor; being an aggressor does not stop you from identifying with the victim' – we can suggest that in such an approach there is, so to speak, a tendency for antimetabole to slide into antinomianism; for a reversal of positions to imply a remission of sins. Of course, there is a crucial distinction between identifying with an aggressor as a victim and being an aggressor oneself; but it is a more difficult distinction to draw than the kind which, after the fashion of Genet's Judge, cuts the world in two like an apple. If Rose's argument for the importance of fantasy is correct – and much of it does seem to account for matters which are not otherwise easily understood – is there any possibility that it could be widely accepted? Indeed, is it not the case that if fantasy does have the importance with which she credits it, the psychic economy which sustains it will not be easily changed?

If it were changed to any significant extent, it would clearly involve a major political, legal, social, civil, cultural and ethical transformation – and, of course, a transformation in gender roles and relations. In this latter area, Rose, in this book, is arguing for – and, in her analysis of Plath, exemplifying – an intellectually, ethically and politically strenuous feminism – an élite feminism, in a sense – which none the less has resonances in popular culture, as her discussion of Plath's involvement in that culture indeed suggests. It is Rose's achievement to suggest the ways in which a range of phenomena – such as high art, popular culture, fascism, fantasy, identification and feminism interact. One of her most daring moments is her reading of those lines in 'Daddy' which have proved so difficult for feminism: 'Every woman adores a fascist,/The boot in the face, the brute/Brute heart of a brute like you':

> Who is putting the boot in the face? The fascist certainly (woman as the recipient of a sexual violence she desires). But, since the agency of these lines is not specified, don't they also allow that it might be the woman herself (identification *with* the fascist being what every woman desires)? (p.233)

Rose's interpretation of 'Daddy' leads her, almost at the end of *The Haunting of Sylvia Plath*, tentatively to raise a question which, in its general form, has been very important for feminism, but which in this book she has hitherto avoided: the question of whether women have got something men haven't. She suggests that 'Daddy' allows us 'to ask whether the woman might not have a special relationship to fantasy' and whether we could not read, in the line 'Every woman adores a fascist', 'a suggestion, or even a demonstration, that it is a woman who is most likely to articulate the power – perverse, recalcitrant, persistent – of fantasy as such'. For Rose, it is this – which she sees as not incompatible with woman's legitimate protest against patriarchy – which is 'finally, the wager of Plath's work' (pp.237-8). Rose's peroration thus boldly rewrites Pascal's *pari*: the woman's wager exceeds the stake of both the male metaphysical gambler and God.

17 New World Maps: Edward W. Said

Culture and Anarchy (1869); *Culture and Society* (1958); *Culture and Imperialism* (1993). The conjoined terms in the titles of three books by, respectively, Matthew Arnold, Raymond Williams and Edward Said represent different ways, which developed at different historical moments, of understanding culture and its significance. Culture as the antidote to anarchy; culture as conceptually split from, yet integrally related to, society; culture as inseparably bound up with imperialism. There is a fourth conjunction which, like a dark trace scrawled in dried blood, underlies all of these, and which is indicated in Walter Benjamin's famous statement, quoted by Said in his book, that 'there is no document of civilization which is not at the same time a document of barbarism' (*Culture and Imperialism*, p.373). This fourth conjunction is culture and barbarism: culture seen not as the antithesis of barbarism but as its accomplice. That conjunction bears a particular relationship to the coupling of culture and imperialism made by Edward Said; for Said makes the trace of barbarism appear beneath that of imperialism. as if he were making visible the earlier writing of a palimpsest, and he causes the blood in which it is written to flow again. Moreover, the link between imperialism and barbarism, if one thinks of the etymology of the latter term, is peculiarly intimate: barbarian was the term the Greeks gave to those whose language they did not understand and which they heard as 'bar-bar'. Imperialism depends on a construction of those it subjugates as barbarians while in some ways behaving like a barbarian itself.

Culture and Imperialism is a work that will reshape thinking about culture as surely as *Culture and Anarchy* and *Culture and Society* did. But it is more explosive than either of those texts, and more international in its reach. The English reader, even a liberal-minded one, might well feel his red, white and blue hackles starting to rise; and the red of indignation, of anger, of hot denial, will soon start to spread across the other colours of the flag. The French reader could see the tricolour fluttering over a steadily diminishing domain and finally shrivelled and shamed by the blinding sun of torture that reached its zenith in the Algerian war. The American reader might see the Stars and Stripes expanding into the monstrous garment of a huge, hi-tech bully, a flabby Rambo with smart bombs. Ngugi wa Thiong'o, the Kenyan novelist, once called the impact of imperialism a cultural bomb. Said lobs a few cultural bombs back, and they're smart ones too.

The explosive image is unfortunate, in a sense, because it could seem to reinforce a hostile caricature of Said as a terrorist sympathizer: he is an ardent supporter of the Palestinian cause which, as he complains, has often been represented, particularly in the American media, as merely, mindlessly terroristic. Said is a Palestinian who was born in Jerusalem, of a Jerusalem family, in 1935. His family were Anglicans and thus, as Said himself puts it, 'a minority within the Christian minority in an Islamic majority setting' (Imre Salusinszky, *Criticism in Society*, p.128). Due to his family's business, he lived as a child in both Jerusalem and Cairo, and after 1948 settled in Egypt; he also spent some time in the Lebanon. As a boy, he spoke both English and Arabic, and now includes French and German in his linguistic arsenal. Because of his family's mobility, he went to a number of schools in Egypt, and in the early 1950s, he left the country in disgrace – 'I had been at a colonial English public school, and was effectively asked not to return because I was a troublemaker' (*Criticism in Society*, p.128). He then went to boarding school in Massachussetts, and on to Princeton and Harvard. He is now University Profesor of English and Comparative Literature at the University of Columbia.

This background, combined with his intellectual abilities, his present academic position and his political commitment, gives him a lot of what Pierre Bourdieu calls symbolic capital: to be of 'colonial' and/or ethnic provenance, if one also occupies a prestigious academic chair, gets a higher rating today than being of working-class provenance. (In England, Terry Eagleton, now Warton Professor of English Literature at Oxford, has recently been stressing his Irish rather than his proletarian origins.) This is not just a matter of fashion; it is, rather, that the presence of those from the 'periphery', from what were once the domains of empire and/or 'underdevelopment', has come to serve as a focus for the problems of contemporary civilization as the working class once seemed to do (which is not to deny the continued existence or importance of the latter). Moreover, the Palestinian cause gives Said a very specific commitment which other intellectuals yearning for commitment might envy (though they are probably glad to be spared the death threats Said has received). Said combines ethnic provenance, an academic chair and political commitment with more than a trace of that old-style humanism which travelled from Central Europe to North America; he is well-read in, and deeply appreciative of, the canonical European literary texts, and a lover and amateur performer of music. Said is ironically aware of the unease and attraction aroused by the combination of different elements which he embodies: 'the notion of being both a Palestinian and a literary critic is for some people an oxymoron: you can't be. To others, I gather that it's a thrilling and a rather peculiar pleasure to watch somebody who is supposedly a terrorist carrying on in a fairly civilized way' (*Criticism in Society*, (p.131).

Said's first book, *Joseph Conrad and the Fiction of Autobiography* (1966), was, in J. Hillis Miller's words, 'excellent but still relatively conventional' (*Theory Now and Then*, p.133). The book which followed, *Beginnings* (1975), was a much more unusual and wide-ranging exploration of 'the problem of beginnings' – moving over, for instance, Vico, Milton, Swift, Flaubert, Renan, Marx, Hopkins, Hardy, Conrad, Mallarmé, Valéry, Freud, Wittgenstein, Foucault, Barthes and Derrida. It served, among many other things, as an implicit riposte to Frank Kermode's *The Sense of an Ending* (1967). The big breakthrough came with *Orientalism* (1978), in which Said brought his immense erudition and intense intellectual and political passions to the study of the scholarly and aesthetic discourses which had constructed 'the Orient' as an object of representation and, in doing so, had in effect furthered the project of Western imperial domination. *Orientalism* fostered a whole new field of study: the analysis of colonial discourse. It was a hard act to follow, but *Culture and Imperialism* may well make even more impact.

Culture and Imperialism has the hybrid quality which Said himself finds in Frantz Fanon's *The Wretched of the Earth* (1961). In Said's case, the elements which his book brings together include literary and cultural analysis, broad historical generalization, impassioned polemic, oblique autobiography, and utopian envisioning. Although there is a certain linear movement – from *Mansfield Park* to CNN on the Gulf War – the book does not display a clear, cumulative unfolding: not least, perhaps, because that is the very way a certain kind of imperialist narrative unfolds. Instead it switches channels, doubles back, repeats with variations, to create an immense cornucopia of fertile fruits. Here the attempt will be made to draw out its central ideas and to pose some of the questions which they provoke.

What definitions for his two central terms does Said propose? He sees 'culture' as having two meanings in particular. One is 'all those practices, like the arts of description, communication, and representation, that have relative autonomy from the economic, social, and political realms and that often exist in aesthetic forms, one of whose principal aims is pleasure' (p.xii). The term 'relative autonomy' is Althusser's, but it has, rather in the manner of those elements of the 'travelling theories' which Said discusses in *The World, the Text and the Critic* (1983; 1984 edn, pp.226-47), floated free of its Parisian-Marxist base. Said largely leaves aside the conceptual difficulties of the idea of 'relative autonomy' and the issue of whether the economic level is to be taken as finally determining; he sometimes draws on Marxist perspectives and terminology but he is not a Marxist, and indeed in *Culture and Imperialism* he points to the imperialist assumptions of Marx himself and of the 'Western Marxist' tradition (pp.183, 336).

The second particular sense which 'culture' has in this book is that of 'a concept that includes a refining and elevating element, each society's reservoir of the best that has been known and thought, as Matthew Arnold put it in the 1860s' (p.xiii). Said points out that this concept of culture becomes bound up with national identity, with the differentiation of 'us' from them, and the assertion of 'our' superiority. It can serve to endorse aggressive collective definition: sweetness and light turn dark and sour, become a rancorous assertion of superiority. One might instance here, though Said does not use the example himself, the case of F.R. Leavis, with his increasingly strident assertion of an 'essential Englishness' represented by certain literary texts. More recently, as Said notes, it has been evident in the United States (and, we might add, in England) in calls for the imposition of a list of books that students should read in order to reinforce a sense of national identity.

Said tells us that he uses the term 'imperialism' in the sense of 'the practice, the theory, and the attitudes of a dominating metropolitan centre ruling a distant territory; "colonialism", which is almost always a consequence of imperialism, is the implanting of settlements on distant territory'. In the present day, colonialism has largely ended, but imperialism remains in 'a kind of general cultural sphere as well as in specific political, ideological, economic, and social practices' (p.8). It is also crucial to Said's definition that imperialism produces *resistance* on the part of those it subjugates. He feels that in *Orientalism* (1978) he left out the response of resistance which was to culminate 'in the great movement of decolonization all across the Third World' (p.xii).

Said's account of imperialism is not a fully-developed one. He does not really engage with the question of *why* imperialism occurred – why should a metropolitan centre *want* to rule a distant territory? He says, for example, that 'the main battle in imperialism is over land' (p.xiii), but this only resites the question – why should land be important? We noted earlier that he uses the term 'relative autonomy' but largely avoids the question of determination, of what it is that culture is 'relatively autonomous' of and of how far that autonomy extends. This avoidance is also evident in his definition of imperialism. What, precisely, is the role of economic forces in imperialism, and what are the relations of those forces to culture? What are the relations between imperialism and other possible historical motors like capitalism and war? These issues are not fully explored. In a sense, imperialism, as Said defines it, is a given phenomenon, and its dynamics are not investigated in any sustained way.

What relationship, then, is implied by that 'and' which, in Said's title, links 'culture' with 'imperialism'? His argument is that culture prepares the intellectual and aesthetic framework which makes imperialism acceptable and even admirable, even before the pace of imperial expansion accelerates later in the nineteenth century; culture then promotes, develops and sustains imperialism, and does not offer any real deterrent to it until resistance starts to develop among the colonized themselves. Culture provides and maintains what Said calls 'a structure of attitude and reference' – the term is related to Raymond Williams's concept of 'structure of feeling' – which helps to legitimate empire; empire is seen as necessary, even if sometimes, as in Conrad's *Heart of Darkness* (1902), corrupt; the 'natives' are perceived as inferior, needing to be kept in their place, prodded into work, pulled out of their backwardness, sometimes beaten into submission. They are not regarded as agents in their own right but objects in the imperialist discourses who none the less sometimes trouble those discourses and must be brought into line with them.

This 'structure of attitude and reference' is not static: rather it is mobilized in the form of *narrative*. The 'structure of attitude and reference' is to a very significant extent produced, dramatized and elaborated in *stories*, stories of conquest, of *la mission civilizatrice*. These stories occur in a wide variety of fictional and ostensibly non-fictional forms: government reports, travel books, histories, even maps. For Said, one of their primary modes in nineteenth-century England and France was the novel, and, in the America of the later twentieth century, television news reporting. It is thus through the production and elaboration of structure in narrative that culture prepares for, ratifies and promotes imperialism.

This is not to claim, however, that culture is a mere reflex of imperialism, that it is, so to speak, the 'superstructure' of which imperialism is the 'base'. There are two reasons for this. One is that the 'relative autonomy' of culture enables cultural productions such as the novel to generate, at certain historical moments, implicit and explicit criticisms of some aspects of imperialism – once again, *Heart of Darkness* comes to mind, and also *Nostromo*. This is not to say that novels can wholly transcend their context of production: Conrad's fiction remains locked in imperialist perspectives to some extent, but it is not wholly enclosed by them. As Said puts it:

> Conrad was both anti-imperialist and imperialist, progressive when it came to rendering fearlessly and pessimistically the self-confirming, self-deluding corruption of overseas domination, deeply reactionary when it came to conceding that Africa or South America could ever have had an independent history or culture, which the imperialists violently disturbed but by which they were ultimately defeated. (p.xx)

The second reason why culture is not a mere reflex of imperialism is that just as imperialism produced resistance, so the culture which promoted but sometimes criticized imperialism also produced resistance. This resistance took two forms. One was the appropriation of the languages, forms, structures, narratives, stereotypes, concepts and methodologies of the imperial culture in order to challenge and criticize it: we see this, for example, in the work of the Caribbean writers George Lamming and Sam Selvon (the latter not mentioned by Said) and of African writers such as Achebe, Ngugi and Soyinka, as well as in the work of scholars such as C.L.R. James and George Antonius. The second form of resistance, often interrelated with the first, was the maintenance, rediscovery and development of those indigeneous languages, forms, structures, narratives, stereotypes, concepts and methodologies which imperialism and colonialism had disrupted, denied, suppressed, ignored or exploited: the production of counter-structures and counter-narratives. As Said puts it: 'stories are at the heart of what explorers and novelists say about strange regions of the world; they also become the method colonized people use to assert their own identity and the existence of their own history' (p.xiii).

Given these general propositions about the relationship between culture and imperialism, how is it to be explored? Clearly the field is so vast that considerable delimitation is necessary if the project is not to take on an encyclopaedic scope far exceeding the powers of one person, even someone as able as Said. Moreover, the encyclopaedic project is, in its ultimate ambition, unrealizable – phenomena will always outstrip it – and it is also suspiciously imperialist in its pretensions: it recalls the encyclopaedic projects conducted by Western scholars in relation to the Middle East which, in *Orientalism*, Said saw as serving the ends of imperialist domination. Said's method is, therefore, 'to focus as much as possible on individual works, to read them first as great products of the creative or interpretative imagination, and then to show them as part of the relationship between culture and empire' (p.xxiv). It is notable that Said is willing to retain the concept of the 'great' work/author – he reiterates the adjective unashamedly – and also to retain the concept of the author him/herself, an author who is seen as part of society and history but not as wholly determined by them. Said does not therefore follow the line of argument which would see notions of 'greatness', the 'work', and the 'author' as themselves constructions of a culture of domination which help to maintain that domination. Nor does he follow the kind of 'cultural studies' approach which would regard a supposedly trivial or popular or marginal text as being as revealing, or even more so, than conventionally valued texts.

Said selects a number of culturally valued English and French nineteenth and twentieth century texts which he holds to be both aesthetically valuable and particularly significant in what they can be made to reveal about the relationship between culture and imperialism. These texts are *Mansfield Park* (1814); *Heart of Darkness* and *Nostromo*; Kipling's *Kim* (1901); Forster's *A Passage to India* (1924); Gide's *The Immoralist* (1902); Camus's *The Outsider* (1942); and – Said's musical passion surfacing here – Verdi's opera *Aida* (1871). His discussions of each of these texts, mixing formal analysis with social, cultural and political history in what he calls a 'contrapuntal' way, are extremely interesting. Consider, for example, his discussion of *Mansfield Park*. The imperial connection has not usually come to the foreground in interpretations of this novel, but there are a small but not insignificant number of direct references to it and there is a sense in which the action and themes turn on Sir Thomas's absence in, and return from, Antigua (where slavery was still in force). Said's overall argument is that the novel articulates a relationship, an interdependence, between Sir Thomas's proper management of his imperial spaces and his proper management of the domestic spaces of Mansfield Park. This relates to a more general concern of Said's in his analysis of culture and imperialism: that imperialism is to be understood as a matter of spatial control, as the domination and ordering of territory, and that this may find its analogues in domestic and metropolitan forms of social control.

Said's interpretation of *Mansfield Park* has been available for some time – it was first published in *Raymond Williams: Critical Perspectives* (1990) and reprinted in K.M. Newton's reader in modern literary criticism, *Theory into Practice* (1992) and Francis Mulhern's reader *Contemporary Marxist Literary Criticism* (1992). One small error should be noted, which persists in *Culture and Imperialism* from the Raymond Williams volume, although it was corrected in the Newton book: Maria Bertram is referred to as Lydia (*Culture and Imperialism*, p.104). The interpretation had thus already began to penetrate into discussions of Jane Austen's novel: appearing in the context of the more general argument of *Culture and Imperialism*, it will now be unignorable. Like Chinua Achebe's famous or notorious attack on *Heart of Darkness* as a racist book (see *Hopes and Impediments*, pp.1-13), it will change the way we see a classic, forever; for all the pertinence and provocative force of Achebe's attack, Said's analysis is conducted at a more theoretically sophisticated level. Moreover, Achebe's attack arguably exhibits what Said calls 'the rhetoric of blame, so often now employed by subaltern, minority, or disadvantaged voices [which] attacks [Austen], and others like her, retrospectively, for being white, privileged, insensitive, complicit' (p.115) and which can fall into 'a kind of retrospective vindictiveness' (p.xxiv). That rhetoric may have its place, but, Said suggests, it can repeat the exclusiveness which characterizes imperialism itself.

Said's interpretation of *Mansfield Park* bears out his general claim that an awareness of the relationship between culture and imperialism can *enhance* our readings of texts. Indeed, it may also enhance our appreciation of authors. There is a sense in which Said's account of *Mansfield Park* elevates Jane Austen, not by turning her into a mid-twentieth-century liberal, but by making her appear to be a rather more astute conservative political thinker than had been realized. It certainly challenges the notion, summed up in the misconception that she never mentions the Napoleonic wars, that her attention was confined to the domestic and moral sphere and did not extend to the wider political world.

He does not, however, want to offer a linear narrative in which European texts from *Mansfield Park* to *The Outsider* inscribe, with varying degress of unease, versions of empire that meet no resistance. Though there is, as we noted above, a certain linear movement in Said's text, his overall approach aims to be not so much linear as contrapuntal, breaking up the smooth narrative of imperial rise and decline with the intrusions of the subjugated peoples themselves, who are not blank slates for the imperialists to write on. As the book proceeds, Said thus moves increasingly to consider the culture of resistance to imperialism. His approach, as he suggests, has large implications for thinking about modernism: 'a huge and remarkable adjustment in perspective and understanding is required to take account of the contribution to modernism of decolonization, resistance culture, and the literature of opposition to imperialism' (p.293). W.B. Yeats is provocatively recruited into 'a tradition not usually considered his, that of the colonial world ruled by European imperialism during a climactic insurrectionary stage' (p.266). Said also looks at a number of writers from the colonized world who took what he calls '*the voyage in*' (p.295) who, as it were, invaded the metropolitan cultural space and used its intellectual tools to criticize the metropolis and to give the periphery a voice.

He discusses two works from an older generation of non-metropolitan intellectuals, C.L.R. James's *The Black Jacobins: Toussaint L'Ouverture and the San Domingo Revolution* (1938) and George Antonius's *The Arab Awakening: The Story of the Arab National Movement* (1938), and compares these with two books by intellectuals of a later generation, *A Rule of Property for Bengal: An Essay on the Idea of Permanent Settlement* (1963) by a Bengali political economist, Ranajit Guha, and *The Myth of the Lazy Native: A Study of the Image of the Malays, Filipinos, and Javanese from the 16th to the 20th Century and Its Function in the Ideology of Colonial Capitalism* (1977) by a Malaysian Muslim historian and social theorist, S.H. Alatas. The titles tell part of the story: James and Antonius offer narratives which present alternative stories to that of Western imperial triumph but they do so in some of the terms of the Western cultural tradition, and on the assumption that their alternative stories have some continuity with the Western narrative; for instance, C.L.R. James argues that the discourse of the French *encylopédistes* and of the French Revolution gave Toussaint the language and concepts with which to articulate his challenge. Furthermore, James and Antonius address a relatively wide audience – Western and non Western, specialist and general. Guha and Alatas, on the other hand, give a sense of the discontinuity between European and indigeneous cultural modes and of the constant conflict between the forms of imperial control and the forms of the colonized society: narrative is replaced by irony. Their audience is a narrower, specialist one: many readers will have heard of James, some of Antonius; comparatively few, outside their specialisms, will have heard of Guha and Alatas (though their appearance in Said's book will doubtless change this!).

Said's point, however, is not to privilege the James-Antonius kind of writer over the Guha-Alatas kind, or *vice versa*; he wants, rather, to suggest that their respective kinds of work emerge at different historical moments. James and Antonius wrote at a time when movements towards independence had been launched and were gaining strength, but had still to come to fruition; Guha and Alatas wrote at a time, still our own, when formal independence had largely been achieved, but when imperial attitudes persist and form part of what Said calls 'the post-colonial predicament' (p.309).

A writer who foresaw something of that predicament was Frantz Fanon (1925-61), the psychiatrist from Martinique who supported the Algerian Revolution and wrote two powerful books, *Black Skin, White Masks* (1952) and *The Wretched of the Earth* (1961). The posthumous trajectory of Fanon has been an interesting one. He became fashionable, not least among white metropolitan intellectuals, in the 1960s, but then rather fell from view. David Caute's vivid and informative study of him, published in 1970 in the 'Modern Masters' series, went out of print, and it is perhaps significant that Frank Kermode, recalling that his work as editor of that series meant that he retained little memory of the contents of the books, recently remarked: 'There was a book on Fanon. I couldn't tell you anything about Fanon now; I think he's completely out of my head' (*Poetry, Narrative, History*, 1990, p.93). In fact, Fanon was by this time enjoying a revival among intellectuals of 'peripheral' provenance, such as Said himself, and Homi Bhahba, and he is likely – not least as a result of Said's account in *Culture and Imperialism* of the complexities of his texts – to become increasingly important in the 1990s. In the 1960s, Fanon was identified primarily – by some of his metropolitan supporters as well as detractors – with the romantic exaltation of revolutionary violence as a cleansing and restorative force; it may be that Sartre's Preface to *The Wretched of the Earth*

– an endorsement but also an appropriation of Fanon – played its part in this (see 'Sartre/Barthes' above). That identification continues among some of Fanon's hostile critics, as Said points out, but while it would be wrong to minimize the stress on violence, there is, as Said shows, much more to Fanon than that. The stress on violence occurred, in any case, in the context of a specific anti-colonial struggle, that of the FLN in Algeria. An important aspect of Fanon today is that, as Said suggests, he foresaw some of the dangers and tasks that would face post-colonial societies, as well as offering a vision of what those societies, and all societies, might become.

Said is painfully aware of the harsh realities of many post-colonial societies; he is also well aware of the way in which those realities have reinforced neo-imperialist perceptions in the West: look at what happened to them when we gave them their 'freedom'! Said contends, however, that those realities should be seen as the continuation of imperialism by other means: as the consequences of the disorder and violence produced by the original imperialist incursion itself; as the result of neo-imperialist policies which serve to keep the formerly colonized countries in a state of dependence and tutelage; and as a result of the persistence of the core concept of imperialism itself – the concept of a unitary, monolithic identity which is superior to other identities – the very 'them'/'us' division by which imperialism was ideologically and culturally sustained. Said identifies two particular forms of this concept in post-colonial societies: nationalism, the notion of a unified, essential, and superior national identity, and nativism, the notion of a unified, essential and superior native or ethnic culture (as in the idea of *négritude*). Said does not deny the value of these notions in providing a sense of identity, especially in a time of anti-colonialist struggle, but when they become essentialized in the pressures of the post-colonial phase, they are likely to contribute to oppression.

In the last chapter of his book, Said tackles two major issues: the persistence of imperialist attitudes in the United States, especially as exemplified in the Gulf War; and the possibility summed up in the title of the chapter: Freedom from Domination in the Future. In taking up the first issue, Said becomes an angry polemicist. He has three main targets: the American decision to fight the Gulf War; the restriction of public debate on the issues in America; and the reproduction of ignorant stereotypes of the 'Arab world' and of 'Islam', which were particularly manifest during the Gulf Crisis, but are elements of an ongoing misrepresentation. Part of Said's attack strikes home, but it has to be said that he sometimes lets his anger get the better of him and does his case less than justice. Given that the bulk of the American (and European) public are as ill-informed on the War itself and on 'the Arab world' as Said claims, it might have been appropriate to use the opportunity this book provides to give an informed account of the issues. At one point he laments, with an echo of T.S. Eliot's 'Gerontion': 'With such information about Iraq, what forgiveness, what humanity, what chance for humane argument?' (p.360). Yet Said does not really provide much more information, and the reader who might be sympathetically disposed towards his views, or at least be prepared to consider them, is left little the wiser. In relation to the Gulf War, there is, for instance, no extended discussion of alternative policy options: Said cites Theodore Draper's argument in a *New York Review of Books* article of 16 January 1992 that, as Said puts it, 'some acknowledgement of Iraq's claim against Kuwait might have staved off a war' (p.358). But the implications of this view – its credibility, its possible consequences if acted upon – are not really explored. Said becomes as heated in his polemic as some supporters of the war, and thus, like those supporters, loses sight of the more difficult and complex questions. Moreover, he comes close at times to producing an image of 'America' which is as monolithic and stereotyped as the image of 'the Arab world' which he berates 'America' for maintaining.

Angry polemic, however, gives way to utopian vision when Said adumbrates a world free from domination. This would be a world not of warring, separated essences, or of rigidly enclosing systems, but of hybrid, mobile, provisional, anti-systemic identities, intercrossings and interminglings. It is an inspiring vision, but is it any more than a pipe dream? One question to be asked is: what kinds of material conditions would be required for such a world, and how would those material conditions be achieved? Said does not really address this question; his vision, like other recent projections of hybridity and difference, seems to involve an over-estimation of the power of culture to effect social and political change: it is inspiring partly because it implies that to jettison essentialist ideas is to take a fast jet towards utopia. But what if the ideas of hybridity and difference were themselves a kind of imperialism, the products of the empire of global capitalism? And what if the material conditions which made them possible for a few could not be made available to everybody? Said's ideal sometimes sounds suspiciously like a generalization of his own privileged position as a well-heeled, well-known, fast-moving American professor.

A further question is implicitly raised by Said himself in his

Conclusion to his earlier book *The World, the Text and the Critic*, when he remarks on 'what seem to be necessary features of human life, the need for certainty, group solidarity, and a sense of communal belonging' (p.290). Does he still believe that these needs are 'necessary features of human life' and if so, how would they be satisfied in the nomadic, hybridic world Said envisages? If he does not now believe that they are necessary, why is it that certain people at certain times seem to have such needs, and how might they be able to move beyond them? Again, more attention to material conditions – and to the intimations of psychoanalysis – might be helpful here.

There can be no doubt, however, that Said, with *Culture and Imperialism*, has set an agenda which will revolutionize not only the reading of literature but also the reading of verbal and visual texts in general. For some time to come, there will be much interpretation of texts in terms of the approach which he summarizes near the end of the book:

> I have been proposing the contrapuntal lines of a global analysis, in which texts and worldly institutions are seen working together, in which Dickens and Thackeray as London authors are read also as writers whose historical influence is informed by the colonial enterprises in India and Australia of which they were so aware, and in which the literature of one commonwealth is involved in the literatures of others. Separatist or nativist enterprises strike me as exhausted; the ecology of literature's new and expanded meaning cannot be attached to only one essence or to the discrete idea of one thing. But this global, contrapuntal analysis should be modelled not (as earlier notions of comparative literature were) on a symphony but rather on an atonal ensemble; we must take into account all sorts of spatial or geographical and rhetorical practices – inflections, limits, constraints, intrusions, inclusions, prohibitions – all of them tending to elucidate a complex and uneven topography. (pp.385-6)

This kind of approach will generate a wide range of new readings and new 'knowledges' and such intellectual and cultural production will have much wider repercussions on attitudes to, concepts of, and ways of representing and exploring, the changes now taking place in the world. They may also have effects on political and social action, but these are difficult to envisage or estimate. How far Said's vision of a world freed from domination can be translated into reality remains an open question; but our new world maps need their utopias.

Bibliography

Achebe, Chinua. *Hopes and Impediments: Selected Essays 1965-1987*. London: Heinemann, 1988.

Adam, Ruth. *I'm Not Complaining*. London: Virago, 1983.

Alatas, Syed Hussein. *The Myth of the Lazy Native: A Study of the Image of the Malays, Filipinos, and Javanese from the Sixteenth to the Twentieth Century and Its Functions in the Ideology of Colonial Capitalism*. London: Frank Cass, 1977.

Althusser, Louis. *Lenin and Philosophy and Other Essays*, trans. Ben Brewster. 2nd edn. London: New Left Books, 1977.

Anderson, Perry. *A Zone of Engagement*. London: Verso, 1992.

—— *English Questions*. London: Verso, 1992.

—— *In the Tracks of Historical Materialism*. London: Verso, 1983.

—— *Lineages of the Absolutist State*. London: New Left Books, 1974.

—— *Passages from Antiquity to Feudalism*. London: New Left Books, 1974.

Antonius, George. *The Arab Awakening: The Story of the Arab National Movement*. Beirut: Librairie du Liban, 1969.

Armstrong, Paul B. *Conflicting Readings: Variety and Validity in Interpretation*. Chapel Hill: University of North Carolina Press, 1990.

Austen, Jane. *Mansfield Park*. London: Penguin, 1966.

Barnett, Correlli. *The Audit of War: The Illusion and Reality of Britain as a Great Nation*. London: Macmillan, 1986.

Barthes, Roland. *Camera Lucida*, Trans. Richard Howard. London: Flamingo, 1984.

—— *Critique et vérité*. Paris: Seuil, 1966.

Barthes, Roland. *Empire of Signs*, trans. Richard Howard. London: Cape, 1982.

—— *Image-Music-Text*, selected and trans. Stephen Heath. London: Fontana, 1977.

—— *Mythologies*, selected and trans. Annette Lavers. London: Paladin, 1970.

—— *Roland Barthes by Roland Barthes*, trans. Richard Howard. London: Macmillan, 1977.

—— *Sade, Fourier, Loyola*, trans. Richard Miller. New York: Hill & Wang, 1976.

—— *The pleasure of the text*, trans. Richard Miller. London: Cape, 1976.

—— *S/Z*. Paris: Seuil, 1970. Trans. Richard Miller. Oxford: Blackwell, 1990.

—— *Writing Degree Zero and Elements of Semiology*, trans. Annette Lavers and Colin Smith. London: Cape, 1984.

Bayley, John. 'The uncommon pursuit'. Review of Terry Eagleton, *Literary Theory*, (1983). *Times Literary Supplement*, no. 4184, 10 June 1983, pp.587-8.

Beauvoir, Simone de. *Adieux: A Farewell to Sartre*, trans. Patrick O'Brian. London: André Deutsch and Weidenfeld and Nicolson, 1984.

—— *All Said and Done*, trans. Patrick O'Brian. London: André Deutsch and Weidenfeld and Nicolson, 1974.

Belsey, Catherine. *Critical Practice*. London: Methuen, 1980.

—— 'Literature, history, politics'. *Literature and History*, vol. 9, no. 1, 1983, pp.17-27.

—— 'Problems of Literary Theory. The Problem of Meaning'. *New Literary History. A Journal of Theory and Interpretation*, vol. 14, no. 1, 1982, pp.175-182.

Boswell James. *The Life of Samuel Johnson LL.D.* 2 vols. London: Dent, 1906.

Bradbrook, M.C. 'Queenie Leavis: the dynamics of rejection'. *The Cambridge Review*, vol. 103, no. 2265, 20 November 1981, pp.56-9.

Brooke-Rose, Christine. *Stories, theories and things*. Cambridge: Cambridge University Press, 1991.

Camus, Albert. *Essais*. Paris: Gallimard, 1965.

Carey, John. 'Queenie Leavis – a help or hindrance to her husband?'. *The Listener*, vol. 108, no. 2781, 7 October 1982, pp.15-17.

Caute, David. *Fanon*. London: Fontana, 1970.

Cioffi, Frank. 'Wittgenstein's Freud'. *Studies in the Philosophy of Wittgenstein*, ed. Peter Winch, pp.184-210. London: Routledge and Kegan Paul, 1969.

Cixous, Hélène. 'The Laugh of the Medusa'. *Signs*, vol. 1, no. 4, 1976, pp.875-99, trans. Keith Cohen and Paula Cohen. Reprinted in *New French Feminisms: An Anthology*, eds. Elaine Marks and Isabelle de Courtivron, pp.245-64. New York: Schocken, 1981.

Cockburn, Alexander and Blackburn, Robin, eds. *Student Power/ Problems, Diagnosis, Action*. London: Penguin Books in association with *New Left Review*, 1969.

Cranston, Maurice. *The Mask of Politics and other essays*. London: Allen Lane, 1973.

Culler, Jonathan. *Barthes*. London: Fontana, 1983.

—— *On Deconstruction: Theory and Criticism after Structuralism*. London: Routledge & Kegan Paul, 1983.

—— *Structuralist Poetics: Structuralism, Linguistics and the Study of Literature*. London: Routledge & Kegan Paul, 1975.

Davey, Kevin. 'Communities: the novels of Raymond Williams'. *PN Review* 51, vol. 13, no. 1, 1986, pp.40-2.

De Man, Paul. *Wartime Journalism, 1939-1943*, eds. Werner Hamacher, Neil Hertz, Thomas Keenan. Lincoln, USA: University of Nebraska Press, 1988.

Derrida, Jacques. *Of Grammatology*, trans. Gayatri Chakravorty Spivak. Baltimore: Johns Hopkins University Press, 1976.

—— *Positions*, trans. Alan Bass. London: Athlone Press, 1981.

—— *Writing and Difference*, trans. Alan Bass. London: Routledge and Kegan Paul, 1978.

Eagleton, Terry. *Criticism and Ideology: A Study in Marxist Literary Theory*. London: New Left Books, 1976.

—— *The Ideology of the Aesthetic*. Oxford: Blackwell, 1990.

—— *Literary Theory: An Introduction*. Oxford: Blackwell, 1983.

—— 'Literature and History'. *Critical Quarterly*, vol. 27, no. 4, 1985, pp.23-6.

—— ed. *Raymond Williams: Critical Perspectives*. London: Polity Press, 1989.

Eagleton, Terry. *The Significance of Theory*. Oxford: Blackwell, 1990.

—— 'The Subject of Literature'. *Cultural Critique*, no. 2, 1985-6, pp.95-104.

Easthope, Antony. Letter under heading 'If Marx saw us now', *Guardian*, 16 March 1983, p.12.

—— *Poetry as Discourse*. London: Methuen, 1983.

Fanon, Frantz. *Black Skin, White Masks*, trans. Charles Lam Markmann. London: Pluto Press, 1986.

—— *The Wretched of the Earth*, trans. Constance Farrington. London: Penguin, 1967.

Fish, Stanley. *Doing What Comes Naturally; Change, Rhetoric and the Practice of Theory in Literary and Legal Studies*. Oxford: Oxford University Press, 1989.

Fraser, G.S. *Poems of G.S. Fraser*, eds. Ian Fletcher and John Lucas. Leicester: Leicester University Press, 1981.

Freud, Sigmund. *Case Histories I: 'Dora' and 'Little Hans'*, trans. Alix and James Strachey, ed. Angela Richards. London: Penguin, 1977.

Fuss, Diana. *Essentially Speaking: Feminism, Nature and Difference*. London: Routledge, 1990.

Genet, Jean. *The Balcony*, trans. Bernard Frechtman. London: Faber, 1965.

—— 'Jean Genet in Conversation'. Interview with Pierre Vicary. *PN Review* 32, vol. 9, no. 6, 1983, pp.45-51.

Gilbert, Sandra M. and Gubar, Susan. *The Madwoman in the Attic: The Woman Writer and the Nineteenth-Century Literary Imagination*. New Haven: Yale University Press, 1979.

Greene, Graham. *The Power and the Glory*. London: Penguin, 1971.

Guha, Ranajit. *A Rule of Property for Bengal: An Essay on the Idea of Permanent Settlement*. Paris and The Hague: Mouton, 1963.

Heath, Stephen. *Vertige du Déplacement: lecture de Barthes*. Paris: Fayard, 1974.

Hewison, Robert. *The Heritage Industry: Britain in a climate of decline*. London: Metheun, 1987.

Hughes, Ted. Letter under heading 'Ted Hughes and the Plath Estate', *Times Literary Supplement*, no. 4647, 24 April 1992, p.15.

James, C.L.R. *The Black Jacobins: Toussaint L'Ouverture and the San Domingo Revolution*. New York: Vintage, 1963.

Jameson, Fredric. *Late Marxism: Adorno, or, The Persistence of the Dialectic*. London: Verso, 1990.

—— *Marxism and Form*: Twentieth-Century Dialectical Theories of Literature. Princeton: Princeton University Press, 1971.

—— *The Political Unconscious: Narrative as a Socially Symbolic Act*. London: Methuen, 1983.

—— *Postmodernism, or, The Cultural Logic of Late Capitalism*. London: Verso, 1991.

Jameson, Storm. *Journey to the North*. London: Collins and Harvill Press, 1970.

Johnson, Barbara. *The Critical Difference*. Baltimore: Johns Hopkins University Press, 1980.

Johnson, R.W. *Heroes and Villains: Selected Essays*. Hemel Hempstead: Harvester Wheatsheaf, 1990.

Kermode, Frank. *Poetry, Narrative, History*. Oxford: Blackwell, 1990.

Lawrence, D.H. *Complete Poems*, eds. Vivian de Sola Pinto and Warren Roberts. 2 vols. London: Heinemann, 1972.

Leavis, F.R. *The Critic as Anti-Philosopher: Essays and Papers*, ed. G. Singh. London: Chatto and Windus, 1982.

—— *The Great Tradition*. London: Penguin, 1972.

—— *The Living Principle. 'English' as a Discipline of Thought*. London: Chatto and Windus, 1975.

—— *Thought, Words and Creativity: Art and Thought in Lawrence*. London: Chatto and Windus, 1976.

Leavis, Q.D. 'Caterpillars of the commonwealth unite!'. Review of Virginia Woolf, *Three Guineas* (1938). *Scrutiny*, vol. 7, no. 2, 1938-9, pp.203-14.

—— *Collected essays: Volume I: The Englishness of the English novel*, ed. G. Singh. Cambridge: Cambridge University Press, 1983.

—— *Collected essays: Volume 2: The American novel and reflections on the European novel*, ed. G. Singh. Cambridge: Cambridge University Press, 1983.

—— *Collected essays: Volume 3: The novel of religious controversy*, collected and ed. G. Singh. Cambridge: Cambridge University Press, 1989.

Leavis, Q.D. 'The Englishness of the English Novel'. *New Universities Quarterly*, vol. 35, no. 2, 1981, pp.149-71. Reprinted in Leavis, Q.D., *Collected Essays: Volume 1*, pp.303-27.

—— 'Femina Vie-Heureuse Please Note'. Review of Ruth Adam, *I'm Not Complaining* (1938), *Scrutiny*, vol. 7, no. 1, 1938-9, pp.81-5.

—— *Fiction and the Reading Public*. London: Penguin, 1979.

—— 'Introduction' to Oliphant, Margaret *Autobiography and Letters of Mrs Margaret Oliphant*. Leicester: Leicester University Press, 1974. Ed. Mrs Harry Coghill. Reprinted in Leavis, Q.D., *Collected essays: Volume 3*, pp.159-81.

—— 'Introduction' to Oliphant, Margaret *Miss Marjoribanks*. London: Chatto and Windus, 1969. Reprinted in Leavis, Q.D., *Collected essays: Volume 3*, pp.135-58.

—— 'Lady Novelists and the Lower Orders'. *Scrutiny*, vol. 4, no. 2, 1935-6, pp.112-32.

—— Untitled review of Dorothy Richardson, *Clear Horizon* (1935). *Scrutiny*, vol. 4, no. 3, 1935-6, pp.328-30.

Lerner, Laurence, ed. *Reconstructing Literature*. Oxford: Blackwell, 1983.

Light, Alison. Untitled contribution to Brighton LTP Group, 'Problems of the Progressive Text: *The Color Purple* by Alice Walker'. *Literature Teaching Politics* 6, compiled and ed. Helen Taylor. Bristol: Bristol Polytechnic, 1985, pp.127-32.

Lodge, David. *After Bakhtin: Essays on fiction and criticism*. London: Routledge, 1990.

Macksey, Richard and Donato, Eugene, eds. *The Structuralist Controversy: The Languages of Criticism and the Sciences of Man*. Baltimore: Johns Hopkins University Press, 1970.

Malcolm, Norman. *Ludwig Wittgenstein: A Memoir*. 2nd edn. Oxford: Oxford University Press, 1984.

Masson, Jeffery. *Freud: The Assault on Truth – Freud's Suppression of the Seduction Theory*. London: Faber, 1984.

Miller, J. Hillis. *Fiction and repetition: seven English novels*. Oxford: Blackwell, 1982.

—— *Theory Now and Then*. Hemel Hempstead: Harvester Wheatsheaf, 1991.

—— *Tropes, Parables, Performatives: Essays on Twentieth-Century Literature*. Durham, USA: Duke University Press, 1991.

Miller, J. Hillis. *Victorian Subjects*. Hemel Hempstead: Harvester Wheatsheaf, 1990.

The Miner: Journal of the National Union of Mineworkers: Special Issue, 11 December 1984.

Moi, Toril. *Sexual/Textual Politics: Feminist Literary Theory*. London: Methuen, 1985.

Mulhern, Francis, ed. *Contemporary Marxist Literary Criticism*. London: Longman, 1992.

—— *The Moment of 'Scrutiny'*. London: New Left Books, 1979.

Newton, K.M., ed. *Theory into Practice: A Reader in Modern Literary Criticism*. London: Macmillan, 1992.

Norris, Christopher. *Deconstruction: Theory and Practice*. London: Methuen, 1982.

Orwell, George. 'The Lion and the Unicorn: Socialism and the English Genius'. *The Collected Essays, Journalism and Letters of George Orwell. Volume II. My Country Right or Left 1940-1943*, eds. Sonia Orwell and Ian Angus, pp.74-134. London: Penguin in association with Martin Secker and Warburg, 1970.

Parrinder, Patrick. *The Failure of Theory: Essays on Criticism and Contemporary Fiction*. Brighton: Harvester, 1987.

Pinkney, Tony. *Raymond Williams*. Bridgend, Mid Glamorgan: Seren Books, 1991.

Plath, Sylvia. *The Bell Jar*. London: Faber, 1966.

—— *Collected Poems*, ed. Ted Hughes. London: Faber, 1981.

Richards, I.A. *Science and Poetry*. London: Kegan Paul, Trench, Trubner, 1926.

Rose, Jacqueline. Letter under heading 'Ted Hughes and the Plath Estate', *Times Literary Supplement*, no. 4645, 10 April 1992, p.15.

—— *Sexuality in the Field of Vision*. London: Verso, 1986.

—— *The Haunting of Sylvia Plath*. London: Virago, 1992.

Said, Edward W. *Beginnings: Intention and Method*. 1975.

—— *Culture and Imperialism*. London: Chatto and Windus, 1993.

—— *Orientalism*. London: Routledge and Kegan Paul, 1978.

—— *The World, the Text, and the Critic*. London: Faber, 1984.

Salusinszky, Imre. *Criticism in Society: Interviews with Jacques Derrida, Northrop Frye, Harold Bloom, Geoffrey Hartman, Frank Kermode, Edward Said, Barbara Johnson, Frank Lentricchia, and J. Hillis Miller*. London: Methuen, 1987.

Sartre, Jean-Paul. *Critique of Dialectical Reason: I: Theory of Practical Ensembles*, trans. Alan Sheridan-Smith, ed. Jonathan Rée. London: Verso, 1982.

—— *The Family Idiot: Gustave Flaubert 1821-1857*, trans. Carol Cosman. Vol. 1. Chicago: University of Chicago Press, 1981.

—— *Iron in the Soul*. Vol. 3 of *Roads to Freedom*, trans. Gerard Hopkins. London: Hamish Hamilton, 1950.

—— 'Itinerary of a Thought'. *New Left Review* 58. 1969, pp. 43-66.

—— 'Jean-Paul Sartre répond'. *L'Arc* 30, 1966, pp.87-96.

—— *Nausea*, trans. Robert Baldick. London: Penguin, 1965.

—— 'Preface' to Frantz Fanon, *The Wretched of the Earth*, trans. Constance Farrington, pp.7-26. London: Penguin, 1967.

—— *The Problem of Method*, trans. Hazel Barnes. London: Methuen, 1963.

—— *Sartre by himself*, trans. Richard Seaver. New York: Urizen, 1978.

—— *Sartre in the Seventies: Interviews and Essays*, trans. Paul Auster and Lydia Davis. London: André Deutsch, 1978.

—— *Sartre on Theater*, eds. Michel Contat and Michel Rybalka, trans. Constance Farrington. London: Quartet Books, 1976.

—— *Situations*, trans. Benita Eisler. London: Hamish Hamilton, 1965.

—— *Situations, II: Qu'est-ce que la littérature?* Paris: Gallimard, 1948.

—— *Situations, IX: Mélanges*. Paris: Gallimard, 1972.

—— *Situations, X: Politique et autobiographie*. Paris: Gallimard, 1976.

—— *Sketch for a Theory of the Emotions*, trans. Philip Mairet. London: Methuen, 1962.

—— *What is Literature?*, trans. Bernard Frechtman. London: Methuen, 1967.

—— *Words*, trans. Irene Clephane. London: Penguin, 1967.

Scholes, Robert. *Protocols of Reading*. New Haven: Yale University Press, 1989.

—— *Textual Power. Literary Theory and the Teaching of English*. New Haven: Yale University Press, 1985.

Scriven, Michael. *Sartre's Existential Biographies*. London: Macmillan, 1984.

Selden, Raman. *A Reader's Guide to Contemporary Literary Theory*. Brighton: Harvester, 1985.

Sharratt, Bernard. 'Tressell and the Truths of Fiction'. *The Robert Tressell Lectures 1981-88* ed. David Alfred, pp.93-113. Rochester: Workers Educational Association, 1988.

Steiner, George. *Language and Silence: Essays 1958-1966*. London: Faber, 1967.

—— *On Difficulty and Other Essays*. Oxford: Oxford University Press, 1980.

Stevenson, Anne. *Bitter Fame: A Life of Sylvia Plath*. London: Viking, 1989.

Strickland, Geoffrey. *Structuralism or Criticism? Thoughts on How We Read*. Cambridge: Cambridge University Press, 1981.

Tredell, Nicolas. *Uncancelled Challenge: the work of Raymond Williams*. Nottingham: Paupers' Press, 1990.

Ungar, Stephen. *Roland Barthes: The Professor of Desire*. Lincoln, Nebraska: University of Nebraska Press, 1983.

Walsh, William. *F.R. Leavis*. London: Chatto and Windus, 1980.

Widdowson, Peter, ed. *Re-Reading English*. London: Methuen, 1982.

Wiener, Martin J. *English Culture and the Decline of the Industrial Spirit 1850-1980*. Cambridge: Cambridge University Press, 1981.

Williams, Raymond. *Border Country*. London: Chatto and Windus, 1960.

—— *The Country and the City*. London: Paladin, 1975.

—— *Culture*. London: Fontana, 1981.

—— *Culture and Society 1780-1950*. With 'Postscript'. London: Penguin, 1963.

—— *Drama from Ibsen to Brecht*. London: Chatto and Windus, 1968.

—— *Drama from Ibsen to Eliot*. Revised edn. London: Penguin Books in association with Chatto and Windus, 1964.

Williams, Raymond. *Drama in a Dramatised Society*. Cambridge: Cambridge University Press, 1975.

—— *Drama in Performance*. London: Muller, 1954.

—— *Drama in Performance*. Revised and expanded edn. London: Pelican, 1972.

—— *The Fight for Manod*. London: Chatto and Windus, 1979.

—— *The Long Revolution*. London: Penguin, 1965.

—— *Loyalties*. London: Chatto and Windus, 1985.

—— *Marxism and Literature*. Oxford: Oxford University Press, 1977.

—— *Modern Tragedy*. London: Chatto and Windus, 1966.

—— *Orwell*. With 'Afterword'. London: Flamingo, 1984.

—— *People of the Black Mountains I: The Beginning*... London: Chatto and Windus, 1989.

—— *Politics and Letters: Interviews with New Left Review*. London: New Left Books, 1979.

—— *Problems in Materialism and Culture: Selected Essays*. London: Verso, 1980.

—— *Resources of Hope: Culture, democracy, socialism*, ed. Robin Gable. London: Verso, 1989.

—— *Second Generation*. London: Chatto and Windus, 1964.

—— *Television: Technology and Cultural Form*. London: Fontana, 1974.

—— *Towards 2000*. Pelican, 1985.

—— *The Volunteers*. London: Eyre Methuen, 1978.

—— *Writing in Society*. London: Verso, 1983.

Wilson, Simon. *Pop*. London: Thames and Hudson, 1974.

Index

Compiled by Angela Tredell